the menu toronto

the
menu
TORONTO

the best restaurants and a sample of their menus

JEREMY FERGUSON

TEN SPEED PRESS
Berkeley | Toronto

Ten Speed Press
P.O. Box 7123
Berkeley, California 94707
www.tenspeed.com

Distributed in Australia by Simon and Schuster Australia, in Canada by Ten Speed Press Canada, in New Zealand by Southern Publishers Group, in South Africa by Real Books, and in the United Kingdom and Europe by Airlift Book Company.

Design by Betsy Stromberg
Cover photo by Xavier Bonghi / Getty Images
Back cover photo by Ryan McVay / Getty Images

Library of Congress Cataloging-in-Publication Data

Ferguson, Jeremy, 1943-
    The menu Toronto: the best restaurants and their menus/Jeremy Ferguson.
        p. cm.
    ISBN 1-58008-278-5 (alk. paper)
        1. Restaurants—Ontario—Toronto—Guidebooks. 2. Menus. I. Title.

TX907.5.C2T67 2003
647.95713'541—dc21

                                                                2003048447

First printing, 2004
Printed in Canada

1 2 3 4 5 6 7 8 9 10 — 07 06 05 04

To Carol, the best cook—and woman—in the world.

contents

introduction

I love restaurants, which explains why I watch my waistline as a spectator sport. I'm never happier than when, marinating in anticipation, I settle into a restaurant. I'm not sure life would be worth living without restaurants. Food writers are always comparing restaurants to good sex. The truth is, restaurants are probably better, for they will pleasure you all your life, even when sex has become the fluff of haunting dreams.

I'm deeply pleased to see Toronto's restaurant scene, fueled by a healthy local economy and still healthier appetites, defining and refining its horizons, nurturing adventurous talents and catering to a public eager to experiment and learn. In fact, I'm amazed at the distances Torontonians will go to learn: Once I wrote an April Fool's Day newspaper column in which I fabricated a restaurant specializing in owl soup, baked skunk, and tenderloin of squirrel. My poor editor was hounded by readers pleading for the telephone number to make reservations.

The Origins of Toronto's Cuisine

The story of Toronto's restaurants is the story of immigrants, the poor and dispossessed from all over the world, who arrived in search of the proverbial pot of gold and inadvertently brought it with them. In Toronto, everyone comes from someplace else. When I was growing up here in the 1950s, the city was dominated by English, Irish, and Scots who'd forged its history. But even before then, Toronto was not a culturally homogenous city. The Chinese, for instance, had been here since the railway-building era of the 1870s. Italians had been here as early as the Rebellion of 1837, which came undone when the ruling bigwigs were tipped off by one Filippo de Grassi, who ratted on the rebels. One of the city's most enduring enterprises is Pasquale Bros., which has been bringing virgin olive oils and divinely stinky cheeses to Toronto Italians since 1917.

The great wave of immigration after World War II remade the city. Wave upon wave of new Canadians arrived on the shores of Lake Ontario. Always on the run—from the hardship of postwar Europe, the Soviet tanks of the Hungarian Revolution, the maelstrom of Southeast Asian history, Ethiopian famine and war, the Hong Kong takeover—they came, settled, worked, built, begat, and cooked. When they took their cooking out of the home kitchen and into the streets and opened restaurants, the rest of us were giddy with pleasure. It was Toronto's era of discovery, and it was great.

Unlike the melting pot experiment south of the border, the Canadian approach encouraged newcomers to maintain their identities, culture, customs, and, thankfully, *cuisine*. This is where it all started, the hothouse for everything that makes Toronto the most cosmopolitan city in Canada and, according to UNESCO, the most multicultural city in the world.

Everyone, even suburban politicians who would like nothing better than razing downtown and paving it over with blacktop, acknowledges Toronto's eighty-plus ethnic groups as the wellspring of its vitality. Torontonians rightly view their city as a grand tour through the global village kitchen, a gastronomic tour of the planet.

Toronto Restaurants Today

Over the past twenty-five years, I've had the privilege of making my living as a travel writer. I've seen and eaten my way through at least 150 countries. It's a joy to know that I can find most of these cuisines in my own backyard. Pad thai wafting with sweet basil whisks me to the emerald fire of rice paddies and toppled Buddhas in Thailand's temple ruins. Halfway through a bistro take on confit de canard, I'm back in Paris, lunching in the Marais. Spooning some spicy stuff on to a floppy chunk of *injera*, I return to Ethiopia, scrambling up misted hills to the source of the Blue Nile. My elbows on the table, I am forever journeying.

At the same time, I find myself questioning to what extent Toronto restaurants actually reflect the cooking fires of those faraway lands. What has been lost on the journey? How authentically do the world's cuisines perform on Toronto plates for Toronto palates?

FRENCH

French cuisine is the gold standard. We measure any city by the quality of its *gastronomie*, but Toronto has always been something of an anomaly: The city has never really had terrific French restaurants until fairly recently. Now we're playing catch-up: High-profile restaurants such as Scaramouche, Truffles, and the Fifth dispense haute cuisine, while Bouchon defines the bistro with high-flying standards.

ITALIAN

If the city has seemed bereft of great French cuisine, it's because Torontonians think Italian. Toronto has the largest population of Italians outside of the Boot. Ristorantes and trattorias are all over town, and Little Italy has never been as fashionable as it is today. Initially, the Toronto connection was to the impoverished south of Italy, to the lusty tomato-based cooking of Naples and Calabria and Sicily. Northern Italian food followed, with velvety risotto, osso buco whose flesh cascaded from the bone, and the sublime cheeses Asiago and Gorgonzola.

CAL-ITAL

Cal-Ital swept into town with Franco Prevedello, the man from Asolo, whose restaurants so blissfully married Italian and California sensibilities. This is the sunny, high-spirited style that to this day epitomizes Toronto at its most energetic and worldly, its trademarks the open kitchen, sizzling grill, boozy pastas, mittfuls of herbs—and no qualms about picking the pocket of any passing cuisine and claiming the booty as its own.

GREEK

Although less populous than the Italians, Toronto's Greeks do their bit for Zorba. Greektown unfurls along the Danforth east of the Don River. I like to wander the street in the blue air of a summer night, listening to the thrum of bouzouki and sucking in the aroma of charcoaled calamari. This sense of the Aegean can be heady stuff, yet only a few Danforth eateries actually reach beyond incinerated souvlaki and squid fit for recycling as bungee cords. The siren palette of the eastern Mediterranean remains largely untapped.

SPANISH AND PORTUGUESE

Some Toronto restaurants seem frozen in time, like the biblical Lot's wife turned into a pillar of salt. I lived in Spain for almost a year in the late 1960s. The fare I find in Toronto's Spanish restaurants today is exactly the same food that I was eating on the Costa Blanca thirty-five years ago: gazpacho, paella, zarzuela, flan. We don't see Spanish *neuva cucina* here because Spain is thriving in the European Union, and Spaniards stopped moving to Toronto decades ago.

Conversely, the Portuguese contingent from the Iberian Peninsula is undergoing a startling resurgence driven by one man, Albino Silva, and trumpeting a new era in Toronto Portuguese. I can only hope some culinary conquistadores from Spain will look at Silva's achievement and follow his lead.

EASTERN EUROPEAN

Decidedly unfashionable these days, Eastern European cooking skulks in the wings, awaiting the renovation that defines modern cooking as light and lovely. The kickline of Hungarian restaurants along Bloor Street West in the Annex is mostly gone, but goulash houses are warming up suburban strip malls, and Polish cooks are still dishing out piroshki and kishke on Roncesvalles in the west end.

CHINESE

In the twenty-first century, Chinese has outstripped Italian as Toronto's second language. Toronto's Chinese community is the largest on this continent, with at least five Chinatowns. The most vibrant Chinatown has grown up around Spadina and Dundas, steadily devouring the old Jewish garment district. China on Spadina is a wonderful place to shop, providing fresh fish, dried lotus leaves, preserved duck eggs, and Southeast Asian fruits, even the foul-smelling durian. Yet most of its restaurants—Cantonese, Peking, Swatow, Shanghainese, Szechuan, and Hunan—are little more than purveyors of grease and MSG.

A second Chinatown at Gerrard and Broadview is known as Chinatown East. It caters to often Mandarin-speaking immigrants from the Republic of China, but it knows how to feed the masses: One restaurant, the Pearl Court, offers 140 items on the main menu plus another 60 on a supplementary menu and 46 posted specials and another 18 on the blackboards. It also serves the best dim sum in the city.

The affluent Chinatowns that thread the city's northeastern suburbs, reflect the exodus of Hong Kongese with the takeover jitters in the early 1990s. This territory is more Great Mall than Great Wall, aglow with neon Chinese characters, dim sum instead of doughnut shops, and monster homes built to accommodate feng shui. But it's here—the moon to downtowners—that you find shark's fin, bird's nest, and gossamer deep-fry, the icons of Cantonese sophistication, subtlety and finesse.

JAPANESE

Toronto can't get enough of Japanese food. Good Japanese is easy to find. Great Japanese can be had at Hiro Sushi, Omi, and Kaji, where the art of the raw soars into the stratosphere. What sushi-lovers don't know is that most Japanese restaurants are operated by Koreans, whose own pungent cooking, in spite of a spate of kimchi-bulgogi houses in the Bloor and Christie district, has little popular appeal beyond the Korean community.

THAI

Thai food is as ubiquitous as Japanese. This racy Southeast Asian cuisine was a little slow getting here, but when it did, it swept in with the force of a tropical storm. Thai is the Starbucks of Asian cooking: Just when you think you've reached the saturation point, another one opens right across the street. Golden Thai is a perennial favorite; Vanipha Lanna, specializing in palate-popping northern Thai and Lao cooking, has some of most original Thai food in town.

VIETNAMESE

It confounds me, but Toronto's burgeoning Vietnamese population has yet to produce a first-rate restaurant worthy of this complex and magical Southeast Asian cuisine. A smattering of Vietnamese eateries, most of them very basic, have sprouted up in the Spadina Chinatown. I remember fleeing one as a kitchen fire sent flames to the ceilings. The staff paid no attention and kept right on dispensing greasy spring rolls and overflowing bowls of pho to horrified eaters. Still, the pho is excellent at Pho Hung, and that's a start.

PAN-ASIAN

The new wave is pan-Asian, in which a single kitchen, in a flurry of woks and pans, sizzle and smoke, turns out the edible culture of several countries. Spring Rolls on Yonge has Chinese-Vietnamese brothers cooking Cantonese, Szechuan, Thai, and Vietnamese all at once, if blandly. Lalot takes a higher road to a similarly adventurous territory.

INDIAN

Toronto's Indian cuisine, alternately delights and frustrates. With a South Asian population exceeding 100,000, all that's missing from Little India in the city's east end are carefree cows wandering through rush-hour traffic. Yet the restaurant scene is a pandemonium of inconsistency. Toronto has few Indian restaurants evoking either the great hotel dining rooms of the mystic subcontinent or London's fiery Indo-Pakistani curry houses. Toronto settles for good enough.

AMERICAN AND LATIN AMERICAN

The enduring restaurant for American regional cuisine is Southern Accent, fixing New Orleans Cajun and Creole in Mirvish Village. Enough Mexican restaurants have opened for the law of averages to give us a couple of good ones. Latin American, a relatively new immigrant force is so far confined to an outbreak of hole-in-the-wall beaneries offering cooking heavy enough to send you through the floorboards.

CANADIAN

The most challenging among recently arrived cuisines is Canadian. Toronto has three boldly Canadian restaurants, all wrestling with the vexing question of what constitutes CanCuisine. Their menus cast spotlights on the quality and variety of indigenous produce—surprising for so inhospitable a land—including Bay of Fundy salmon, Quebec foie gras, Manitoba golden caviar, Alberta beef, British Columbia oysters, caribou from the Northwest Territories, and the incomparable fish known as Arctic char.

Canadian also has to do with a new breed of homegrown chefs who embrace these ingredients and infuse them with personal alchemy, transforming them into contemporary cuisine of startling hauteur. Welcome to Canuck chic. One restaurant stuffs a baked apple with foie gras, if you can believe it.

FUSION

Toronto multiculturalism swirls in the urban blender. I hesitate to use the f-word, fusion, because the concept has been so mauled by untalented chefs. In some quarters, fusion is the cuisine chefs and critics love to hate. But it seems to me much more thrilling than that, at its finest rising above the sum of its parts.

If France has French and China has Chinese, fusion is a phenomenon natural to New World countries such as Canada, the United States, Australia, and New Zealand. It demands a worldly affinity for food, for how food works, for what bright and beautiful new marriages may be negotiated. Great fusion kickstarts your sense of wonder. Then it is the most exciting food Toronto has ever seen. There is genius at work here: at Susar and Sen5es, anyway.

The Menu Toronto

When I was approached to write *The Menu Toronto,* I welcomed the format simply because, as my wife, Carol, is always telling me, I'm a menu addict. I'm a sucker for anything that informs me about what to eat and how most enjoyably to eat it. I won't even contemplate a restaurant that fails to post a menu: It must have something to hide.

Carol reminds me of cities in which she practically collapsed with hunger as I scoured every menu on the street before making a decision. She reminds me of streets in which she came close to collapsing as I scoured every menu *after* a meal. She reminds me of stays in Paris, when I spent more time looking at menus than at great paintings in the Musée d'Orsay or fussing in the nooks and crannies of Notre Dame. She reminds me of the time I mistook a sign reading "Bonnes Fetes" for "Pommes Frites." At such moments, we both know I am lost forever.

Guilty, guilty, guilty. But after a while, people who love food develop a sixth sense about menus. We learn to read between the lines. Here, in front of you, are the ingredients that tell you whether a chef is conventional or creative or simply crazy, how sensible or silly the marriages of flavors are—I'll pass on any restaurant which puts strawberries in green salad, thank you—and whether or not the prices will send you scurrying for a second mortgage.

Writing this book became a question of choosing restaurants that best represent the Toronto scene—which restaurants, in pleasing their own constituents, please the world at large. I began with all the restaurants I knew to be excellent from my own experience. I asked chefs where they liked to eat on their nights off. I talked to other foodies, followed reviews, plumbed the Internet for fragments of knowledge.

Eventually, a core list emerged: the visionaries who open your eyes and deliver the thrill of the new, making their marks with distinct ambience and memorable signature dishes; the solid restaurants that settle for quality and consistency, bless them; neighborhood restaurants that transcend neighborhood standards; and the originals that fix on one thing and do it better than anyone—like the Chinese eatery offering fifty different kinds of congee or the South Indian "hut" with a dozen kinds of *dosa;* the Baskin-Robbins of exotica.

Regrettably, as I assembled these restaurants, some of our best chefs were out of the business. They include Arpi Magyar, who founded Splendido and made it better than splendid, and the awesomely talented Andrew Chase and Camilo Costales, who at Youki brought all of Asia to our doorstep and had the gall to serve Chinese bull's penis soup for Valentine's Day. I can only hope they're all back in the kitchens as you read this.

ETHNIC CATEGORIES

I was also hoping to unearth a terrific restaurant in every ethnic category. This ideal didn't quite materialize, but I've included some restaurants that may be less than great but still represent the best of their ethnicity. This way, the reader with a craving for Turkish, Tibetan, Ethiopian, or Polish will be able to eat reasonably well—hopefully *very* well—at some reliable establishments.

NEIGHBORHOODS

Geographically, I've located restaurants by well-known neighborhoods such as Little Italy, Chinatown, the Danforth, and so on. Let's call Downtown the area north from the waterfront to Bloor Street, west to University/Avenue Road, and east to Sherbourne. Downtown West is downtown from University west to Bathurst; West Toronto is anything beyond. Downtown East is downtown from Sherbourne to the Don River; East Toronto is anything beyond. North from Bloor to Eglinton is Midtown. Uptown is Eglinton north to Sheppard. Suburban North, Suburban Northeast, and Surburban Northwest are the suburbs of Thornhill, Richmond Hill, Markham, and Mississauga.

MY PREFERENCES

Finally, it would be unfair of me not to warn you about my own biases and preferences. When it comes to food, I'm an omnivore who has taken pleasure in dishes from roast armadillo to prosciutto of camel. I've never met a cuisine I didn't like. I love strong, clean, honest flavors—and spice, and heat, and deep-fry. Not for nothing am I known as a gastro-gnome. But you wouldn't trust someone who likes everything, would you? I dislike plenty. This includes most fast food, which is little more than grease and salt and slurry. I have no use for the bland: Life is too short. Nor am I fond of the towering cuisine that manifests itself in skyscrapers of food and topples and crashes at the touch of a fork.

I have uneasy feelings about the resurgent steakhouse, the bricks of beef bigger than ever, the price of USDA prime edging up into the caviar and truffle league. I enjoy a steak as much as the next person, but the new carnivorous feeding frenzy seems to me akin to the denial of smokers.

I buckle at arrogant chefs who put no salt and pepper on the table; everyone has a different tolerance in this matter, and if I'm footing the bill, I want to decide for myself. I'm amused at the inescapable phenomenon of the "peppier," the gaunt server who dutifully arrives at every table with a pepper grinder the size of a blunderbuss, dispensing token sprinkles.

I love dinner. Like the proverbial Frenchman, I wake up in the mornings pondering, "And what will I eat tonight?" This is very bad for my waistline and very good for my sense of being alive. I call my theory DTLF (dinners to live for) quotient.

To determine your own DTLF quotient, do this: Calculate your own life expectancy. Deduct the years you've already lived. Take the figure—say, twenty years—and multiply that by 365. What you come out with is the number of dinners you have left. Well, isn't it plain? Doesn't it scream at you? You can't afford another bad dinner, not tonight, not tomorrow, not ever.

This guide is dedicated to that principle. You should be able to walk into every restaurant in these pages and show your DTLF quotient a good time. I hope you'll have as much fun as I did, only without the extra twenty pounds.

restaurants

360 Restaurant

CN Tower
301 Front Street
Toronto
416-362-5411
www.cntower.ca

**Global
DOWNTOWN**

Wheelchair
access

V / MC / AmEx /
D / DC

Sunday brunch

lunch

dinner

beer/wine

cocktails

high chairs

private parties

non-smoking

reservations
recommended

dress business
casual

menu changes
seasonally

Conventional wisdom says that the better the view, the worse the cuisine. But the powers in the Tower—still the world's tallest building and freestanding structure—occasionally attempt a revolution bigger than the one the restaurant makes every seventy-two minutes and surprise you with decent food. The menu strikes a balance between the bottom line (yes, Aunt Mabel can handle Caesar salad and prime rib) and a notch up (smoked salmon with deep-fried sage leaves, osso buco with saffron risotto). Reasonable dining assured, the magnificent view is free to steal the breath away, especially when you're peering down into a phalanx of skyscrapers at dusk.

THE RESTAURANT AT THE CN TOWER
360
TORONTO · CANADA

APPETIZERS

Hearts of romaine with pancetta curls, garlic croutons and caesar vinaigrette
$12
Daily soup or mixed greens with garden vegetables tossed in shallot vinaigrette
$8
East coast mussel chowder with saffron, caramelized onions and parsley toast
$12
Sage and ricotta ravioli with pecorino cheese, roasted squash and French beans
$17
Foie gras and chicken liver terrine with toasted brioche and Newfoundland partridge berry relish
$18
Parma Ham and French beans with mustard seed vinaigrette and parmesan tuille
$17
Mussels, clams and shrimp tossed with tagliatelle, smoked wild boar bacon and parsley leaves
$22

MAINS

Maple glazed **boneless half chicken**, sweet potato mash and natural jus
$31
Braised **lamb shank** with white bean and turnip puree, roasted root vegetables
$33
Sage and ricotta ravioli with pecorino cheese, roasted squash and French beans
$27
Canadian AAA **prime rib of beef** with baked potato, seasonal vegetables & natural jus
10oz - $40   •   16oz - $55
Seared fillet of St. Stevens **salmon** with wild rice, potato hash, oranges, grapes and almonds
$32
Braised **beef short ribs** with flask cooked great northern beans and mashed potatoes
$31

Accents

Sutton Place Hotel
955 Bay Street
Toronto
416-924-9221

**Global
DOWNTOWN**

Wheelchair
  access
valet parking
V / MC / AmEx
breakfast
lunch
dinner
beer/wine
cocktails
high chairs
private parties
non-smoking
reservations
  required
dress informal
menu changes
  seasonally

Sutton Place saw the writing on the wall, gave up on fine dining, and jumped on the bistro bandwagon with the resources of a luxury hotel. Accents is all scaled-down swank, a 100-seat room of distinct European character and space to hear yourself think. The pragmatic all-day menu gallivants, and Nigel Didcock cooks, easily delivering fat sea bass blanketed in breadcrumbs, duck with Le Puy lentils, and risottos every which way. Graciousness is a holdover from another era. I witnessed servers scurrying to rescue some tall, gangling guy who forgot his room number: the somebody was Jack Palance.

APPETIZERS

Cured Atlantic Salmon
with Cucumber Noodles, Ginger Coriander Mousseline

Foie Gras Terrine
Jasmine Glazed Peaches and Brioche Points

Grilled Chicken Salad "Multicolor"
Horseradish, Fresh Ginger and Arugula Salad

Seared Crab Cakes
Celeryroot Slaw, Roasted Pepper Coulis and Chive Oil

MAIN COURSES

Potato Basket of Seared Scallops and Lobster
Tomato Coolant and Basil Points

Pan Seared Filets of St. Pierre
Parsley and Lemon Forked Potatoes and Chive Fondue

Pan Seared Veal Medallions and Sweetbreads
Buttered Corn and Fava Bean Succotash

Acqua

BCE Place
10 Front Street West
Toronto
416-368-7171
www.acquacatering.com

Global
FINANCIAL DISTRICT

Wheelchair
 access

V / MC / AmEx / DC

lunch

dinner

late supper

beer/wine

cocktails

high chairs

private parties

non-smoking

reservations
 recommended

dress casual

menu changes
 seasonally

Acqua, the last of the restaurants launched by
Franco Prevedello, lives up to its name with styl-
ized masts and sails jutting into the skylit atrium
of BCE Place. Suits from the towers powerlunch,
and after dark, the Hummingbird and Street
Lawrence Centres deliver the theatergoers—which
is just as well, because the cavernous public space
calls for a large and boisterous throng. Chef Robert
Buchanan's menu navigates the mainstream
adroitly, as in rack of lamb, perhaps preceded by
a dozen Malpeque oysters fresh off the ice. Maple
crème brûlée makes for a patriotic finish.

RISTORANTE E BAR

APPETIZERS & SALADS

BABY LETTUCES & COOKSTOWN ORGANIC SEEDLINGS with pear & ginger vinaigrette and toasted pinenuts	$6.95
FRESHLY SHUCKED EAST COAST OYSTERS with a selection of traditional garnishes	12.00
ACQUA'S CAESAR SALAD with romaine hearts and fresh shaved parmagiano	7.50
SAUTÉED CALAMARI SALAD soya ginger dipping sauce and Asian vegetable slaw	10.50
APPLEWOOD SMOKED SALMON with warm shrimp cake, lemon crème fraîche and shaved Bermuda onion	11.95
WILD MUSHROOM & TOMATO MINESTRONE with mascarpone ravioli, truffle oil & parmesan	10.95
PISTACHIO CRUSTED TUNA TARTARE with green apple & shallots, organic seedlings & nappa salad	11.95
WOOLWICH GOAT CHEESE GRATINÉE with arugula, prosciutto & Portobello mushrooms	10.95
ACQUA'S CHERRYSTONE AND LITTLENECK CLAM CHOWDER	5.95
ACQUA'S DAILY SOUP.......... no butter or cream	5.50

PASTA

PENNE with roasted plum tomato sauce, basil & roasted garlic	15.95
LINGUINE with Manila clams, garlic, white wine, shallots, extra virgin olive oil, red chilies & parsley	17.50
FETTUCINE CARBONARA	16.95
CAPPELLINI with seared shrimp, tomato concasse, julienne of snow peas tossed in lemon butter	22.95

SQUASH RISOTTO with duck confit & gorgonzola	Appetizer	11.95
	Main	19.95

MAIN COURSES

SEARED SUSHI GRADE FLUKE with a curried shrimp crust, coconut basmati rice with roasted almond soy emulsion	25.00
GRILLED SALMON with lobster & chive whipped potatoes, asparagus & roasted tomato-tarragon butter sauce	26.00
ROASTED FRESH AUSTRALIAN RACK OF LAMB provencál vegetable tian, seared Portobello mushrooms and rosemary grain mustard reduction	33.00

Across the Road

679 Mount Pleasant Road
Toronto
416-486-1111

Global
MIDTOWN

Valet parking

V / MC / AmEx / DC

dinner

late supper

take out

beer/wine

cocktails

private parties

non-smoking

reservations
recommended

dress casual

menu changes
seasonally

When restaurateur Peter Costa sold Pronto—the historic hothouse where Torontonians learned to love Cal-Ital and brilliant chefs Mark McEwan and Arpi Magyar earned their toques—to the Oliver Bonacini juggernaut (now it's Steakfrites), he took his food across the road and called it Across the Road. It's no groundbreaker, but the room is pretty and comfortable, servers pay attention, and chef Scott Stubbins is right at home with both fashionable Asian touches and gusts of garlic and rosemary. The antipasto platter, generous with grilled shrimps and squid, is a perennial favorite among the locals.

ACROSS THE ROAD

APPETIZERS

P.E.I. Mussels *in a ginger, coriander broth tossed with slivers of green mango* **9.95**

Charred Calamari *with anchiovies, capers, Gaeta olives, roasted garlic, tomato and fresh lemon* **9.95**

Grilled Mahogany Quails *on a bed of wild rice risotto* **9.95**

Grilled Tiger Shrimps *on a bed of baby greens with an eggplant, roasted pepper and goat cheese roulade* **10.95**

Baked Crab Cakes *served on a fennel, orange salad with grilled red onions* **10.95**

Phyllo Wrapped Brie *with a garlic, basil crostini and an apricot glaze* **10.95**

Antipasto Platter *for two or more, changes daily and **priced daily***

MAIN COURSES

Mushroom Stuffed Chicken Breast *with Truffle mashed potato and broccoli spears* **18.95**

Roasted Grain Fed Cornish Hen *on oven roasted root vegetables with a spicy jus* **19.95**

Herb Crusted Ontario Lamb Rack *oven roasted and served with garlic mashed potato, vegetables, natural juices and with fresh mint* **34.95**

Black Angus Striploin *served with a Cambozola potato Rosti, assorted vegetables and a port shallot jus* **30.95**

Baked European Sea Bass *with wild rice pilaf, sautéed spinach, and sundried tomatoes* **26.95**

Pistachio Crusted Salmon *with Asian greens, pineapple basil rice and a soya vinaigrette* **21.95**

Lamb Shank *with apple braised rice, assorted vegetables and rosemary gremolada* **18.95**

Grilled Veal Medallions *on a bed oven roasted sweet potatoes, swiss chard, oyster mushrooms, and a Pommery mustard jus* **24.95**

Adega

33 Elm Street
Toronto
416-977-4338
www.adegarestaurant.ca

Portuguese
DOWNTOWN

V / MC / AmEx / DC

lunch

dinner

beer/wine

cocktails

private parties

non-smoking

reservations
recommended

dress casual

menu changes
weekly

A downtown partnership for Portuguese wizard Albino Silva, Adega sits in a lovely ochre house, its interior glowing with stuccoed walls, rain-washed terra-cotta hues and a prize collection of paintings from Picasso contemporary René Marcil. Concessions to the mainstream location (Caesar, pastas, risottos) take nothing away from co-owner Manny Botelho's fix on intensely grilled sardines, salmon, and squid with a rainbow of Mediterranean accents. Three-term former Canadian Prime Minister Jean Chrétien has chosen to nosh at the pizza joint next door, while his RCMP bodyguards dined so much better here—as have actresses Meryl Streep, Rachel Ward, and Salma Hayek.

Pastas & Risotto's

Penne with Grilled Chicken & Portuguese Chourico Sausage
in a tomato basil sauce $12.95
Fettuccine & Smoked Salmon
in a tomato vodka cream with grilled leeks $13.50
Seafood Linguini
in a fresh tomato sauce $16.50
Wild Mushroom & Seasonal Vegetable Risotto $13.50
Risotto of Fresh Fish & Seafood $16.75

Entrees

Grilled Atlantic Salmon
crusted with fresh herbs & marine salt $16.95
Grilled Squid
with lemon , coriander, garlic & olive oil $16.95
Grilled Octopus
with a tomato, red onion & olive salsa $18.25
Grilled Salted Cod
with roasted garlic & olive oil $17.95
Pan Roasted Capon Breast
spiced with Piri Piri hot peppered olive oil sauce $15.95

Adriatico

14 Dupont Street
Toronto
416-323-7442

Seafood
MIDTOWN

Valet parking

V / MC / AmEx / DC

lunch

dinner

beer/wine

cocktails

private parties

reservations
  recommended

dress informal

menu changes
  daily

Millennia living off the fruits of the Adriatic pay off in Toronto's only Italian fish and seafood house. Octopus, the fleshy whitefish known as branzino, and marvelous grills in clouds of herbs are siren calls in a lovely room with flickering candles in whitewashed niches and flamboyant Majolica dinnerware. Here's to chef Eduardo Deberardinis for groundbreaking courage: the restaurant serves no beef, lamb, veal, or chicken. It only serves fish—the freshest fish, some all the way from the Adriatic, some unfamiliar, some (like the giant scampi) leaving us wide-eyed—on a menu that trounces silly landlubber prejudices. Now where are the fresh anchovies?

RISTORANTE|ADRIATICO

crostini misti
assorted seafood bruschetta   *7.00*

ostriche crude al limone
raw oysters with lemon - half dozen   *ea. 1.85*

vongole in umido
sauté of clams in a white wine sauce   *8.50*

cozze in umido rosate
steamed mussels in a light tomato sauce   *8.50*

carpaccio di tonno con olio d'oliva, capperi e limone
blue fin tuna carpaccio drizzled with extra
virgin olive oil, capers and lemon   *10.50*

seppie alla griglia con olio d'oliva, prezzemelo e aglio
grilled cuttlefish drizzled in extra virgin olive oil,
parsley and garlic   *19.00*

brodetto di pesce alla silvarola
assorted fish and seafood in a fresh tomato broth   *24.00*

tranci di palombo in umido al pomodoro e capperi
slices of shark in a light tomato sauce with capers   *20.00*

pescatrice con olive e finocchi infornate
monkfish broiled with olives and fennel   *21.00*

Agora

Art Gallery of Ontario
317 Dundas Street West
416-979-6612
www.ago.net

Global
DOWNTOWN WEST

Wheelchair
 access

V / MC / AmEx / DC

Saturday and
 Sunday brunch

lunch (T- F)

beer/wine

cocktails

high chairs

private parties

non-smoking

reservations
 recommended

dress informal

menu changes
 with exhibit

The restaurant of the Art Gallery of Ontario is suitably vast and airy, part gallery, part sanctuary—and contrary to rumor—not just for ladies who lunch. I can't think of a classier or more civilized milieu for old-fashioned conversation. Menus change according to featured exhibitions: for Matisse, they served Provençal and Moroccan with appropriate music. My god, what will they do for the Dalí? Chef Anne Yarymowich focuses on upscale ingredients and artful plating—a "still life" starter is almost too beautiful for knife and fork—and standards slip only as servers turn to Keystone Kops under the pressure of a full house.

appetizers

seasonally inspired soup $8

composition in blue and green: warm blue potato salad on green leaf lettuce and mustard cress, with braised leeks and crumbled stilton cheese $12

spinach salad in a warm bacon and red wine-shallot vinaigrette, garlic croutons, poached organic egg $10

still life with mushrooms: roasted oyster, shiitake and honey mushrooms with crisp parmesan tuile, white truffle oil and balsamic glaze $10

poached oak island choice oysters served warm on baguette crouton with brandade de morue and ocetra caviar $15

seared quebec duck foie gras on toasted brioche with crabapple gelée and pickled crabapples $15

entrées

butternut squash and extra old cheddar soufflé with caramelized apples and squash, toasted walnuts and apple cider-walnut oil vinaigrette $16

chicken pot pie served with plum chutney and salade vinaigrette $16

grilled trout fillet with warm french lentil, pancetta and frisée salad, garlic aïoli and fingerling potato crisps $16

duck leg confit with sour cherry compote, sweet potato mash and watercress salad dressed with sour cherry vinaigrette $17

Ambassador

280 West Beaver Creek Road
Richmond Hill
905-731-5570

Chinese
SUBURBAN NORTH

Wheelchair
  access
V / MC / AmEx
lunch
dinner
late supper
take out
beer/wine
cocktails
high chairs
private parties
non-smoking
reservations
  recommended
dress casual
menu changes
  seasonally

The bright and brassy Ambassador specializes in high-end banquets focused on such icons as shark's fin, abalone, and clawless rock lobster, with the ten-person, ten-course Deluxe Royal, on sale at a mere $888. Some accents baffle—why bother with such foolishness as jumbo shrimps with fruit salad or maraschino cherries?—but Cantonese refinement kicks in with hot-and-sour soup festooned with seafood, succulent black cod done in a hot pot with pork and five-spice, and one of Toronto's great, crispy-skinned, juicy-fleshed Peking ducks. The dim sum slate, rhyming off eighty items, packs in the lunch crowd seven days a week.

湯羹類
Soup

	例 Regular	每位 Per person
麗華彩棠羹 *Rainbow broth* *a colorful selection of fresh market seafood in* *a thick chicken stock, crowned with caviar*	$ 24.00	$ 6.00
蟹肉魚肚羹 *Fresh Alaska king crab bisque with fish maw*	$ 48.00	$ 12.00
瑤柱花膠鴨絲羹 *Aromatic broth* *studded with fish maw, julienne of duckling,* *mushrooms and sun-dried mandarin peel*	$ 32.00	$ 8.00
雞茸粟米羹 *Diced chicken in a thickened soup flattered with* *sweet corn and drops of egg white*	$ 22.00	$ 5.50
海皇酸辣湯 *Hot and sour soup* *with diced seafood and deep forest mushrooms*	$ 22.00	$ 5.50

Anatolia

5112 Dundas Street West
Toronto
416-207-0596
www.anatoliarestaurant.ca

Turkish
WEST TORONTO

V / MC
lunch
dinner
take out
beer/wine
high chairs
private parties
non-smoking
reservations
  recommended
dress casual

Unquestionably one of the world's great crossroads cuisines, Turkish renders Greek witless by comparison. Toronto's only Turkish restaurant sits in a dreary strip mall in the megacity's west end, but owner Ayse Aydemir compensates with warmth and authenticity. Her meze, a procession of appetizers, includes deeply smoked eggplant puree; feathery boreks or phyllo "cigars" stuffed with feta and patties of minced beef, cracked wheat, walnuts, and spices. Main dishes tend towards massive kebabs of charred chicken, beef, and lamb, but Anatolia busts out on the month's first Friday, when a belly dancer gyrates and off-menu wonders may prove worthy of the Istanbul sultans.

Anatolia
Traditional Turkish Cuisine

Mantı
House specialty, mini dumplings filled with seasoned ground beef, topped with yogurt, mint, melted butter and ground red pepper.......................$7.95

Shish Kebab
A skewer of marinated lamb or chicken grilled to perfection and served with rice and a garden salad.
chicken..$10.50
lamb......$12.95

Ali Nazik Kebabı
Squares of succulent grilled lamb served on a bed of pureed eggplant and garlic yogurt, topped with warm butter and a light tomato sauce........$12.95

Talaş Böreği
Puff pastry filled with zuccini, eggplant, potatoes and onions, ovenbaked and served with a garden salad...$8.50

Adana Kebabı
Named after the city of origin, spicy ground beef & lamb shish kebab, bar-b-qued and served with rice, domates ezmesi, and a garden salad............... $11.95

Yoğurtlu Adana
This variation of the kebab is served on a bed of toasted pita bread with a hearty side of yogurt, topped with a light tomato sauce.....................$12.50

Beyti
Lightly grilled spicy ground beef and lamb wrapped in a pastry topped with savoury tomato sauce. Served with lettuce, yogurt, and sauted onions...........$12.95

Karışık Isgara
Mixed grill including lamb chops, adana kebab (chicken) shish kebab (lamb) served with rice, domates ezmesi and garden salad................ $19.50
2 people $35.95
4 people $69.95

Weekend Specials - Iskender, Döner & Midye Tava (Mussels)
Ask your server!

Annona

Park Hyatt Hotel
4 Avenue Road
Toronto
416-925-1234
www.parkhyatt.com

Global
MIDTOWN

- Wheelchair access
- valet parking
- V / MC / AmEx / D / DC
- Saturday and Sunday brunch
- breakfast
- lunch
- dinner
- beer/wine
- cocktails
- private parties
- non-smoking
- reservations recommended
- dress informal
- menu changes seasonally

Gone is the celebrated Rooftop restaurant (now the preserve of private functions) and its beloved panoramic view. The Annona, a $1 million, street-side restaurant at the Park Hyatt Hotel hasn't set the world on fire, but it's been winning friends steadily with clubby blue-and-gold surroundings, moderate prices (for a hotel dining room) and chef Joan Monfaredi's snappy take on cooking that falls somewhere on the high side of bistro. On a good day, this translates as a juicy slab of tuna grilled just-so and served under a tony mop of crisply frizzled vegetables.

R E S T A U R A N T

Lobster Bisque	Coral cream, brandy, straw potato	9
Sautéed Foie Gras	Quatre épiced quail breast, grilled pear, spinach with warm bacon citrus vinaigrette, rhubarb dark side chutney	17
Curry Spiced Shrimp	Steamed thin cut vegetables, coriander white wine sauce, coconut chutney	10
Grilled Venison Chop	Butternut squash puree, arugula with preserved lemon vinaigrette	13
Seared Tuna	Salad of avocado jicama, orange segments, spicy cilantro lime vinaigrette, lotus root crisps	11
Sautéed Crab Cakes	Avocado salsa, aged balsamic reduction	12
Arugula and Spinach Salad	Black olive crisp, chilled ratatouille, smoked tomato vinaigrette	9
Tequila Cured Salmon	Chili polenta crisps, mixed seedlings, black bean relish	12
Lobster Ravioli	Truffle tarragon cream sauce, crisp carrots, sauteed spinach	12
Crisp Slow Roasted Duck	Corn and wild rice waffle, braised rapini, orange infused tarragon jus	26
Seafood Risotto	Seasonal mushrooms and asparagus, parmesan-reggiano, tarragon	19
Rummo Spire pasta	Light tomato sauce, oven roasted garlic and sweet peppers, mushrooms, red onions, goats cheese, fresh herbs	17
Pan Seared Rainbow Trout	Gingered carrot mash, chili verjus beurre blanc, baby bokchoy	23
Grilled Salmon Fillet	Caper parsley vinaigrette, potato gratinée, warm watercress and mushroom salad	22
Pan Seared Sea Bass	Aged balsamic reduction, roast sweet potato, sautéed spinach	24
Roasted Chicken Breast	Queso manchego, oven dried tomato, pan juices, braised lentils, sauteed rapini	23
Roast Rack of Lamb	Cloudberry shallot sauce, chive mash, herbed vegetable spears	29
Grilled Provimi Veal Chop	Truffle Yukon gold mash, mushroom ragout, steamed French beans	32

Arax

1966 Queen Street East
Toronto
416-693-5707

Bistro
THE BEACH

V / MC / AmEx

dinner

late supper

take out

beer/wine

cocktails

private parties

non-smoking
section

reservations
recommended

dress casual

menu changes
seasonally

My neighborhood, the village known as the Beach or Beaches—the name is a controversy among the cranky urban hermits who inhabit the vicinity—has rarely been lucky with restaurants (possibly because cranky urban hermits don't eat out). A cheerful exception is the exuberant Raffi Asperian's pocket-sized dining room specializing in mezes, the Eastern Mediterranean answer to Spanish tapas and Chinese dim sum. On weekends, expect a party, with Asparian, his persona wavering somewhere between Zorba the Armenian and mad monk Rasputin, haranguing customers to boogie atop the bar and whirling around the room with cunningly orchestrated platters of lemon-infused, garlic-scented exotica.

A R A X
MEDITERRANEAN   CUISINE

CALAMARI $6.95
Crispy Pan Fried served with Special Garlic Dip

CAESAR SALAD $6.75
Romaine lettuce tossed in creamy garlic dressing, Pita Croutons

GARLIC SHRIMPS $9.95
Peel & Eat Shrimps, sauteed in a Creamy Garlic Parsley Sauce

GREEK SALAD $6.95
Feta Cheese, Lettuce, Tomato, Onion, Cucumber, Oregano Dressing

GARLIC ZUCCHINI $5.95
Crispy Pan Fried in Tempura-like Batter with Lemon Garlic Sauce

ARTICHOKE SALAD $6.75
Hearts of Artichoke, Tomato, Onion, Parsley, Garlic and Olive Oil

GRAPE LEAVES $6.95
Vine Leaves, Stuffed Rice, Onion, cooked in Olive Oil and Herbs

Auberge du Pommier

4150 Yonge Street
Toronto
416-222-2220
www.oliverbonacini.com

French
UPTOWN

Wheelchair
  access
V / MC / AmEx / DC
lunch
dinner
late supper
beer/wine
cocktails
private parties
non-smoking
reservations
  recommended
dress jacket/tie
menu changes
  seasonally

Just beyond the roar of the sixteen-lane Highway 401 lies a French country restaurant that recalls that dreamy afternoon in Provence or Dordogne: walls of honeyed stone, beamed ceilings, vested and aproned servers, and a dappled terrace render it a resplendent bauble in the Oliver Bonacini crown. Auberge delivers sophisticated French cuisine hallmarked by inventive pairings and barely a trace of nouvelle silliness. Veal breast takes an Asian turn and veal tenderloin a French one on the same plate. Pan-seared scallops atop braised oxtail seamlessly redefine surf 'n' turf. Corporate wheeling and dealing and intimate tête-à-têtes blissfully coexist.

PAN FRIED MEDITERRANEAN SARDINES
on roasted red peppers and a fig and nut compote
$15.00

CRÈME DE HOMARD
creamed lobster soup with white beans and a parsley chantilly
$11.50

TORCHON OF FOIE GRAS
marinated in Muscat de Beaumes de Venise with an orange, lingonberry and pine nut salad
$19.00

HAND PICKED SWEET AND BITTER GREENS
With a sherry Dijon vinaigrette
$9.50

GRENOUILLE À LA PROVENÇAL
black peppered boneless frog legs with ratatouille
$16.00

BUTTER POACHED LOBSTER "À LA NAGE"
in a laurel and Riesling broth with paysanne vegetables
$39.00

GRILLED ENTRECÔTE FORESTIÈRE
10oz. striploin steak and frites, sautéed wild mushrooms,
*and béarnaise sauce or à la **Tradition du Chef***
$38.00

BRAISED VEAL SHANK "AU PISTOU"
with root vegetables, northern bean jus and basil purée
$34.00

ALMOND CRUSTED GROUPER FILLET
with pommes croquette, grilled mushrooms and a cauliflower truffle velouté
$37.00

Avalon

270 Adelaide Street West
Toronto
416-979-9919

Global
DOWNTOWN WEST

V / MC / AmEx / DC

lunch on
  Thursdays only

dinner

beer/wine

cocktails

private parties

non-smoking

reservations
  required

dress business
  casual

menu changes
  daily

Much-acclaimed chef Chris McDonald took a doomed space (it used to be Coco Lezzone, which used to be Hot Gossip) in the Entertainment District and, with consummate skills and attention to detail, transformed it into the solid gold of Avalon. No list of the city's top ten ignores this one, despite McDonald's admirable disregard of fashion: The Avalon faithful don't rave about fusion and fantasia, but about the perfect roast chicken from the wood-burning oven, the perfect steak, the perfect mashed spud, and the untrendy presence of offal—not just obligatory seared foie gras, but calf brains and sweetbreads sauced in chanterelles.

AVALON

FIRST COURSES

KUMAMOTO OYSTERS ON THE HALF~SHELL WITH CHAMPAGNE MIGNONETTE
2.75 / PIECE
BABY GREENS WITH SHERRY VINAIGRETTE
8.75
GRILLED SARDINES WITH A PRESERVED LEMON, GREEN OLIVE
& FENNEL SALAD
9.00
DUCK CONSOMMÉ WITH DUCK CONFIT RAVIOLI
10.00
GRILLED PORTOBELLO MUSHROOM CROSTINO WITH CHÈVRE NOIR,
EGGPLANT & WHITE BEAN PURÉE, RAPINI AND ROASTED RED PEPPERS
13.50

MAIN COURSES

ROAST BREAST OF GRAIN~FED CHICKEN WITH ASPARAGUS, WILD RICE
AND JERUSALEM ARTICHOKE SAUCE
28.00
CHOUCROUTE OF ATLANTIC SALMON WITH PETIT GRIS ESCARGOTS,
ROAST GARLIC AND FINES HERBES
29.00
PAN~ROASTED SKATE WITH A BEET GREEN GRATIN AND CHILPACHOLE SAUCE
29.00
rLY SMOKED MOULARD DUCK BREAST WITH POMMES ANNA, BRAISED RED CABBA
ROAST PEARL ONIONS AND BLACK CURRANT SAUCE
30.00
AVALON POT-AU-FEU WITH A TRIO OF SAUCES
30.00
YELLOWFIN TUNA, GRILLED RARE, WITH ARTICHOKE FRITTERS, WILTED FRISÉE
AND HORSERADISH SAUCE
34.00

Avenue

Four Seasons Hotel
21 Avenue Road
Toronto
416-928-7332
www.fourseasons.com

Global
YORKVILLE

Wheelchair
access

valet parking

V / MC / AmEx / DC

Sunday brunch

lunch

dinner

late supper

beer/wine

cocktails

live
entertainment

private parties

non-smoking
section

reservations
recommended

dress informal

menu changes
seasonally

Designer Brian Gluckstein's onyx bar (more like an altar to the goddess of Yorkville), serendipitous glimpses of movie stars (Denzel Washington, Ethan Hawke) at play, a crowd dressed (or undressed) to turn heads, extravagant drinks (fifteen takes on the martini, including lychee, mango, and chocolate), tony munchies (vegetable chips, dried beans), and the most ambitious "bar" food in town all make Avenue the sizzler among Toronto watering holes. Executive chef Lynn Crawford's menu caters to grazers and sharers: oysters on the half-shell, lobster Caesar, pizza with truffle oil, first-rate steak tartare; thank heavens she's gotten rid of the silly foie gras burger.

AVENUE

⌘ SINKU OYSTERS FROM BRITISH COLUMBIA ON THE HALF SHELL,
CHAMPAGNE MIGNONETTE, CLASSIC COCKTAIL SAUCE.....18.00

•

SUMMER VEGETABLE MINESTRONE, TORTELLINI OF HAM HOCK
AND ROASTED SWEET GARLIC.....8.00

•

"AVENUE" BEEF BURGER OR GRILLED CHICKEN BREAST
WITH LETTUCE, TOMATO AND PICKLES.....15.00
CHOICE OF ROASTED ONIONS, MUSHROOMS AND AGED CHEDDAR CHEESE

•

◆ ROCKET PIZZA WITH SUNCHOKES, REGGIANO AND TRUFFLE OIL.....14.00

•

⌘ GRILLED RARE AHI TUNA SANDWICH, TOASTED SESAME ROLL
ASIAN SLAW AND PRESERVED GINGER......18.00

•

CLASSIC CAESAR SALAD.....9.00
WITH CHICKEN.....16.00   WITH LOBSTER.....24.00

•

NEW YORK STEAK SANDWICH, GRILLED ROSEMARY SOUR DOUGH
"BEEFSTEAK" TOMATOES AND BUTTERMILK ONION RINGS.....21.00

•

⌘ VIETNAMESE SHRIMP SALAD ROLLS
SWEET AND SOUR DIPPING SAUCE.....12.00

Avli

401 Danforth Avenue
Toronto
416-461-9577
www.avlirestaurant.com

Greek
DANFORTH

V / MC / AmEx / DC

lunch

dinner

late supper

take out

beer/wine

cocktails

booster seats

live
   entertainment

private parties

non-smoking

dress casual

There is a sense that, among Danforth tavernas, Avli works a little harder for its regulars. Owners Lambros Vassiliou, who fronts the room with Zorba-like largesse, and Sharon Murray, a Newfoundlander, show a preference for the grill over the deep fryer. The fish is fresh (reliable snapper, red mullet from Greece, soft-shell crab in season). Juicy lamb shank is a signature, as are the hefty rabbit–pearl onion and chicken-rosemary pies, whose flaky olive-oil pastry sends you home feeling like a stuffed goose. Vegetarians, falling back on moussaka piled with eggplant, zucchini, and chickpeas, do not go without.

AVLI
r e s t a u r a n t

Lamb Shank...*slowly baked with sun dried tomato & wine served over orzo pasta (a house favorite)* $16.95

Small Lamb Shank... *served the same as above but a smaller portion* $11.95

Meat Moussaka...*baked layers of eggplant, zucchini & potatoes filled with ground beef topped with béchamel cream, served with a green salad* $12.95

Half Free Range Stuffed Chicken...*½ chicken deboned & stuffed with cashews, dates, apples & rice finished with a light cream sauce served with potatoes & vegetables* $15.95

Quarter Free Range Stuffed Chicken... *served the same as above but a smaller portion* $9.95

Rabbit & Pearl Onion (stiffado) Pie...*deboned rabbit & pearl onions simmered in port wine, cinnamon, cloves, rosemary, and garlic* $15.95

Seafood Feta Tomato Pie...*shrimp, scallops, mussels, and fish of the day baked in a spicy tomato sauce with feta cheese* $14.95

Chicken Mushroom Rosemary Pie...*free range chicken, fresh rosemary, and pinenuts simmered in white wine & butter* $12.95

Grilled Lamb chops *with tzatziki, wedge homefries & vegetables* $16.95

Vegetarian Specialities

$5.50 each or any three for $12.95

Baked Eggplant & Pine nuts	Grilled Leek & Sweet Pepper
Giant Beans & Tomato Casserole	Grilled Zucchini & Goat Cheese

Vegetarian Moussaka...*baked layers of eggplant, zucchini & potatoes filled with chickpeas, green beans, carrots, and celery in a tomato sauce topped with béchamel cream, served with a green salad* $12.95

Fettuccini... *with your choice of a tomatoes with herbs or white cream sauce* $8.95

41

Babur

273 Queen Street West
Toronto
416-599-7720

Indian
QUEEN WEST VILLAGE

Wheelchair
access

V / MC / AmEx / DC

Sunday brunch

lunch

dinner

late supper

take out

beer/wine

cocktails

high chairs

private parties

non-smoking

reservations
recommended

dress casual

menu changes
seasonally

Babur's marble walls recall the Taj, the glassed-in tandoor pit presents a turbaned chef tossing chapatis and kebabs, tables come set with copper flagons of drinking water, and the kitchen sends out spicy, layered flavors worthy of the Moghuls who ruled India in the name of Allah. Babur's fluffy samosas are the best in town. I've never eaten a finer chicken curry in Delhi or Bombay and the daily lunch buffet is an affair of such abundance, I need a winch to get me out the door. Kingfisher beer comes imported from India, but where are my favorite Indian labels, Guru, Thunderbolt, and Stud?

BABUR
INDIAN CUISINE

Tandoori   *(Barbecued in clay ovens and served on sizzlers)*

Tandoori Chicken	*Chicken marinated in yogurt, garlic, ginger and cooked in Tandoor*	*full*	$ 21.50
		half	$ 10.95
Anarkali Bahar	*Boneless chicken marinated in yogurt, garlic and ginger and cooked in Tandoor with vegetables*		$ 11.95
Fish Tikka	*Boneless fish marinated in yogurt and cooked in Tandoor*		$ 12.95
Seekh Kabab *(Full)*	*Minced lamb meat blended with spices and herbs. Cooked on skewers in Tandoor*		$ 10.95
Shashlik Paneer	*Home-made cottage cheese marinated in yogurt and cooked in Tandoor. Served with vegetables*		$ 11.95

Chicken

Butter Chicken	*Boneless chicken marinated in yogurt and spices, barbecued in Tandoor and cooked in cream sauce*	$ 11.95
Chicken Vindaloo	*Boneless chicken cooked with potatoes in hot and sour sauces*	$ 9.95
Murgh Bhoona	*Boneless chicken stir-fried with spices*	$ 10.95
Murgh de Gama	*Chicken marinated for a day, fried in batter and cooked with herbs and spices*	$ 10.95
Murgh Nawabi	*Boneless chicken cooked in cream sauce with nuts*	$ 11.95
Pili-Pili Chicken	*Boneless chicken stir-fried with hot spices, pepper and chili. Served on a sizzler*	$ 11.95
Mango Chicken	*Chicken marinated for a day, fried in batter and cooked with mango*	$ 12.95

Meat

Rhogan Josh	*Aromatic lamb stir fried and cooked in whole spices in yogurt*	$ 10.95
Mutton Tikka Masala	*Lamb simmered and cooked in a piquant sauce with tomatoes and onions*	$ 10.95
Beef Masala	*Beef simmered and cooked in a piquant sauce with tomatoes and onions*	$ 10.95

Ban Vanipha

638 Dundas Street West
Toronto
416-340-0491

Southeast Asian
DOWNTOWN WEST

V / MC

lunch

dinner

take out

beer/wine

cocktails

high chairs

non-smoking

reservations
recommended

dress casual

menu changes
seasonally

Peter Thavone's Lao–Northern Thai restaurant is cousin to Vanipha Lanna and proffers the same addictive spicy cuisine found in the backstreets of Vientiane or Chiang Mai. In the sticky heat of summer, such fare brings a gentle rain of lemongrass, kaffir lime, and chiles; in winter bluster, seething Southeast Asian memories. The kitchen can be fastidious at the expense of speed—don't plan on a movie afterwards—but it's worth the wait. I'll go the distance for *mee grob,* which combines chicken and shrimp with vermicelli noodles soaked in sweet-and-sour sauce, then deep-fried to delectable crunchiness. Yes, it sounds like a mess, but I'd go back for it.

THAI NOODLE

Pad Thai_____$9.25
-Stir-fry of soft rice noodles w/ chicken &
shrimps topped w/ peanuts

Khao Soy Hoe_____$9.25
-Northern Thai style egg noodles served w/ rich
coconut beef curry sauce

Mee Grob_____$9.25
-Crispy vermicelli noodles tossed w/ chicken &
shrimp in sweet & sour sauce

Mee Hank_____$9.25
-Stir-fried egg noodles w/ chicken & shrimps in
spicy lime coriander sauce topped w/ peanuts

Khao Poon Garee Nuar_____$9.25
-Laotian style soft vermicelli noodles w/ beef
curry lemongrass sauce topped w/ peanut

Vientiane Noodle_____$9.25
-Stir-fried vegetables w/ rice noodles in spicy
yellow curry sauce

THAI CURRY

Gang Ped Gai_____$9.25
-Chicken in spicy red coconut curry sauce

Gang Hung Lay_____$9.25
-Northern Thai spicy beef yellow coconut curry

Gang Kheao Goong_____$10.95
-Shrimps in spicy green coconut curry sauce

Gang Kheao Phed_____$10.95
-Duck pineapple in spicy green coconut sauce

POULTRY

Ping Gai_____$8.95
-Laotian marinated B.B.Q. chicken served w/
spicy coriander sauce

Pad Gai Holapha_____$9.25
-Chicken stir-fry w/ vegetables, hot chilies &
fresh Thai basil

Larp Gai_____$8.95
-Laotian style chicken w/ mint, garlic, onion,
lemongrass, coriander & chili rice powder

Pad Gai Mark Moung_____$9.25
-Chicken stir-fry w/ fresh mango, chilies &
assorted vegetables

Bangkok Garden

18 Elm Street
Toronto
416-977-6748
www.bangkokgarden.ca

Southeast Asian
DOWNTOWN

V / MC / AmEx / DC

lunch

dinner

take out &
  delivery

beer/wine

cocktails

high chairs

private parties

non-smoking

reservations
  recommended

dress casual

menu changes
  weekly

The racy cuisine of the Land of Smiles sizzles across town, but Bangkok Garden, in business for more than two decades, remains the Dowager Empress of Toronto Thai. I eat here simply because it's a gorgeously authentic room, a two-level teak palace that manages to evoke memories of shimmering temples, serene Buddhas, dazzling spice markets, and voyages up the Maekok River in long-necked canoes. The kitchen proves adroit with lemongrass-infused soups and red and green curries silken with coconut milk, but disappointing with dishes that should call for five-alarm chile fires.

THAI CURRIES

Vegetable Curry - Choice of Emerald Curry
with vegetables or Red Curry w/ vegetables
and pineapple. *$15.95*

Tamarind Beef Curry - Curry of beef with
potatoes & whole unroasted peanuts. *$19.25*

Pineapple Shrimp Curry - Curry w/ fresh lime leaves,
plump shrimp & fresh pineapple. *$19.25*

FROM THE WOK

Cashews with Chicken Stir-Fry *$16.95*

Ramwong Scallops - Scallops stir-fried
w/ spring onions, chillies, sweet peppers
& fresh herbs. *$17.95*

Demon's Dare - Slices of beef stir-fried w/
fresh chillies, basil & Thai spices. *$15.95*

Ginger Chicken Stir-Fry - *$15.95*

Barberian's

7 Elm Street
Toronto
416-597-0335

Steakhouse
DOWNTOWN

Wheelchair
  access
V / MC / AmEx / DC
lunch
dinner
late supper
take out
beer/wine
cocktails
high chairs
private parties
non-smoking
reservations
  recommended
dress casual

Toronto's most venerated testosterone temple is
not the work of barbarians, but an Armenian
named Barberian. The steakhouse to beat since
the late Harry Barberian opened the room in 1959,
it's neither changed nor franchised, maintaining a
carnivorous continuum of juicy, charred steaks
(a twenty-four-ounce porterhouse looks about the
size of a Volkswagen) and baked potatoes dolloped
with sour cream and chives. The restaurant seems
to call for a time machine—Burton and Taylor
first got engaged here in 1964—but limos are more
the order at the Elm Street landmark. Barberian's
twenty-first century wrinkle is wine, a thirty-three-
page list of more than a thousand labels.
Cheers, Harry.

BILL OF FARE
ENTREES

Centre Cut Top Sirloin (9oz)	26.50
Rib Steak (16oz)	33.00
Rib Steak (24oz)	46.00
Filet Mignon Wrapped In Bacon (8oz)	35.50
Filet Mignon Wrapped In Bacon (12oz)	49.00
New York Sirloin Steak (10oz)	33.00
New York Sirloin Steak (16oz)	49.00
Roast Prime Rib of Beef	33.00
Porter House Steak (24oz)	48.00
Chateaubriand For Two	74.75

• Pepper Steak Version for Any Steak 4.00
• Béarnaise Sauce 4.00

Lemon Grilled Free Range Capon	24.50
Barbecue Baby Back Ribs	28.75
Grilled Atlantic Salmon Steak	24.75
Double Thick Pork Chop	25.50
Fresh Fish of The Day	26.00
Beef Tenderloin Brochette	29.00
Grilled Rack of Lamb	39.50
Surf & Turf *(Filet Mignon & 1/2 Live Lobster)*	*Market Price*
Nova Scotia Lobster *(Steamed Or Broiled)*	*Market Price*

Garlic Bread, Delicious Kosher Dills and Crisp
French Fries, Baked Potato or Rice served with each order.

ACCOMPANIMENTS

Sauté Onions	4.00
Sauté Mushrooms	4.00
Onion Rings	4.00
Mashed Potatoes	4.00
Fresh Vegetable of the Day	5.00
Fresh Spinach	5.00

Bb33 Bistro+ Brasserie

Delta Chelsea Hotel
33 Gerrard Street West
Toronto
416-585-4319

Canadian
DOWNTOWN

Wheelchair
  access
valet parking
V / MC / AmEx /
  D / DC
Sunday brunch
breakfast
lunch
dinner
beer/wine
cocktails
high chairs
private parties
non-smoking
reservations
  recommended
dress casual
menu changes
  seasonally

A daring move for middle-of-the-road Delta Hotels, Bb33 seems a tad precious (the "brasserie" still looks like a hotel coffee shop to me), but the much more intimate Canadian bistro better lives up to its promise with candelight, knowledgeable servers, and diligent cooking from chef Margaret MacKay. MacKay has the most fun with game dishes: venison carpaccio drizzled with tangerine oil, deer osso buco, and flaky *tortiere* that manages to do something useful with wild boar and bison, a couple of beasts that constantly disappoint on most plates. MacKay goes clear over the top when she stuffs foie gras into a baked apple. Surprisingly, it works.

Soups, Salads & Beginnings

SLOW ROASTED CARROT AND GINGER SOUP - 8

FRENCH CANADIAN STYLE ONION SOUP WITH AGED QUEBEC CHEDDAR - 8

RED OAK LEAF SALAD WITH SMOKED CAESAR DRESSING AND SHAVED REGGIANO -9

ROASTED ASPARAGUS AND YOUNG SPINACH SALAD WITH WARM BACON AND PEARL ONION DRESSING -10

SEARED SEA SCALLOPS WITH SWEET MINERS LETTUCE, ORGANIC RED CARROT AND BALSAMIC GLAZE-14

P.E.I MUSSELS STEAMED WITH PIMENTON, VQA CHARDONNAY AND ROASTED RED PEPPER -10

B.C. HOUSE CURED SABLEFISH COUPLED WITH SMOKED ATLANTIC SALMON WITH ROASTED BEET
SALAD, HORSERADISH AND DILL CRÈME FRAICHE-14

ESCARGOT BAKED WITH QUEBEC BENEDICTON BLUE CHEESE-11

SHRIMP MARTINI
WITH ALL-CANADIAN COCKTAIL SAUCE - 14

"New Canadian" Main Course

BAKED SALMON IN MUSTARD CRUST WITH RED PEPPER JUS - 26

APPLE BLOSSOM HONEY AND MINT MARINATED ONTARIO RACK OF LAMB -34

PAN-SEARED ARCTIC CHAR WITH ONTARIO WILD MUSTARD BEURRE BLANC -28

MARITIME LOBSTER AND SCALLOP HOTPOT SIMMERED IN BRANDIED BISQUE SAUCE-34

ROAST PORK TENDERLOIN STUFFED WITH SOUR CHERRY AND CHESTNUT WITH CIDER GLAZE -26

"STEAK FRITES", 8 OZ ALBERTA AAA STRIPLOIN AU JUS WITH FRESH CUT YUKON GOLD FRITES -29

HOMEMADE LEMON GNOCCI WITH SAGE BUTTER -21

ROASTED RED DEER CHOPS WITH YUKON SALMONBERRY GLAZE -33

SAFFRON LINGUINI WITH SMOKED CHICKEN AND NICOISE OLIVES IN PLUM TOMATO SAUCE-24

WILD BOAR AND BISON TORTIERE WITH SASKATOON BERRY CHUTNEY-39

GRILLED BONELESS CHICKEN WITH FRITES OR YUKON GOLD MASH POTATO -24

18 OZ CHAUTEAUBRIAND FOR 2, CARVED TABLESIDE WITH ORGANIC VEGETABLES AND ROASTED POTATO
SERVED WITH CABERNET JUS AND BEARNAISE WITH ORGANIC TARRAGON-65

Benihana

The Fairmont Royal York
100 Front Street
Toronto
416-860-5002

Japanese
DOWNTOWN

Wheelchair
  access
valet parking
V / MC / AmEx / DC
lunch
dinner
take out
beer/wine
cocktails
high chairs
private parties
non-smoking
reservations
  recommended
dress informal

Teppanyaki is the gastronomic sidekick to karaoke, which was conceived in Japan for Western tourists, and when it succeeded beyond imagination, it became entrenched in the bedrock of Japanese pop culture. At Benihana in the Royal York Hotel, *gai jin* hordes huddle around stainless steel teppan grills as toqued samurai slice and dice, sear and sizzle seafood, chicken, and beef, much of it flying through the air. There's a big sushi bar, too, but Benihana's prevailing charm is its raucous party atmosphere. The sake cocktail list speaks of a new liquid dimension in East-West fusion.

Benihana Onion Soup   4.50
Japanese consommé with onions, mushrooms and scallions

Miso Soup   5.00
Tofu, green onion and wakame seaweed in bonito broth

Age Nasu   7.00
Tender eggplant with a creamy sesame dressing

Sunomo Salad   8.50
Sweet baby shrimp, sea leg, wakame seaweed, cucumber, daikon and rice vinegar dressing

Asparagus & Kinoko Tempura   8.50
Crispy fresh asparagus and kinoko mushrooms served with tempura sauce

BC Soft Shell Crab   12.50
Savory ponzu sauce, fresh lemon

Kakiage Tempura   9.00
Crispy diced shrimps, scallops and shredded vegetables with tempura sauce

Shrimp Tempura   9.50
Two crispy jumbo shrimp and vegetables with tempura sauce

Sashimi ~ Starter   13.00
Selection of fresh fish with white radish and wasabi mustard (3 types)

California Roll   8.50
Crab stick, flying fish roe, avocado & cucumber rolled with nori (6 pieces)

Sushi Sampler   11.50
Tuna, salmon & shrimp sushi with California roll

Sashimi "Kaede" fresh market selection with 7 types of fresh fish   37.00 *

Sashimi " Momiji" fresh market selection with 5 types of fresh fish 30.00 *

Bertucci's

630 College Street
Toronto
416-537-0911

Italian
LITTLE ITALY

Wheelchair
  access

V / MC / AmEx / DC

dinner

late supper

take out

beer/wine

cocktails

high chairs

live
  entertainment

private parties

non-smoking

reservations
  recommended

dress casual

menu changes
  seasonally

Domenico Bertucci likes to call his thirty-two-seat ristorante "old-fashioned" because it plays plain sister to the high-kicking hotties of Little Italy's seething restaurant strip. Bertucci built the place, "every nail, every screw," with his own hands. He shops for his groceries—by now he's given up on the bicycle—and fusses over picking his wines (500 labels, 10,000 bottles). On weekends, he's head waiter, and on weeknights the only waiter. On a good night, the flavors not only sing, they do opera, with unctuous salmon carpaccio, fluffy gnocchi tossed with gorgonzola, and blackboard specials tending toward game and ancestral Sicilian fare steeped in chiles, anchovies, and sunshine.

Bertucci's

Antipasto

Sufflé di Zucca
Butternut and spaghetti squash soufflé,
topped with smooth tomato-herb sauce, sprinkled with Parmigiano Reggiano
8.50

Funghi Saltati
Organic mushrooms sautéed with lemon, thyme and sherry
on a bed of salad greens, drizzled with truffle oil
11.00

Quaglia con Polenta
Grilled boneless quail marinated in sage and garlic,
served with grilled polenta and braised endive
10.00

Pasta

Gnocchi al Gorgonzola e Noce
Home made potato dumplings in creamy gorgonzola sauce
with toasted walnuts
15.00

Conchiglie di Ricotta e Spinaci
Baked pasta shells stuffed with fresh ricotta and spinach
in light tomato basil sauce
14.00

Maltagliati con Fagioli Freschi e Funghi
"Badly cut" egg pasta with fresh romano beans, roasted red peppers
and portobello mushroom in light tomato broth
14.00

Biagio

157 King Street East
Toronto
416-366-4040
www.biagio.tordine.com

**Italian
DOWNTOWN**

Wheelchair
  access
V / MC / AmEx / DC
lunch
dinner
take out
beer/wine
cocktails
live
  entertainment
private parties
non-smoking
reservations
  recommended
dress casual
menu changes
  weekly

Power lunches and power dinners—pictures of Ontario provincial politicos festoon one corner of the restaurant and could put you off the veal—remain a driving force in this grandly formal dining room in the 1850 Street Lawrence Hall. Biagio Vinci follows a well-beaten northern Italian path and boasts a raft of awards (including a *Wine Spectator* award of excellence); not bad for an immigrant from dirt-poor Calabria. Biagio has his standards; order the tuna well done, and he won't serve you. In summer, the courtyard is a Tuscan twirl.

RISTORANTE

Fish

Salmone Atlantico al basilico
Grilled or poached fresh Atlantic salmon,
mounded on braised red onions and emulsified
green basil sauce   19.50

Gamberoni con zucchine
Grilled prawn shrimps wrapped in a zucchine with
a reduced brandy cream paprika sauce   29.50

Tonno con pepperoni e salmoriglio
Fresh tuna, flash fried in a stone pan completed with
yellow red pepper salsa and aromatic herbs   24.00

Capesante con ragu di vegetali
East coast seared scallops with poppy seeds arranged
on a fresh garden vegetable ragu and saffron
scented sauce   26.50

Grigliata assortita di pesce
A variety of fresh grilled fish, drizzled in oil essence
    26.00

Calamari alla Barese
Garlic flavored, sautéed calamari rings in a spicy
tomato sauce, rapini and orecchiette pasta   18.00

Entrees

Tagliata di manzo al balsamico e asparagi
Grilled and sliced beef striploin, placed on green
asparagus carpaccio, laced with balsamic aroma,
rosemary and thyme   26.00

Sella di Agnello
Oven roasted rack of Australian lamb, coated with
honey mustard, herbed bread crumbs with braised
garlic cloves and lamb jus   38.50
(allow 30 minutes)

Nodino di vitello alla salvia
Pan fried provimi veal chop deglazed with white
wine, sage and reduced veal jus   32.50

Rognone fiammeggiato al brandy
Provimi calves kidney flamed with garlic and brandy
sauce   18.50

Filetto di manzo al vino rosso e tartufo
Grilled beef tenderloin, crusted with dried herbs,
reduction of red wine and truffle essence   29.50

Galletto ai ferri
Seared, free-range Cornish hen, infused with
rosemary and garlic jus
 (**allow 30 minutes**)   22.00

Medaglioni di vitello ai funghi
Grilled provimi veal medallions, presented with a
variation of mushrooms, garlic and red wine
deglazed veal jus   26.50

Fegato verdure croccanti
Sauteed provimi liver in a julienne of tender crisp
fresh vegetables   18.50

Costoletta milanese classica
Provimi veal cutlet breaded and pan fried in butter
and veal jus drizzle   28.50

Ossobuco con risotto
Provimi veal shank with braised vegetable and tomato,
dry mushroom sauce with creamy saffron risotto   28.00

Biff's

4 Front Street East
Toronto
416-860-0086
www.oliverbonacini.com

French
DOWNTOWN

Wheelchair
  access
V / MC / AmEx / DC
lunch (M-F)
dinner Saturday
late supper
beer/wine
cocktails
private parties
non-smoking
reservations
  recommended
dress informal
menu changes
  seasonally

Biff's, which sits facing the Hummingbird Centre, is a surge in the unstoppable Oliver Bonacini empire, which includes Auberge du Pommier, Canoe, Jump, and Steakfrites. Gorgeous leather and crescent banquettes, classic French posters, and aproned servers suggest a fashionable stretch of, say, the Marais or Boulevard Saint-Germain. Redefining luxe bistro in Toronto, Biff's is an easy room to love. Pâté maison upgraded to silken terrine of rabbit and Quebec foie gras dressed in truffle signify a kitchen delivering much more oomph than it did after its lackluster start. Reserve for after eight, when the theater crowd is well out the door.

BIFF'S

HORS D'ŒUVRES

Biff's Caesar salad with romaine hearts, lentilles du Puy and a creamy Parmesan dressing   9.00

Sautéed escargot with a green peppercorn pastis and parsley compote on thyme toast   10.50

Biff's fruits de mer; oysters, little neck clams, shrimps, mussels   Grande   24.00
and our daily St. Lawrence special   Petite   16.00

Hearts of Boston Bibb salad dressed with a creamy Dijon sherry vinaigrette   8.50

Steamed mussels à la mariniére, julienne of leeks and a splash of Chablis   9.25

Chicken liver parfait with pear chutney and sourdough toast   10.75

Spinach, endive and pear salad with toasted walnuts and Roquefort cheese   9.75

POTAGES

Mediterranean style fish and lobster soup   9.00

Wild mushroom and tarragon soup   7.00

Soupe a' l'oignon gratinée   7.00

ENTREES

Braised Provimi veal roulade with sweetbreads, roast garlic pomme purée   26.50
and a lemon caper relish

Laurel grilled tiger prawns with baked aubergine ratatouille and potato aïoli   25.50

Braised lamb shank on a white bean and tomato cassoulet   24.00

Poached Atlantic salmon fillet on a warm new potato salad dressed with salsa verde   24.00
and steamed asparagus

Grilled entrecôte steak frites with sautéed mushrooms and a shallot sauce   28.00

Roast Rock Cornish hen with Yukon potatoes, bacon lardons and pan jus   22.00

Bistro 990

990 Bay Street
Toronto
416-921-9990

French
DOWNTOWN

Wheelchair
  access
V / MC / AmEx / DC
lunch
dinner
late supper
beer/wine
cocktails
private parties
non-smoking
reservations
  recommended
dress informal
menu changes
  seasonally

With its French doors, tiled floors, and abundant flowers, Bistro 990 looks far more the genteel auberge than anybody's notion of bistro. Maybe this explains it being the gastronomical hub of the star-studded Toronto Film Festival, *the* restaurant in which to catch gaggles of movie stars. In the festival's ten days, Bistro 990 serves two months' worth of food and wine. Critics suggest the bistro is vacant the rest of the year, but it generally pleases with its everyday French cuisine and unrelenting prettiness.

BISTRO 990

Hors d'Oeuvres

Soupe du jour .. 7.00

Consommé aux chanterelles, tortellini au ricotta .. 8.00
Winter chanterelles in consommé and ricotta filled tortellini

Truite et saumon en terrine, raifort à la crème .. 8.50
Smoked salmon and trout terrine with horseradish, dill and green peppercorns

Pâté de campagne .. 9.00
Country style pâté with a quince marmalade, wine preserves and cornichons

Brie en feuilleté .. 9.00
Baked Brie in phyllo with pickled ginger, pistachios and concord grape sauce

Homard frais, melon, menthe et vinaigrette .. 17.50
Fresh lobster and melon with mint and rice wine vinaigrette

Calmars frits aux deux sauces .. 12.00
Calamari, deep-fried served with spicy yogurt and Mediterranean sauces

Viandes

Poulet rôti au jus, purée de pommes de terre .. 20.00
Crispy roasted half chicken in an herbed jus with garlic mashed potatoes

Steak Frites, sauce échalote ou Roquefort .. 22.00
Sirloin with a shallot or Roquefort sauce, served with frites

Magret de canard, cuit saignant, gratin Savoyard .. 26.00
Breast of duck served rare with apple galette and scalloped potatoes

Foie de veau, échalotes, vin blanc .. 21.00
Calf's liver sautéed with shallots, garlic, white wine and herbs

Carré d'agneau farci au Camembert .. 36.00
Rack of lamb au jus, stuffed with Camembert and roast garlic pâté

Osso bucco / Braised veal shank served with its cooking jus .. 23.00

Filet mignon, sauce Stilton-Porto (6 oz.) .. 29.00 **(8 oz.)** .. 34.00
With a Stilton and port jus

Bistro Tournesol

406 Dupont Street
416-921-7766
Toronto
www.bistrotournesol.com

French-Italian
ANNEX

V / MC

dinner

beer/wine

cocktails

non-smoking

reservations
  recommended

dress informal

menu changes
  daily

Tournesol is the French word for sunflower, and the motif and sensibility of this little bistro is so cheery that many would happily clone it for our own neighborhoods. Granted, the space between tables might prompt Celine Dion to suck it in, the room is as packed as a Tokyo subway train, weekends verge on the raucous, and the waiters couldn't go faster on rollerblades. But the two-course, fixed-price menu is a deal. Even traditionally hapless vegetarians are delighted with the smartly assembled slate. French onion soup, Caesar salad, and anything with escargots are happy staples, and the wine du jour is often worth getting to know.

BISTRO TOURNESOL

<u>Prix Fixe Menu</u>:
<u>First and Second Course for $25.00</u>

First Course:
- Just a little green salad with sunflower seeds in a Tournesol champagne vinaigrette
- Frisee salad with Danish blue cheese, croutons and roasted walnut dressing
- Caesar Salad with roasted garlic croutons and shaved Grano Padano cheese
- Escargots " a la Bourguignonne" garlic, parsley and Pastis butter
- Mussels steamed in white wine with sweet red onion and roasted garlic

Second Course:
- Roasted Chicken Breast with melted French Brie, raspberry cabernet reduction
- Grilled Atlantic Salmon with an orange ginger vinaigrette
- Rare roasted Duck Breast served with blackberry - red wine reduction
- Black Angus Sirloin Steak, with pink and green peppercorn glaze   +$2.50
- Bouillabaisse: scallops, mussels, salmon and shrimp in a saffron tomato broth
- Barbequed Shrimp brochette over Capellinni pasta in a light herbed cream sauce

Blowfish

668 King Street West
Toronto
416-860-0606
www.blowfishrestaurant.com

Fusion
DOWNTOWN WEST

V / MC / AmEx / DC

dinner

late supper

take out

beer/wine

cocktails

live
   entertainment

private parties

non-smoking

reservations
   recommended

dress smart
   casual

menu changes
   seasonally

Blowfish is known as *fugu* to Japanese who hanker for a soupçon of death with dinner. Its toxin is reputedly 279 times more powerful than cyanide, and it has left my chopsticks shuddering in Tokyo, but don't fret. Although legal in Canada, the beak-faced fish is too expensive to thrive on Toronto tables. The scary aspect of Blowfish is "blue snow," a tuna-based sushi roll slathered with blue Curaçao. Still, there is much to like about the cool interior mockingly hung with chandeliers, a menu that takes Japanese two steps beyond and a slate of 15 chilled sakes and *sojus,* plus saketinis.

blowfish

- **asari miso** *stone clams in a sake-infused miso broth* — **4.00**
- **hana ebi** *clear soup with tiger shrimp in wonton dumpling and hon-shimeji mushrooms* — **5.00**
- **korean-style tofu** *with pickled bamboo shoot, cucumber, and chili-soy dressing* — **7.00**
- **baby asian mix** *asian pear, mango, grapefruit, walnuts and baby greens with ginger dressing* — **7.00**
- **aspara-spinach raft** *blanched asparagus & baby spinach with sesame toasted dressing* — **8.00**
- **snow crab spring roll** *and summer vegetables wrapped in rice paper* — **9.00**
- **bbq salmon skin salad** *assorted greens and bbq salmon skin with serrano pepper dressing* — **9.00**
- **kushiyaki platter** *skewered scallop, shrimp, beef & vegetable brushed with teriyaki* — **10.00**
- *seared* **cape scallops** *baked in a salmon wrap with wasabi-crab mayonnaise* — **16.00**
- *grilled* **chicken breast** *with panko-encrusted miso-mustard sauce and asian vegetables* — **17.00**
- *charbroiled* **black cod** *with sweet miso marinade on a bed of baby spinach chips* — **18.00**

Boba

90 Avenue Road
Toronto
416-961-2622

Global
YORKVILLE

V / MC / AmEx / DC

dinner

beer/wine

cocktails

private parties

non-smoking

reservations
  required

dress informal

menu changes
  weekly

In the Yorkville area house that was for years Auberge Gavroche, Boba—an acronym for chefs Bob Bermann and Barbara Gordon—is a rock-solid favorite among Toronto diners. Vested servers usher tipplers through a scholarly wine list while Bo and Ba gallivant through a global village repertoire that plants creamy little falafel croutons on Caesar salad and playfully sides beef tenderloin (is nothing sacred?) with macaroni and cheese. But Bo's steady hand at the grill is a sure thing with colossal tiger shrimp and ostrich (do they clean the sand from the head?) and Ba's all-out desserts are justly famed.

RICE PAPER WRAPPED CHICKEN BREAST ON BLACK THAI RICE
SPICED RICE WINE VINEGAR SAUCE
19.95
RARE GRILLED TUNA FILET WITH COCONUT NOODLES
AVOCADO/MANGO SALSA,BLACK BEAN SAUCE
(Market Price)
GRILLED GIANT TIGER SHRIMP
LEMON SCENTED ISRAELI COUS-COUS
28.95
GRILLED ATLANTIC SALMON
ROAST RED PEPPER SAUCE
22.95
GRILLED PROVIMI VEAL LOIN,SQUASH PUREE
VERMOUTH SAUCE
30.95
ROAST RACK OF LAMB
BLACK OLIVE SAUCE
33.95
GRILLED FRESH ONTARIO OSTRICH
GUAVA-PEPPERCORN GLAZE
27.95
MUSCOVY DUCK- TWO WAYS
27.95
GRILLED AURORA ANGUS NEW YORK STEAK
CHIPOTLE CREAM SAUCE/YUKON GOLD FRITES
29.95
GRILLED FILET MIGNON,ASIAN B.B.Q. GLAZE
NOODLE CAKE,SPICY CASHEW SAUCE
28.95

Bouchon

38 Wellington Street East
Toronto
416-862-2675

French
DOWNTOWN

V / MC / AmEx / DC

lunch

dinner

late supper

take out

beer/wine

cocktails

high chairs

private parties

non-smoking
  section

reservations
  recommended

dress casual

menu changes
  daily

Jean-Pierre Challet forged a reputation for originality and delight at the Inn at Manitou and
Auberge du Pommier, but as chef-owner of the
cozy, subterranean Bouchon, he's at the impas-
sioned top of his game. His is a splendidly real-
ized repertoire—foie gras daringly paired with
Quebec goat cheese, powerhouse bouillabaisse
risotto draped with grilled fish, lamb encrusted in
black tea—that simply doesn't exist anywhere else.
What's more, all dishes are delivered in appetizer—
generous appetizer—portions. Toronto bistro
cuisine has never been this playful, sophisticated,
or richly satisfying. The prices are modest, too:
Bouchon is the gastronomic equivalent of getting
a Picasso at black velvet prices.

Bouchon

BISTRO | WINE BAR

From the Pot

The Daily Soup	6.
Traditional Fish Soup with Garlic Croutons and sauce Rouille	7.
Lobster Bisque with Shrimp and Pickled Ginger	8.

From the Garden

Simply Greens with Many Fresh Herbs	8.
Vine ripe Tomatoes with a Goat Cheese and Caramelized Shallot Tart	9.
Avocado Salad with Vanilla Shrimp, Squid and Scallop	13.

From the Field

Sun dried Tomato Risotto with Red Pepper Ketchup and Tomme	13.
Beef Tenderloin and Braised Salsify with Chanterelle Ravioli	16.

Tartare & Co.

Vine Ripe Tomato Tartare on Prosciutto, Marinated Moroccan olives and Artichokes	11.
Top Meadow Farm Steak Tartare with "Gratin Dauphinois"	13.
J.P.'s Smoked Salmon and Bay of Fundy Salmon Tartare with Pickled Ginger & Frisée	13.

From the Water

Bay of Fundy Salmon Tournedos with Salmon Quenelle and Yukon Gold Gnocchi	13.
Bouillabaisse Risotto draped with grilled Fish	15.

On Earth

Top Meadow Farm dry aged NY Striploin in Bordelaise with "Dauphines"	15.
Beef Bourguignon on Potato Purée with a Wild Mushroom Strudel	16.

Heaven

Foie Gras Terrine with Pineapple and Red pepper Chutney	16.
Seared Foie Gras with "C'est boncheese" Millefeuille and Liquorice Jus	16.
"Whispering Heaven" tea encrusted Rack of Lamb and Lemongrass Lyonnaise Potatoes	19.

Boujadi

999 Eglinton Avenue West
Toronto
416-440-0258
www.boujadi.com

Moroccan
MIDTOWN WEST

Wheelchair
  access

V / MC

dinner

take out

beer/wine

cocktails

high chairs

private parties

non-smoking

reservations not
  taken except
  for groups of
  8 or more and
  for Saturday
  5 P.M. – 7 P.M.

dress casual

Charles and Dahlia Obadia's Boujadi is Toronto's single oasis for an Arabian Nights cuisine as fantastical as a whirl on a flying carpet. The caravansary sensibility shines in leaded-glass lamps, crockery, and gorgeous conical tagine pots. The authentic menu ensures diners get the real thing, from pickled lemons and the fiery sauce known as *harissa* to phyllo pastry "cigars" and six kinds of couscous—the essential Berber staple of billowing steamed semolina—piled high with vegetables, fowl, meats, or the spicy lamb sausage merguez.

BOUJADI

ENTREES

*All entrees are served with mediterranean salad, black olives, harissa sauce
and whole wheat Moroccan style bread.*

COUSCOUS FAMOUS

*Couscous is the national dish of Morocco, consisting of semolina (durham wheat) enriched with
vegetables, bouillon and fresh herbs.*

Chicken Couscous   11.50
Cooked with green olives and pickled lemons.

Merguez Couscous   12.95
With three homemade Moroccan sausages.

Kafta Couscous   11.50
With three sizzling burgers spiced with various herbs.

Meatball Couscous   11.50
Meatball and tomato meat sauce.

Couscous Pasha   13.95
Chicken enrobed with our famous prune sauce.

Lamb Couscous *Now Available*   18.95

Most of our meals are sprinkled with grilled almond slivers, fresh parsley and/or coriander.

THE TAJINES	MEDINA TAJINES

*The word "Tajine" simply means pot, composed
of a large deep dish and a lid of a conus shape:
both made from red clay. All the cooking,
simmering and serving were
done in the same Tajine.*

*The thick spicey onion/tomato sauce enriched with
saffron and fresh coriander has earned the name"
medina" which makes the surrounding quarters of
the souk. It is generously poured on the meat of
your choice with a bed of couscous or rice.*

Chicken Olive Tajine	11.50	**Chicken Rice Medina**	11.50
Meatball Olive Tajine	11.50	**Meatball Rice Medina**	11.50
With your choice of rice or couscous.		**Liver Rice Medina**	11.50
Chicken Onion Tajine	12.50		
Meatball Onion Tajine	12.50		

Rice or couscous on the side.

Watch for our "Tajine of the Day" featuring vegetables of the season and our chief's creativity of the
moment.

Brasserie Aix

584 College Street
Toronto
416-588-7377
www.brasserieaix.com

French
LITTLE ITALY

Wheelchair
  access

V / MC / AmEx / DC

dinner

late supper

beer/wine

cocktails

private parties

smoking section

reservations
  required

dress informal

menu changes
  seasonally

From innovative restaurateur David Bowen, who made originality pay with the pan-Asian Monsoon, comes yet another flashy Yabu Pushelberg design statement, this time set in Little Italy, of all places. The area around the zinc-and-Douglas fir bar seems the epicenter of the hip universe, magnifying the shock when you step into a knockout dining room, with its towering painted-tin ceiling, glowing terra-cotta hues, and terrazzo floor. It evokes the feeling of a twenty-first century cathedral, its hymns murder on the ears, its worshippers a noisy throng of hearing-impaired twenty-five-year-olds, and its communion over food—think rosemary sweetbreads and terrific steak frites—joltingly good.

Brasserie Aix

Salade de Saumon Fumé et Maquereaux   *8.65*
Smoked salmon and mackerel salad with apple, frisée and horseradish crème fraîche

Salade de Chèvre Chaud   *9.25*
Marinated ripened goat cheese wrapped in eggplant, with baby lettuces, tomato confit and blood orange vinaigrette

Salade d'Escarole et Ris de Veau   *9.10*
Sweetbreads roasted with rosemary, smoked bacon with escarole, hazelnuts and Champagne vinegar

Moules à la Provençal   *8.95*
Mussels steamed in white wine with tomato, garlic, lemon and parsely

Jarret d'Agneau Braisé avec Coco   *21.45*
Braised lamb shank with country sausage and haricot bean ragoût

Omble Chevalier Poêlé   *23.85*
Pan seared Arctic char with spinach, basil, garlic confit, wild mushrooms and roasted grape tomatoes

Entrecôte Grillée et Frites*   *19.25*
Grilled ribeye steak with crisp frites, red wine shallot butter and lemon mayonnaise

Coquelet Rôti à la Bourguinonne   *19.95*
Cornish Hen roasted in a clay oven with pearl onions, button mushrooms and lardons, served with garlic mashed potatoes and roasted vegetables

Foie de Veau Grillé   *16.95*
*Grilled Calf's Liver with onion marmalade, frites, Pommery mustard and parsley vinegar sauce**

Confit de Canard   *19.95*
Duck Confit with roasted potatoes, prune and Armagnac jus

Poisson du Jour
*Market fresh fish**   *Market**

Bravi

40 Wellington Street East
Toronto
416-368-9030

Italian
DOWNTOWN

V / MC / AmEx /
D / DC

lunch

dinner

beer/wine

cocktails

private parties

non-smoking
section

reservations
recommended

dress casual

Bravi is the plural of *bravo*, in a nod to the
St. Lawrence and Hummingbird Centres that send
the customers across the street for dinner. Bravi
is also a restaurant with literal ups and downs:
You can book the freight elevator and spend the
evening going up and down four floors, *the*
booked-out table for trysts, engagements, and
weddings. The greater room shows exposed brick,
pillars doubling as chandeliers, and delightful
bistro paintings of aproned, mustachioed waiters.
Duck carpaccio, homemade pastas, and risottos
are signature dishes. Proprietor Rumen Nicola
scurries back and forth between here and his It's
All Good pizzeria, two doors west.

Bravi

r i s t o r a n t e

PASTAS
All Bravi's homemade pastas are prepared daily by hand

Homemade spinach and ricotta gnocchi
In a rich tomato sauce   13.95
Homemade potato gnocchi
With Porcini mushrooms cream sage sauce   14.95
Homemade roasted butternut squash Ravioli
In a carrot apple cream sauce and Arugula   16.95
Homemade Ravioli stuffed with mushrooms leeks and sweet potatoes
In wild mushroom broth, wilted spinach and truffle oil   16.95
Penne with freshly grilled spicy Calabrese sausage
And sautéed leeks in a tomato basil sauce   13.95
Seafood spaghettini
Grilled black tiger shrimp, calamari, mussels in a white wine tomato sauce   19.95
Grilled Chicken Breast Spaghettini
With spinach pistachio pesto and diced Tomato   17.95

RISOTTO
Risotto with bay scallop and grilled shrimp   19.95
Risotto with Butternut squash and Gorgonzola   17.95
Risotto with assorted wild mushroom and truffle oil   18.95

ENTREES

Veal Osso Bucco
With a wild mushroom risotto   24.95
Charbroiled Provimi liver
With caramelized onions, Yukon Gold mash   18.95
Grilled Atlantic salmon
With a sautéed spinach and grilled vegetables in lemon butter sauce   21.95
Tuscany Stake
Angus Beef strip loin marinated in Chianti, mashed potato and grilled vegetable   27.95

Bymark

66 Wellington Street
Toronto
416-777-1144

Global
FINANCIAL DISTRICT

Wheelchair
   access
valet parking
V / MC / AmEx / DC
lunch
dinner
late supper
take out
beer/wine
cocktails
private parties
non-smoking
   section
reservations
   recommended
dress casual
menu changes
   seasonally

When Mark McEwan, the man of North 44, unveiled a subterranean restaurant in the financial district, the buzz was the $33 burger. In New York, such excesses come slathered with foie gras and truffles; Bymark's has melted Brie, porcini mushrooms, truffle-mustard aioli, and the city's best onion rings; it delivers the goods for people whose wallets are fatter than their cerebral matter. Burger aside, the restaurant displays restrained Yabu Pushelberg glamour—the ceiling-high wine cellar, a recommended stocking stuffer for successful suits—while chef Brooke McDougall's kitchen measures up to the boss's impeccable standards: symphonic numbers of players on most plates, fish greatly respected, and wines by the glass recommended for every dish.

Roasted Chicken With Garlic, Sage, Variegated Beets & Frites   29.95
Suggested wine: ENCOUNTER BAY CABERNET SAUVIGNON
                  "NORMAN" 2001, AUSTRALIA

Crisp Skin Salmon With Smashed New Potatoes,
Soy Beans, Braised Onions & Mirin Soy Glaze   30.95
Suggested wine: BELFORD SPRINGS CHARDONNAY 2000, CALIFORNIA

Grilled Texas White Prawns With Pan Seared Mushroom Pot Stickers,
Wilted Greens & Garlic Citrus Sauce   39.95
Suggested wine: MENETOU–SALON "CLOS DES BLANCHAIS" 2001,
                  DOMAINE HENRY PELLE

Grilled Veal Tenderloin With Porcini Mushrooms, Braised Onion Ravioli,
Fine Beans & Natural Reduction   39.95
Suggested wine: DARIOUSH MERLOT 2000, NAPA

Seared Yellow Fin Tuna (Medium Rare-Rare)With Savory Crust,
Cracked Green Olive Tapenade & Frites With Aioli   39.95
Suggested wine: CRANE CANYON CELLARS WHITE CRANE
                  (VIOGNIER / GEWURZTRAMINER) '99, SONOMA

Roasted East Coast Striped Seabass With Field Mushrooms,
Leeks, Scallops, Prawns & Mussels   39.95
Suggested wine: PINOT GRIS GRAND CRU "EICHBERG"2000, WOLFBERGER

Grilled Prime U.S. Burger, 8 oz. With Molten Brie de Meaux Cheese,
Grilled Porcini Mushrooms, Crisp Rosemary Onion Rings
& Truffle Mustard Aioli   33.95
Suggested wine: HAMELIN BAY CAB / SAUVIGNON 2000 MARGARET RIVER

Canoe

Toronto-Dominion Bank Tower
(54th Floor)
66 Wellington Street West
Toronto
416-364-0054
www.oliverbonacini.com

Canadian
FINANCIAL DISTRICT

Wheelchair
   access
V / MC / AmEx / DC
lunch
dinner
late supper
beer/wine
cocktails
private parties
non-smoking
reservations
   required
dress jacket/tie
menu changes
   seasonally

The loftiest outpost in the Oliver Bonacini empire, Canoe paddles excellence to the top, the fifty-fourth floor of the Toronto-Dominion Bank Tower. I go along with the conventional wisdom—the higher the restaurant, the lower the food—but Canoe's cuisine proves as haute as the skyscraping panorama. Canadian accents may include Newfie Screech rum, Saskatoon berries and "canushi" of raw Arctic char, but these playful elements barely hint at the largesse of chef Anthony Walsh's kitchen: Can you resist three caviars atop three kinds of salmon? Ask Elton John or the crown princess of Japan. Pssssst: Table 26 is *it*, but there are no reservations for window tables.

c a n o e

Canoe Seasons

Starters

Carpaccio & Tartar of Alberta Beef
Malpeque Oysters,
Salsify
& Hazelnuts
16.

Wing of Skate
Shallots, Allspice
& Atlantic Lobster
16.

Ravioli of La Ferme Foie Gras
Conquest Hill Organic Squab,
Black Trumpets & Crème Fraîche
17.

Mains

Yukon Gold Gnocchi
Roast Salsify, Honey Mushrooms, Pinenuts
& Porcini Froth
24.

Seared Big Eye Tuna
White Asparagus, Hamachi,
Sunchokes, Winter Kale
& Garlic Caramel
36.

Canoe Fish

Starters

Salmon, Salmon, Salmon
Smoke Salmon Terrine,
Radish Nori Globe,
Spice Cured Salmon Belly
17.

Roast Digby Scallops
Celeriac Apple Purée, Mustard Greens
& Raisin Chutney
18.

Maritime Lobster & Salt Cod Donut
Rocket, Radish & Pelee Island
Whitefish Caviar
21.

Mains

Pan Roast Fillet of Snapper
Yukon Gold & Double Smoked Bacon Hash,
String Beans, Fennel & Aromatic Pepper Jus
36.

Skin Roast Arctic Char
P.E.I. Mussel & Lobster Chowder,
Cookstown Roseval Potatoes & Tarragon
37.

Centro

2472 Yonge Street
Toronto
416-483-2211
www.centrorestaurant.com

Global
UPTOWN

Valet parking
V / MC / AmEx / DC
dinner
late supper
beer/wine
cocktails
high chairs
private parties
non-smoking
reservations
  recommended
dress casual
menu changes
  seasonally

Franco Prevedello's historic monument to the Cal-Ital cuisine that changed the way Torontonians dine, Centro now stands fast as an icon of uptown grandeur, Bruce Woods at the pots and smart Continental cuisine its current mode. The space assumes further glamour with every passing year. Blown-up photos of Prevedello's hometown in Italy contribute a nostalgic touch. Sexy stem lights and remarkable wines (super-Tuscans and California labels beguile oenophiles) extend a high-end hello. Goldie Hawn, Kathleen Turner, Tom Cruise, Nicolas Cage, and others seeking sustenance in Hollywood North dine here.

CENTRO

grill and wine bar

PASTA

RICOTTA AND SPINACH GNOCCHI *with a charred tomato ragu* $14/20

PENNETTE RIGATE *double smoked speck bermuda onions and capers*
in a fresh vine ripened tomato sauce   15/22

LINGUINI *with bay scallops jumbo black tiger shrimps braised leeks*
and baby arugula in a riesling beurre blanc   18/28

HOMEMADE EGG TAGLIOLINI *with smoked chicken portobello mushrooms*
porcini and truffle emulsion   16/24

MAIN COURSES

QUEBEC GRAIN FED SUPREME OF CAPON *farci with a foie gras mousse*
and sundried cherries in an orange and aged balsamic jus $29

PAN SEARED ARCTIC CHAR *glazed with an orange blossom honey*
and a lemongrass and kafir leaf nage   36

AUSTRALIAN RACK OF LAMB *in a honey mustard crust with confit of spring*
vegetables roasted garlic and saffron flan gremolata sauce   39

FILET OF ALBERTA BEEF CHATELAINE *ragout of artichoke hearts and mushrooms*
goat cheese and chervil sauce   39

EMINCE OF CALF'S LIVER *pearl onions speck and granny smith apples*
with a raspberry vinegar jus and creamed polenta   28

STEAMED ALASKAN HALIBUT *fresh pea coulis tomato tartar and homardine sauce*   39

OVEN ROASTED ONTARIO PORK TENDERLOIN *on a bed of barley and pearl vegetables*
with a piquant ginger sauce   28

Chennai Dosa Place

1330 Gerrard Street East
Toronto
416-466-7608

Indian
LITTLE INDIA

V / MC / AmEx / DC
lunch
dinner
late supper
take out
beer/wine
cocktails
high chairs
private parties
non-smoking
reservations
  recommended
dress casual

The dosa is the darling of south India; a billowing rice crepe, here more than two feet long, crisply fried in clarified butter, stuffed with curried potato, and served with symphonically spiced *sambar* (a lentil stew) and a selection of chutneys. The "Place," a large, comfy room in Little India, turns out the best dosas I've eaten outside Madras, with its racy underpinnings of grated ginger, green chiles, and onions. Almost as addictive are the Bollywood production numbers on the giant screen, with dark-eyed beauties in shimmering saris flirting, swooning, gyrating, and crooning through famous international locations.

CHENNAI DOSA PLACE

Rava Dosa...6.95
Fried & spread with ghee, spices (Dosa Hut style only)
Rava Masala Dosa...7.95
Fried & spread with ghee, spices & stuffed with curried potato masala
Dry Fruit Dosa...6.95
Fried & spread with crushed dry fruits
Dry Fruit Masala Dosa...7.95
Fried & spread with crushed dry fruits & stuffed with curried potato masala
Paper Dosa...6.95
Thin crisped extra long dosa
Paper Masala Dosa...7.95
Thin crisped extra long dosa stuffed with curried potato masala
Cheese Dosa...6.95
Fried & spread with shredded cheddar cheese
Cheese Masala Dosa...7.95
Fried & spread with shredded cheddar cheese stuffed with curried potato masala
Onion Dosa...6.95
Fried & spread with fried onions
Onion Masala Dosa...7.95
Fried & spread with fried onions stuffed with curried potato masala
Butter Roast Dosa..7.95
Crisp cone shaped dosa spread with butter

Chiado

864 College Street
Toronto
416-538-1910
www.chiadorestaurant.com

Seafood
LITTLE ITALY

V / MC / AmEx / DC

breakfast

lunch

dinner

late supper

take out

beer/wine

high chairs

live
    entertainment

non-smoking

reservations
    recommended

dress informal

menu changes
    seasonally

Pronounced "she-ad-o," Albino Silva's jewel is
wholly responsible for the resurrection of
Portuguese cuisine in Toronto. The former CIA
(Culinary Institute of America) sage did it his way.
He designed an embracingly lovely room, named
after Lisbon's oldest neighborhood, in peach and
ochre hues. He hung his private collection of Jose
Demarche paintings. He brought in the freshest
sardines, octopus, monkfish, and rarities like
espada—monstrous to behold, blissful to eat—
from the Atlantic depths around Madeira. He
dressed them to kill in olive oil, garlic, and sea
salt. He installed the largest Portuguese wine cellar
outside Portugal. We should build a statue.

First Dishes

Grilled Squid w/ fresh coriander, lemon, garlic, extra virgin olive oil on roasted sweet
peppers, charred tomato & caramelized leeks   9.50

Grilled Quail spiced w/ piri piri, served on a wild mushroom risotto   13.50

Sardines marinated w/lemon, parsley, olive oil, served raw or grilled   9.50

Grilled Tiger Shrimp spiced w/piri piri , jalapenos & banana peppers   21.00

Goat Cheese toasted over grilled eggplant, confit of onion,grilled portabello mushrooms
finished w/compote of pears, honey & champagne vinaiger   12.00

Second Dishes

Lobster & Shrimp Bisque flavored w/ saffron and old oak aged aguardente   8.50

Soup of the Day   7.50

Mixed Seasonal greens, fresh fruit tossed in a balsamic vinaigrette   8.50

Arrugula & fresh Figs w/ slivers of aged Lourais from St. Jorge
drizzled w/fresh lemon & extra virgin olive oil   9.50

Main Dishes

Roasted Breast of Pheasant crusted w/ fresh herbs& garlic, served on a roasted
garlic mashed potato w/ a delicate Madeira wine & caramelized citrus sauce   28.00

Seared & roasted Beef Tenderloin seasoned w/ black peppercorns, served
on saffron roasted potatoes topped w/ an old tawny Port wine sauce   33.00

Seared Striploin finished with a mustard, white wine pan jus served on frites   28.00

Roasted fresh rack of Australian lamb marinated w/ rosemary, bay leaf, garlic & extra
virgin olive oil, crusted w/ golden crumbs , finished w/ a red Douro rosemary sauce   34.00

Risotto of Lobster finished w/ saffron and fresh tomato   32.00

Grilled Tiger Shrimp spiced w/ piri piri, served w/ roasted garlic mash potato & seasonal
vegetables topped w/ a spicy apple, banana pepper chutney   33.00

Grilled Filet of Grouper seasoned w/ fresh herbs & garlic served w/ a salsa of citrus   28.00

Grilled Filet of Atlantic Salmon crusted w/ peppercorns, fresh herbs & marine salt   24.00

Chopan
Kabab House

798 Danforth Avenue
Toronto
416-778-1200
www.chopankabab.com

Afghan
EAST TORONTO

V / MC / AmEx

lunch

dinner

late supper

take out

high chairs

private parties

non-smoking

reservations
  recommended

dress casual

menu changes
  seasonally

Journey east from Greektown and the unpredictable Danforth transports you to a tranquil corner of Afghanistan in which the most formidable weapons are massive beef and chicken kababs. Sizzling in charcoal haze, they recall the simple backstreet eateries of old Kabul, while Chopan's *khassa* conjures up those fantastical flatbreads you find throughout the Muslim world, from Yemen all the way to the Hindu Kush. In accordance with laws of the nearby mosque—this is a Muslim neighborhood, remember—no alcohol is served, so prepare to make do with cardamom-infused green tea. Not to worry, you'll still come away smacking your lips.

Chopan Kabab House & Restaurant

Bolani **1.99**
Pastry stuffed with delicately
special potatoes served with hot sauce

Mantu **2.49**
steamed dough filled with fresh ground beef,
onions and spices topped with special sauce

Ashak **2.49**
A very delightful and common
Afghan recipe, steamed dough with leeks topped
with minced meat and yogurt

Qabeli Pallow **$9.99**
Afghan steam, basmati rice with raisins,
carrots with tender pieces of lamb with two vegetable dishes

Pallow **$9.99**
Afghan steam, basmati rice with tender pieces of lamb
with two vegetable dishes

Challow **$8.99**
Afghan plain, basmati rice served with vegetable dishes

Chainakee **$9.99**
Special Lamb soup, afghan meat soup served with
afghan fresh bread, Chatnee and Salata

Chung King Garden

Market Village Shopping Center
4394 Steeles Avenue East at Kennedy
Markham
905-513-8788

Chinese
SUBURBAN NORTHEAST

Wheelchair
  access
lunch
dinner
take out
beer/wine
high chairs
private parties
non-smoking
reservations
  recommended
dress casual

There's more than one Chung King, but none is as fine as this jewel adjacent to the monstrous Pacific Mall on Markham's fringe. Chung King Garden offers relative intimacy—you don't need shades to protect you from the glare—and sumptuous Mandarin and Szechuan fare. Vegetable rolls, smoky and delicious, are unique to this kitchen. Tradition kicks in with a superstar Beijing duck, the bird splendidly roasted and presented to the table, then served as a first course of crackling skin and juicy meat rolled with hoisin and scallion into feathery crepes, and a second course of minced duckmeat in "crystal fold"—God's justification for iceberg lettuce. Crrunch.

CHUNG KING
GARDEN RESTAURANT
Authentic Mandarin & Szechuan Cuisine

Fried Dumplings (5 pcs.) . . . . $ 3.95

Spring Roll 1.30

Fried Won Ton 3.50

Special Noodles 8.95

Assorted Vermicelli 8.95

Singapore Vermicelli 8.95

Spiced Chicken in Garlic Peanut Sauce 9.95

Spiced Shrimps in Garlic Peanut Sauce 11.95

Tender Beef with Mixed Vegetables 10.95

Stir-Fried Shrimps & Chicken w/ Cashew Nuts 12.95

Sweet and Sour Boneless Fish . . . . Seasonal

Honey Garlic Spareribs 11.95

Teriyaki Chicken 9.95

Lemon Chicken 9.95

Hunan Beef 10.95

Orange Chicken 9.95

Orange Beef 10.95

Orange Shrimps 14.95

Sizzling Chicken in Black Bean Sauce 10.95

Sizzling Beef with Scallions 12.95

Coppi

3363 Yonge Street
Toronto
416-484-4464

Italian
UPTOWN

Wheelchair
  access
valet parking
V / MC / AmEx /
  D / DC
lunch
dinner
beer/wine
cocktails
high chairs
private parties
non-smoking
reservations
  recommended
dress informal
menu changes
  seasonally

Fausto di Berardino—gastronome, former soccer pro, sportsman—dedicated his restaurant to Italian cyclist and national hero Fausto Coppi. Di Bernardo hasn't changed his menu in more than a decade and sees no need: If a dish endured a couple thousand years, a few more decades can't hurt. Emulating the ancient Romans, he buries whole fresh snapper in kilos of salt, roasts it, brings it to the table, skins it, bones it and floors customers with its delicate sea flavor. Spaghetti alla puttanesca, the "whore's pasta" (historically prepared by prostitutes to sate their customers' other appetite) rolls around in tomato, black olives, garlic, and chiles— is my fix.

COPPI
RISTORANTE

Bruschetta · *2.50*

Antipasto della Casa
Mixed daily selection of antipasto · *10.50*

Cozze Gratinate
Mussels with fresh tomato and parmigiano cheese · *8.95*

Acciughe alla Fausto
anchovies, capers, black olives, potatoes & lemon juice · *8.95*

Prosciutto e Melone
Prosciutto with cantaloupe · *9.95*

Carpaccio
*Marinated beef with shavings of parmigiano reggiano cheese
with extra virgin olive oil* · *10.50*

Spaghetti alla Puttanesca
*Spaghetti with garlic, anchovies, capers, black olives,
fresh tomato sauce and hot spices.* · *13.95*

Spaghetti Tirreno-Adriatico
*Spaghetti with mixed sea food, extra virgin olive oil,
garlic & fresh tomato* · *15.95*

Trinette alla Genovese
Trinette with pesto sauce, potatoes, green beans & pine nuts · *14.50*

The Corner House

501 Davenport Road
Toronto
416-923-2604

Global
MIDTOWN WEST

V / MC / DC

dinner

beer/wine

cocktails

private parties
   and corporate
   functions

non-smoking

reservations
   recommended

dress smart
   casual

menu changes
   seasonally

The Corner House has five intimate rooms, and thanks to chef Herbert Barnsteiner, who can cook like nobody's business, it's one of the great charmers on Toronto's restaurant scene. Standards include dreamy lobster bisque, grilled calamari from the chef's previous stint at Jump, and excitingly crusted lamb. Barnsteiner barnstorms on a four-course tasting menu, which may include the high-end likes of foie gras, poached oysters, roast venison, or confit of pheasant. The latter, in his seasoned hands, transcends its usual status as another dumb chicken.

Corner House
RESTAURANT

Appetizers

Asparagus and Artichoke Salad with Parmesan crisps dressed in a champagne, lemon-honey vinaigrette	*9.50*
Caesar Salad with Parmesan croutons, fresh grated Reggiano, smoked bacon, creamy oven roasted garlic dressing	*7.00*
The Corner House Market Soup	*Daily*
Warm toasted Goat cheese on tuscan bread salad with basil, sundried berries, tomatoes and grilled sweet onions with an aged balsamic vinaigrette	*9.50*
Mixed Green Salad with marinated garden vegetables tossed in a pommery mustard white balsamic vinaigrette	*7.00*
Maine Crab Cake with a Caribbean vegetable slaw, smoked chilpotles and sundried tomato aioli	*9.75*

Main Courses

Crackling oven roasted boneless Cornish Hen, with potato wild mushroom gnocchi, peach and apricot chutney and natural pan jus	*19.50*
Oven baked Seabass with coconut basmati pilaf, stirfried vegetables and a spiced mango curry sauce	*22.80*
Atlantic Salmon in a smoked horseradish crust on maple roasted squash, carrots, leeks and apples with a chanterelle broth	*19.50*
Wild Mushroom Risotto with Parmesan cheese, fresh herbs and a white truffle essence	*16.50*
Vegetarian Plate with sweet corn and smoked goat cheese soufflé, wild mushroom ragout, wilted spinach and honey charred vegetables	*17.50*
Oven roasted Rack of Lamb with an herb honey mustard crust and a toasted barley, fava bean and tomato casserole	*23.50*
Grilled Jumbo Shrimp marinated in a soya-ginger glaze on carrot risotto	*19.50*
Grilled 10 oz certified U.S. Black Angus Steak with green string beans, truffle mash and a shallot, five peppercorn sauce	*23.80*

Courthouse Market Grille

57 Adelaide Street East
Toronto
416-214-9379
www.libertygroup.com

**Global
DOWNTOWN**

V / MC / AmEx /
  D / DC

lunch

dinner

late supper

beer/wine

cocktails

private parties

non-smoking
  section

cigar lounge

reservations
  recommended

dress upscale
  casual

menu changes
  seasonally

The 1852 Adelaide Street Courthouse—with jail cells intact, one of which is a cellar for ice wines—is another Heritage property scooped up and grandly restored by the Liberty Entertainment Group. Amid marble walls and towering columns, a please-all kitchen favors spectacularly plated comfort food (corn-and-crab chowder, grilled salmon) and flirts with fusion (salmon tartare cured in tequila, duck confit spring rolls). For the most part, the food is intelligently conceived, skillfully consummated and well matched with a big slate of California wines.

COURT HOUSE
MARKET GRILLE   CHAMBER LOUNGE

Organic Mixed Greens   6.95
With Crisp Duck Crackling & Balsamic Sesame dressing

Crisp Fried Panko Calamari   7.95
with Mustard & Ancho Chili Dip

Romaine Hearts   6.95
Creamy Garlic Dressing, Herb Croutons, Reggiano Shards and Bacon

Chilled Black Tiger Shrimp   12.95
with Housemade Cocktail Sauce

Warmed Foccacia Sandwich   7.95
layered with Grilled Zucchini, Eggplant, Oven Dried Tomato,
Asiago & Spiced Black Bean Mayo and served with Salad

Minute Steak Sandwich   10.95
with an Olive, Basil & Sun-dried Tomato Tapenade and Sweet potato Fries

The Courthouse Club   9.95
Chicken, Avocado, Bacon & Black Bean Mayo on
Multigrain Bread with Fresh Cut French Fries

Quesadilla   7.95
Grilled with Roasted Chicken, Corn, Chilpotle Pepper, Monterey Jack & Salad

Atlantic Salmon   14.95
served on Spicy Stir-Fry Vegetable with Sherry and Garlic Soy Sauce

Barbecue Pizza   8.95
with Fontina Cheese, Crimini Mushrooms, Smoked Chicken,
Pesto, Roasted Pepper and drizzled with Truffle Oil

Provencale Beefsteak Pie   11.50
Beef Tenderloin, Root vegetable, Garlic, Fresh Herbs and Red Wine Sauce

Rotisserie Chicken   1/4 chicken   8.95
served with Organic Mixed Greens   1/2 chicken   11.95

8oz. Filet Mignon   21.00
with Chilpotle Herb Butter, Three-onion Potato Cake
and Red Wine Reduction

Crush Wine Bar

455 King Street
Toronto
416-977-1234
www.crushwinebar.com

French
DOWNTOWN WEST

V / MC / AmEx / DC

lunch (M-F)

dinner

late supper

take out

beer/wine

cocktails

private parties

non-smoking
 section

reservations
 recommended

dress casual

menu changes
 seasonally

After honing his art with Didier Leroy at the Fifth and stellar turns at Rouge and the defunct O-Do, chef Masayuki Tamaru crystallizes his focus on cuisine at Crush. Yes, the exposed brick, hardwood floors, and manic open kitchen seem standard issue now, but the room is handsome, convivial, and expertly staffed. "Small plates" encourage artful grazing and Tamaru whips up great Gallic memories with silken foie gras terrine, pissaladière studded with black olives and anchovies, crispy-skinned Cornish hen and steak frites. Imaginatively chosen wines give you a break, too, no small achievement.

CRUSH

WINE BAR

APPETIZERS

Oysters on the Half Shell **(Market Price)**
Onion and Oxtail Soup $9
Field Lettuces with Banyuls Vinaigrette $9
Crab Croquettes $10
Charcuterie $11
Cured Salmon Terrine $12
Duck Rillette with Lentils du Puy $12
Pear, Celery & Walnut Salad with Roquefort Dressing $12
Mussels with Tomato & Saffron $13
Wild Boar & Foie Gras en Croûte $14

MAINS

Daily Fish **(Market Price)**
Flat Iron Steak with Frites $22
Wild Mushroom Risotto $24
Pork Loin with Walnut Crust $24
Chicken Breast with Brandy Cream $25
Duck Confit with Port Licorice Sauce $26
Halibut with Crab Crust $28
Salmon with Shrimp Bisque $30
Caribou with Chestnut Honey Glaze $30

Dhaba

309 King Street West
Toronto
416-740-6622
www.toronto.com/dhaba

Indian
ENTERTAINMENT
DISTRICT

V / MC / AmEx / DC

Sunday brunch

lunch

dinner

late supper

take out

beer/wine

cocktails

high chairs

private parties

non-smoking

reservations
  recommended

dress casual

The name saluting truck-stop eateries on the byways of the Indian subcontinent, B. K. Singh's Dhaba presents its candidacy for Toronto's best Indian. A copper-framed tandoor kitchen and second-story tables overlooking the circus of the entertainment district are drawing cards. Observe the tandoor chef skewering half chickens and giant shrimp, blushing crimson in clouds of charcoal smoke. Kebabs or curries, Singh's fare stokes sensuous fires along the stations of the palate. The man really wants to please, and he's always there to counsel newcomers on harmonious pairings. Take him up on it.

DHABA

Chicken Tikka Achari $11.95

*Morsels of chicken marinated in pickle flavored
yoghurt and Bar-b'-qued in clay oven.*

Chicken Malai Kebab $11.95

*Breast of chicken marinated with crushed ginger, white
pepper, whipped yogurt and a touch of nutmeg.*

Sheesh Kebab $10.95

*Ground lamb with chopped red onions, cilantro, ginger,
peppers, skewered and bar-b-qued in clay oven.*

Fish Tikka $14.95

*Fish cubes marinated overnight with herbs, Indian
spices and "Ajwain" and cooked over charcoal.*

Tandoori Prawns $18.95

*Juicy prawns marinated with crushed garlic, olive
oil, grated coconut, carom seeds, paprika, and touch
of black pepper.*

Tandoori Tofu $10.95

*Tofu, bell peppers, onions with masala marinade cooked
on a skewer.*

Dragon Dynasty

2301 Brimley Road
Toronto
416-321-9000

Chinese
SUBURBAN NORTHEAST

Wheelchair
  access
V / MC / AmEx
breakfast
Dim Sum lunch
dinner
take out
beer/wine
cocktails
high chairs
private parties
non-smoking
reservations
  recommended
dress casual
menu changes
  seasonally

With a mere 400 seats, Dragon Dynasty ranks as a midsize Cantonese palace in the megacity's Far East. The restaurant is also in a mall where parking doesn't qualify as a form of combat. A restaurant regular urges me to visit for its extra-soft (we're talking jiggle factor) dumpling wraps and spicy sauces, and proves right on both counts. At lunch, a station turns out shrimp-and-coriander dumplings vastly superior to the *har gow* on the prowling dim sum carts. Chicken feet abound; getting at them is a sport worthy of Olympic accreditation. By night, sophistication prevails: Buddha's Delight distills shark's fin, goose web, and sea slug into a consommé of celestial complexity.

龍騰金閣 高級粵菜
DRAGON DYNASTY CHINESE CUISINE

竹笙鼎湖素
Sauteed Bouquet of Seasonal Vegetables
with deep forest mushrooms, crowned with bamboo pith $14.00

花菇燒豆腐
Braised Tofu
with shiitake mushrooms $10.00

銀絲燴雜菜
Seasonal Vegetable Medley and Vermicelli
sauteed and braised in a house sauce $10.00

醬油蒸茄片
Steamed Eggplant
in soya sauce . . . . $ 9.00

西檸脆軟雞
Pan-seared Breast of Chicken in Lemon Sauce
crispy chicken basted in a lemon sauce, with slices of fresh lemon . . . . 半只 Half $10.00
一只 Whole $20.00

雲腿鴛鴦雞
Boneless Marinated Chicken Meat
hugged by Yunnan cured ham and shiitake mushrooms, lightly poached with seasonal vegetables,
Chinese broccoli and oyster sauce . . . . 半只 Half $16.00
一只 Whole $32.00

葡汁焗火鴨
Barbecue Duckling
slowly baked and bathed in a coconut curry cream . . . . 半只 Half $14.00
一只 Whole $28.00

彩虹炒鴨柳
Rainbow Duckling
thin strips of duck, wok-fried with red and green peppers, resting on a bed of deep-fried wheat noodles . . . . $ 12.00

Dynasty

The Colonnade
131 Bloor Street West
Toronto
416-923-3323
www.toronto.com/dynasty

Chinese
DOWNTOWN

Wheelchair
  access

valet parking

V / MC / AmEx

Sunday brunch

lunch

dinner

take out

beer/wine

cocktails

high chairs

private parties

non-smoking

reservations
  recommended

dress casual

menu changes
  seasonally

Dynasty may lack the elegance of Lai Wah Heen and the well-oiled machinery of King's Garden, but it's chic enough for fashionable Bloor Street, its clientele ranging from Chinese families to elderly shoppers with sacks from Holt's and Ashley's. Dynasty proffers consistency to people who want to eat Hong Kong–style food without having to fork out huge bucks or trek to the reaches of the northeastern burbs. Its approach to seafood is classically fresh, light Cantonese. Its spring rolls are among the best in town, and the dim sum slate bowls me over with oh-so-delicate dumplings stuffed with shrimp and Chinese chives.

ENTREES – VEGETABLES

Crabmeat Broccoli	**$ 16.95**
Stir fried Broccoli with Crabmeat	
Snow-pea Leaves with Conpoy (dried scallops)	**$ 19.95**
Baby Bok-Choy with Hunan Ham	**$ 16.95**
Spinich with Spicy Beef	**$ 13.95**
Choice of Chinese Broccoli, Broccoli or Choi Sum with Garlic sauce	**$ 10.95**

ENTREES – VEGETARIAN SUGGESTIONS

Braised Tofu with Mixed Vegetables	**$ 10.95**
Szechuan Eggplant Hot Pot	**$ 14.95**
Twin Mushrooms with Oyster sauce	**$ 12.95**
Stir fried Mixed Vegetables	**$ 11.95**
Eggplant & Tofu Casserole	**$ 12.95**
Enoki with Japanese Egg White Tofu	**$ 13.95**
Braised Enoki w/ Japanese Egg White Tofu in Oyster sauce	

FRIED RICE

Yang Chow Fried Rice	**$ 12.95**
Shrimp & Pork Fried Rice	
Lotus Leaf Fried Rice	**$ 16.95**
Seafood fried rice wrapped in Lotus Leaf	
Ying Yang Fried Rice	**$ 15.95**
Fried rice topped with Shrimps in Tomato sauce; and shredded Chicken in cream sauce	
Hawaiian Fried Rice	**$ 15.95**
Fresh Pineapple & shredded Chicken fried rice served in a whole Pineapple	

Edo

359 Eglinton Avenue West
Toronto
416-481-1370
www.edosushi.com

Japanese
MIDTOWN WEST

V / MC / AmEx /
D / DC

dinner

late supper

take out/delivery

beer/wine/saki

cocktails

high chairs

private dining
room for up
to 20

catering

non-smoking

reservations
recommended

dress casual

Welcome to the restaurant that launched the current wave of hip Japanese bistros. I want to hug restaurateur Barry Chaim—a Westerner who used to live in Japan—for his high-energy fusion of sensibilities: He balances East and West with Canadian content (Arctic char, black cod, salmon caviar) on one hand, and on the other, the swash and buckle of sashimi samurai and the sweetest raw shrimp this side of Tokyo's Tsukiji Fish Market. Chaim's fun, but not irreverent, take on Japanese has just the right feel for Toronto. *Omakase,* the chef's trust-me menu, is always an adventure.

ED●

Fine Japanese Dining

APPETIZERS
(V – All Vegetarian)

EDO Appetizer	Our own shrimp and seaweed dumplings (3 pc)	$ 6.95
Edamame	Boiled soy beans in the pod, sprinkled with salt	$ 4.95
Horenso Goma AE	Spinach blanched, with EDO sesame sauce	$ 4.95
Tsukemono	Japanese Pickled Vegetables	$ 4.95
Nasu Dengaku	Baked Asian or Canadian Eggplant with EDO Dengaku Sauce	$ 6.95
Age Dashi Tofu	Deep fried tofu with EDO Ponzu sauce	$ 5.95
Tofu Steak	Grilled firm Tofu with EDO sesame sauce	$ 5.95
Yaki-Tori	Chicken grilled on skewers, with Teriyaki Sauce (3 pc)	$ 5.95
Gyoza	Pan seared Dumplings – Veal & Ginger or Vegetables (5)	$ 6.95
Chawan Mushi	Chicken & Shrimp steamed in egg custard	$ 8.95
Yaki Kinoko	Assortment of seasonal Grilled Mushrooms	$ 8.95
Sea Treasures	Assorted seafood baked in spicy "Kewpie" (mayonnaise)	$ 9.95
Ebi Almond	Tiger shrimp coated with almond & deep-fried (3 pc)	$ 9.95
Ika Sugata Yaki	Char-broiled squid with assorted vegetables	$ 10.95
Beef Tataki	Thinly Sliced Seared ANGUS Beef ' with ponzu sauce	$ 11.95
Beef-Maki	A roll of thinly sliced ANGUS beef with green onions or asparagus	$ 11.95
Soft Shell Crab	Crisp-Fried Chesapeake Bay Blue Crab, Tangy Ponzu Sauce	$ 11.95
Shrimp Boat	Giant Tiger Shrimp with Tembits, Kani, Ikura, 'Kewpie'	$ 12.95
Kaki-Age	A form of Tempura – Chopped Seafood & Vegetables	$ 12.95
Karashi Sumiso	Seared Tuna in a Japanese mustard-vinegar-Miso dressing	$ 13.95

FISH AND SEAFOOD

		Appetizer	Entrée
Tempura	Deep-Fried Shrimp and Assorted Vegetables	$12.95	$19.95
Salmon	Char-Broiled Salmon with Teriyaki Sauce or Shioyaki (Salt)	$12.95	$19.95
Saikyo Yaki	Grilled Marinated Black Cod or Sea Bass in Saikyo Sauce	$12.95	$19.95
Unaju	Freshwater BBQ Eel Filet with Unagi sauce on rice	-	$16.95
Lobster Tempura	Tempura Style Lobster Tail and assorted Vegetables		$24.95

Ematei

30 Street Patrick Street
Toronto
416-340-0472

Japanese
DOWNTOWN WEST

V / MC / AmEx / DC

lunch

dinner

take out

beer/wine

cocktails

high chairs

non-smoking

reservations
  recommended

dress casual

In spite of quake-like recessionary jitters in Tokyo, Japanese executives stationed in Toronto still put their expense accounts to good use. Frequently their choice for comfort food is this serene room located between the buzz of the Queen Street Village and the Art Gallery of Ontario. On its best days, Ematei offers a greater variety of fresh raw fish than almost any restaurant except for Omi or Hiro Sushi. Everything unfolds with expected precision. A little help from copious flasks of warm sake, and I'm once again wandering the backstreets of Shinjuku in search of easy thrills.

Japanese Restaurant Ematei

🍠 **Yam Tempura**	$3.50	**Ebi Frai**	$7.50
Yam [8pc]		Breaded fried shrimp [3pc]	
🍠 **Kabocha Tempura**	$3.50	**Kaki Frai**	$7.50
Buttercup squash [8pc]		Breaded fried Oyster meat	
🍠 **Veggie Tempura**	$6.00	**Chicken Karaage**	$6.00
Assorted veggie [9pc]		Fried Chicken [6pc]	
Tempura	$6.75	**Chicken Katsu**	$7.00
2 Shrimps and 4 kinds of veggie		Breaded chicken	
Ikageso Tempura	$6.00	**Tonkatsu**	$7.00
Sexy calamari leg [8pc]		Breaded pork	
Gyoza	$5.00	**Kushikatsu**	$7.50
Deep fried dumpling [5pc]		Breaded fried pork and veggie on skewer	
🍠 **Agedashi Tofu**	$5.25	**Soft Shell Crab**	$11.50
Tofu with veggie			
Ebi Shinjyo	$6.75		
Shrimp meat balls [3pc]			

Donburi = a meal of rice with various topping served in a bowl

Oyako Don	$8.00	**Yakiniku Don**	$11.00
Chicken and egg		Pan-fried beef	
Ten Don	$9.50	**Sukiyaki Don**	$11.00
2 Shrimps tempura and 3 Veggies		Sukiyaki beef with raw egg	
Katsu Don	$9.50	**Una Don**	$18.00
Pork cutlet		B.B.Q eel	

107

Epic

The Fairmont Royal York
100 Front Street West
Toronto
416-860-6949
www.fairmont.com

**Global
DOWNTOWN**

Wheelchair
   access
valet parking
V / MC / AmEx /
   D / DC
Sunday brunch
breakfast
lunch
dinner
beer/wine
cocktails
high chairs
live
   entertainment
private parties
non-smoking
reservations
   recommended
dress informal

The city's dowager hotel flashes its crinolines at Epic, which takes a shot at living up to an impossible name with Frette linens, Riedel stemware, Venetian glass chandeliers, and Villeroy & Boch tableware at banquettes in an old-fashioned grill-cum-supper club format. Happily, the cuisine is no afterthought: When the open kitchen is really cooking, it dispenses full-throttle Mediterranean flavors, infusing soups with saffron and garlic, erecting Brittany-style seafood towers, pairing halibut and poached lobster, and hitting the limit with fresh fish in pungent chorizo crust. VQA labels from Ontario and B.C.'s Okanagan dance on the flag-waving wine list—and about time, too.

Herb Encrusted **Australian Lamb Rack**, Stuffed Italian Eggplant, Tomato Chutney, Green Lentil and Lavender Casserole   31

Seared Northern **Arctic Char** with Crushed Peruvian Potato, Warm Long Bean Niçoise Salad and a Black Kalamata Olive Essence   26

Tagliatelle Pasta With a Québec Duckling Confit, Oyster Mushrooms, Tarragon Roma Tomato Cream   22

Charred Alberta **Beef Tenderloin Rossini**, Red Onion Jam, Baby Artichoke, Fondante Potato, Truffle Madeira Jus   32

Pecan Crusted **Halibut Filet**, Fennel and Lemon Thyme Compote, Wilted Arugula, Saffron-Vanilla Sauce   27

Braised Veal Shank "Osso Buco" With Celeriac Purée, Sautéed Cèpes, Natural Jus   28

Epic **Seafood Mosaic** (Salmon, Halibut, Red Snapper, Mussels, Scallops, Clams, Shrimp), Young Leek, Saffron Potato, Bouillabaisse Sauce With Rouille and Fresh Crostini   29

Grilled New York Striploin, Pommes Gratin, Confit Cipollini Onions, Baby Vegetables, Black Pepper Sauce   30

Garlic Roasted Corn Fed Chicken Breast, Pumpkin and Pancetta Risotto Cake, Black Currant Sauce   22

Coriander Rolled **Ahi Tuna**, Sweet Potato Purée, Baby Bok Choy, Ginger and Carrot Emulsion   29

Roast Filet of Venison, Butter Poached Lobster Medallion, Parsnip Purée, Marinated Kumquat   36

Ethiopian House

4 Irwin Avenue
Toronto
416-923-5438
www.ethiopianhouse.com

**Ethiopian
DOWNTOWN**

V / MC / AmEx / DC
lunch
dinner
late supper
take out
beer/wine
cocktails
high chairs
private parties
non-smoking
reservations
  recommended
dress casual

Magnificent photography of the women of Ethiopia (the most beautiful country in all Africa, its glories buried in headlines of war and famine) greets strangers in a downtown house dedicated to an ancient culture and its cuisine. Rustic and robust, Ethiopian cuisine commands you eat with your fingers, scooping up aromatic stews with *injera*, a floppy, sour-tasting, spongelike bread. The food delivers a spice mélange almost Indian in complexity, one of the stellar choices is an *azifa* of lentils, lemons, and green chiles. Stick to vegetables: The beef is tough as Ping-Pong balls. Coffee originated in Ethiopia, so the tableside grinding of the beans is an authentic ritual.

Ethiopian House

1. Azifa...4.75
Whole lentils boiled and mashed with lemon green
chilli and seasonings
(served cold)

2. Timatim Fit-Fit.....................................4.75
Pieces of Injera mixed with tomatoes, onions, green
chillis in oil and lemon dressing (served cold)

3. Sherro Fit-Fit..4.75
Injera mixed with dried pea flour (served cold)

4. Fer-Fer..7.45
Pieces of Injera mixed with berbere sauce.

5. Quanta Fere-Fer....................................8.85
Strips of beef prepared with berbere or awaze* and
salt and pepper, dried and served in small pieces
mixed with Injera

6. Banatu...9.25
Injera sauteed in fried beef with diced hot green
pepper topping

7. Tibs...10.55
Beef sauteed with onions, garlic, green peppers,
tomatoes and awaze* (with Injera)

Far Niente

Commerce Court South
187 Bay Street
Toronto
416-214-9922

**American
FINANCIAL DISTRICT**

V / MC / AmEx / DC

lunch

dinner

late supper

beer/wine

cocktails

private parties

non-smoking

reservations
 recommended

dress casual

menu changes
 seasonally

Saluting that prince of Napa Valley wineries, Far
Niente imbues Financial District concrete with
sunny California sensibility. Lofty ceilings, ram-
pant greenery, cleverly deployed wine crates, and
the scent of the grill highlight the celebratory
room. High-flying vegetarian dishes and a choice
of small or "whole" portions epitomize California
cool for a hipper-than-thou clientele. Grilled scallops with lobster butter atop Yukon Gold mash
and Angus entrecôte with skyscraping onion rings
steal the spotlight. The kindly $10 wine markup
that launched the room is long, long gone, but the
list glitters with Napa and Sonoma labels, and
wine-knowledgeable servers take it from there.

Far Niente

♥ *Grilled Ahi Tuna Steak,* charred green and yellow zucchini,
sweet peppers, Kalamata olives, Bermuda onions,
lemon olive oil 24.00 / 28.00

♥ *Bangkok Style Chicken Breast,* stuffed with ginger, basil and coriander,
Vietnamese vegetable roll, steamed jasmine rice and spicy peanut sauce 21.00

Australian Lamb Rack, honey and pumpkin seed crust,
cassoulet of white northern beans, celeriac, carrots, zucchini,
St. Supéry cabernet sauvignon reduction 37.00

Skillet Seared Seabass, ginger scented vegetables, Yukon gold mashed potatoes,
saffron-vanilla cream sauce and red pepper coulis 24.00 / 28.00

Roast Corn-Fed Chicken Breast, organic spinach, Yukon gold mashed potato,
forest mushroom cream sauce with Remy Martin cognac
and garden tarragon 21.00

♥ *Charred Vegetable Brochette,* almond goat cheese tartlet, zucchini,
portobello mushroom, jasmine rice, roasted red pepper coulis
and basil pesto 21.00

Filet Mignon, certified angus tenderloin, asparagus, field mushroom râgout,
Yukon gold mashed potato, bourbon peppercorn sauce
6 oz 28.00 / 10 oz 36.00

New York Steak, certified angus striploin, asparagus, grilled red pepper, french fries
10 oz 28.00 / 12 oz 34.00

Fat Cat

376 Eglinton Avenue West
Toronto
416-484-4228
www.fatcat.ca

Global
MIDTOWN WEST

V / MC / AmEx / DC

dinner

late supper

beer/wine

cocktails

private parties

non-smoking

reservations
  recommended

dress informal

menu changes
  weekly

From chef Mathew Sutherland's pocket-sized kitchen in this cozy midtown *boîte*, Fat Cat invites indulgence on a menu flagging personal passions. Foie gras from Quebec, wild salmon from B.C., *espada* from Madeira, and lamb from Australia underscore a high-flying global village larder. Meticulously trimmed, crisp-and-silky sweetbreads (the restaurant can't keep up with demand; the sublime gland back with a vengeance) paired with yielding veal tenderloin summon thymus aficionados from the breadth of the megacity. Chronically underrated skate, the ray's wing as dense and sweet as lobster, fetches loving treatment. Wednesday, designated risotto night, sees lemon-garlic-shrimp, sweetbread-smoked bacon-mushroom, and other exuberant rices.

Fat

bar & bistro

Appetizers

Escarole Salad
*with smoked pears, spiced walnuts
and a warm Stilton strudel 10-*

Stir Fried Calamari
*with fresh chillies, lime, olives, red
onion and tomato 9-*

Pan Seared Sea Scallops
*with a leek bacon cream sauce and
citrus juices 10-*

Roasted Quail
*with du puy lentils, beet apple salad
and apple cider cranberry
vinaigrette 9-*

Sautéed Foie Gras
*served on toasted crostini with sour
cherry jam and cloudberry
compote 12-*

**French Goat Cheese and
Carmalised Onion Tart**
*with a salad of frisee and arugula,
toasted hazelnuts and dried
apple 10-*

Entrées

Pan Roasted Breast of Duck
*seasoned with ground pepperberries,
with root vegetable hashbrowns, savoy
cabbage and a wild barberry sauce 24-*

Pan Seared Filet of Skate
*with shellfish, rapini and a brown
butter lemon caper sauce 19-*

Prime Striploin of Beef
*with a potato mushroom croquette,
braised kale and a pommery mustard
green peppercorn sauce 25-*

Filet of Atlantic Salmon
*cooked en papillotte with fennel
tarragon and carrots, served with
sautéed spinach and a saffron pernod
cream sauce 23-*

Tamarind Glazed Rack of Lamb
*with a warm salad of chick pea, mint,
cumin and spinach, spicy curry sauce
and a beet onion chutney 26-*

The Fifth

225 Richmond Street West
Toronto
416-979-3005

French
DOWNTOWN WEST

V / MC / AmEx / DC

dinner

late supper

beer/wine

cocktails

live
   entertainment

private parties

cigar lounge

reservations
   required

dress jacket/tie

menu changes
   monthly

When you have to stumble down a dark alley, run a gauntlet of gorillas in bouncer suits, crawl through a skull-rattling disco, and board a freight elevator to get to your table, dinner had better be something special. At this restaurant and roof garden, it is. For Chef Marc Thuet's exacting cuisine—his oeuvre at Centro was staid by comparison—we'd scale the Eiffel Tower and drop a suitcase of Euros. Pairings such as lamb carpaccio and smoked duck or surf 'n' turf grandeur marrying foie gras and lobster ragout lift you to gastronomic altitudes rarely seen in this town.

T H E 5 F I F T H

Appetizers
Consommé clair d'Orsay
Consommé of squab

Oeuf cocotte Bergère
Shepherd's egg with lamb and mushrooms

Salade cendrillon
Asparagus, celery, artichoke, potato, apples with truffles

Salade des Lords
Salad of lettuce, orange, walnuts and almonds

Sorbet surprise

Main Course
Magret de canard à la menthe
Breast of duck with mint

Tournedos de boeuf Fleuriste
Tournedos of beef with a jardinière of vegetables

Coquelet à la Bourguignonne
Cornish hen in a red wine sauce

Blanc de turbot Hollandaise
Poached turbot with hollandaisc sauce

Le poisson du marché
Fish of the day - market selection

Cheese/Desserts
Sélection de fromages français
Selection of French cheeses

Mont Blanc Mère Jean
Savarin with chestnut cream

Gâteau fromage blanc
White cheese cake with blue berries

Tarte banane et noix de coco
Banana tart with coconut

Members $70.00 / Non-members $80.00

Focaccia

17 Hayden Street
Toronto
416-323-0179

Global
DOWNTOWN

V / MC / AmEx / DC

lunch

dinner

beer/wine

cocktails

private parties

non-smoking

reservations
  recommended

dress casual

menu changes
  seasonally

A pew, with luck, foreshadows a religious experi-ence. This small room welcomes diners with invit-ing earth tones and with Larry Himes, one of the most affable servers in town. Centrally located in the busy, busy Bloor-and-Yonge zone, Focaccia dis-plays a cozy neighborhood sensibility, but surprises with the big-league oeuvre of chef Sam Gassira. Gassira concentrates on near-acrobatic intricacies with occasional fusion—say, translucent sushi-grade tuna scattered with capers and drizzled with truffle oil, with two nicely grilled shrimps on the side and a garnish of wasabi mayo. Now if only portions were only a little more generous, we wouldn't have to snack before bedtime.

focaccia restaurant

Sea scallops, ragout, horseradish, caviar 12.00

Foie gras, scampi, parcels, raspberry 20.00

Provimi sweetbreads, bacon, pearls, asparagus, pomegranate 12.00

Red leaf, radicchio, walnuts, stilton, celery, apple 8.00

Soft shell crab, crab salad, avocado 14.00

Jumbo quail, croquette, artichoke, olives, white wine 18.00

Bison striploin, squash, endive, portobello, Southern Comfort 29.00

Lamb rack, fennel, beet, orange, fused mint 30.00

Tuna filet, clam, Catalan potato, cod, caperberry 25.00

Veal tenderloin, lobster salad, herbs, chevre, pepperonata 26.00

Duck breast, confit, frisee, pear, licorice, red wine 20.00

Artic char, shrimp, spinach, rice, saffron, vanilla 25.00

Fred's Not Here

321 King Street West
Toronto
416-971-9155
www.fredsnothere.com

**Global
ENTERTAINMENT
DISTRICT**

V / MC / AmEx / DC

lunch

dinner

late supper

beer/wine

cocktails

non-smoking

reservations
   recommended

dress casual

The name a play on absentee restaurateurs, Fred's Not Here is the flagship for Fred Luk's steadily helmed Entertainment District restaurant empire: Fillet of Sole (fish and seafood), Whistling Oyster (seafood bistro), Red Tomato (eclectic bistro), and Cha Cha Cha (Latino dinner and dancing). I like Fred's irreverent murals, especially the nude brandishing a ghetto blaster. I like the fury of the open kitchen, in which the brigade toils with the coordination of a SWAT team. I like the way they turn out succulent meats and game dishes with such invention: Really, a *coffee*-marinated rib eye?

FRED'S NOT HERE
SMOKEHOUSE & GRILL

💣 grilled tenderloin of pork "Champion House" w/ sweet & sour
red pepper sauce $18.99

roast medallion of Chilean sea bass w/ horseradish tarragon
crust, littleneck clams, fizzled mustard greens & grapefruit
sherry nage $21.99

pan seared fall mushroom crusted venison medallion w/
baked cranberry & apple chutney over chive & goat cheese
whipped potato $26.99

ravioli di Nona - whipped ricotta cheese in a simple ragout
of roasted tomato, mint, garlic & bread crumbs $18.99

grilled 5-spice flavoured organic filet mignon w/ baby bok
choy, shrimp wonton & Szechwan sauce $29.99

💣 pad Thai - stir fry rice noodles in bean sauce w/ grilled
shitake, young sprouts, peppers, baby bok choy,
asparagus & crushed peanuts $15.99

rabbit cacciatore "slow braised" in buttermilk w/ apricots,
cashews & polenta, crisp fried spinach $21.99

"sexy 7-hour" duck leg w/ Alsatian inspired braised red
cabbage, juniper berries & walnuts, steamed
pancakes $14.99

braised veal osso bucco in chianti w/ porcini gnocchi,
artichokes, kalamata olives & truffle oil $19.99

Fusilli

531 Queen Street
Toronto
416-214-5148

Italian
DOWNTOWN EAST

V / MC / AmEx / DC

lunch

dinner

take out

beer/wine

cocktails

private parties

non-smoking

reservations
  recommended

dress casual

daily specials

For a hit of deeply consoling Italian comfort food, I fly like a homing pigeon to this homespun room obscurely located at Queen Street East and River. Fusilli recalls some inexpensive, unpretentious eatery in Palermo or Calabria. Happily, it follows through with rip-snorting Sicilian fare loaded with tomato, garlic, basil, oregano, and chiles. Chef-owner Giuseppe Pelligra cooks with *lust,* not love: Belting out arias along with the inescapable Andrea Bocelli, he does wonders with garlicky pastas, grilled squid, fork-tender veal, and silken tiramisu. If the dish you crave isn't on the menu, give Giuseppe a couple of days' notice and come on in.

Fusilli
ristorante

Pasta

Fusilli Salmon   10.95

Fusilli in garlic, onion, white wine, fresh salmon, in tomato sauce with a touch of cream.

Penne Boscaiola   9.95

Sauteed with onions, tomato sauce, chopped eggplant and mushrooms.

Tortellini Alla Panna   9.95

Rings filled with cheese in cream sauce.

Gnocchi Melenzane   10.95

Potato dumplings with tomato sauce, basil, cheese and eggplant

Spaghetti Innamorati   12.95

Spaghetti with shrimp and scallops in a white wine tomato sauce and basil.

Pasta Con Salsiccia   9.95

Sliced italian sausage, peppers and tomato sauce and spice

Fettuccine Al Pollo   10.95

Chicken, broccoli, white wine, garlic, fresh tomatoes and basil

Carne

Vitello Del Giorno   13.95

Vitello Pizzaiola   12.95

Veal Scaloppini in white wine sauce, tomato sauce, basil, capers and spices.

Gamelle

468 College Street
Toronto
416-923-6254
www.gamelle.com

French
WEST TORONTO

V / MC / AmEx / DC

lunch

dinner

beer/wine

patio dining

private parties

non-smoking

reservations
   recommended

dress casual

menu changes
   daily

The name *Gamelle* conjures up the solidity and comfort of an old cooking pot, just right for this College Street bistro, which is by now as cozy as an old sock. Framed *New Yorker* covers, a kitchen hung with copper pots and skillets, and an original tin ceiling in lovely rose, blue, and gold hues give the room a French country feel. Regulars arrive for standards from four-onion tart to scrumptious salt-meadow lamb. Wine lover and familiar face Jean-Pierre Centano (formerly of Auberge Gavroche, Fenton's, and Centro) plays matchmaker to food and wine with instincts honed from decades of pleasing Torontonians at the table.

gamelle

Forest Mushroom Risotto
19.00

Mille-Feuilles of Vegetable Ragoût with DuPuys Lentils and Tomato Confit,
Roasted Garlic and Artichoke Coulis
19.00
With Grilled Shrimp Add $ 2.50 Each

Pan-Seared Sea-Bass with Sicilian Blood Orange and Basil Emulsion,
Daily Vegetables
25.00

Roasted Peppercorn and Ginger Crusted Tuna with Soya Glaze and Wasabi
Ginger Sauce, Daily Vegetables
25.00

Grilled Sirloin Steak with Green Peppercorn Sauce, Country Mashed Potatoes
and Daily Vegetables
24.00
with Side of Sautéed Hedgehog Mushrooms $ 5.00

Magret of Muscovy Duck, Arugula, Caramelized Apples and Gamelle's
Potatoes with Oranges and Versinthe Liquor Infusion,
Daily Vegetables
25.00

Roasted Fresh Quebec's Île Vèrte "Pré-Salé" Leg of Lamb with Lavender
Infusion, Rosemary Mustard and Merlot Reduction, Country Mashed Potatoes
and Daily Vegetables
25.00

George Bigliardi's

463 Church Street
Toronto
416-922-9594
www.toronto.com/georgebigliardis

Steakhouse
DOWNTOWN

V / MC / AmEx / DC

lunch

dinner

late supper

beer/wine

cocktails

high chairs

private parties

smoking in bar
area

reservations
recommended

dress informal

menu changes
seasonally

Steak man George Bigliardi has seen it all in more than twenty-five years of serving up slabs of charred prime in a former Church Street funeral parlor. In his immaculately appointed room, framed glossies testify to the parade of celebrity, including not only Frank Sinatra, Anthony Quinn, and Bette Midler, but, good heavens, the pope, photographed waving to Bigliardi from the passing popemobile. Bigliardi stayed the carnivorous course as cholesterol beleagured beeferies, the hockey crowd vanished with the closing of Maple Leaf Gardens, and the big U.S. steakhouse chains moved in from Chicago and New Orleans. A big hand for the little survivor.

FROM THE CHARCOAL BROILER

(All our steaks are U.S. choice)

New York Sirloin - *Maple Leaf Cut* 29.95
Thick New York Sirloin 34.95
Prime Rib Steak 31.50
Filet Mignon - *wrapped in bacon* 31.95
Porterhouse Steak 37.95
Pepper Steak - *N.Y. with peppercorn sauce* 32.95
Châteaubriand Bouquetière for Two - *carved at your table* 68.95
Surf & Turf - *lobster tail & New York sirloin* 39.95
Washington State Grilled Rack of Lamb 34.95
BBQ Spare Ribs 26.95
The above entrées served with choice of baked potato, potato skins, home fries or French fries.

> **STEAK TARTARE 26.95**

VEAL AND CHICKEN

Veal Scaloppine - *light mushroom sauce and white wine* 18.95
Veal Piccata - *sautéed with lemon and white wine* 18.95
Veal Parmigiana - *mozzarella cheese and tomato sauce* 17.95
Thick Veal Chop Provimi Charcoal Broiled 33.50
Grilled Breast of Chicken 16.95
Breast of Chicken Forestière - *light cream and mushroom sauce* 16.95
Breast of Chicken Parmigiana - *mozzarella cheese and tomato sauce* 16.95

SEAFOOD

Dover Sole - *amandine or meunière* 28.95
Grilled Halibut Steak - *with cajun or lemon butter sauce* 22.50
Orange Roughie - *lemon and fine herbs* 22.50
Atlantic Salmon - *broiled or poached with light hollandaise sauce* 23.50
Broiled Swordfish Steak - *lemon and capers* 22.50
Alaskan King Crab - *steamed or broiled, with rice pilaf and lemon* .... priced accordingly
Broiled Lobster Tail - *with rice pilaf and lemon* .... priced accordingly

Golden Court Abalone Restaurant

270 West Beaver Creek Road, unit 22
Richmond Hill
905-707-6628

Chinese
SUBURBAN NORTH

Wheelchair
  access
valet parking
V / AmEx
breakfast
lunch
dinner
take out
beer/wine
cocktails
high chairs
private parties
non-smoking
reservations
  recommended
dress casual
menu changes
  seasonally

In the suburban starkness of a Richmond Hill mall, Golden Court Abalone Restaurant struts its stuff—shark's fin, bird's nest, and sea cucumber—for the multitude, and to gild the Cantonese lily, holds in reserve prime Japanese abalone. The kitchen takes the pucklike shellfish and braises it until it won't yank the crowns out of your teeth and until it actually tastes like something. Abalone-lovers from the north and northeast burbs gather to consume 600 pounds a year. Slathered with oyster sauce, the critter is sweet and subtle, with sea-urchin appeal. It isn't for everybody, but one can always find consolation in fat shrimps and crispy Peking duck.

GOLDEN COURT
ABALONE RESTAURANT

	半只 Half	全只 Whole
京醬扒大鴨 Braised Duck with Spicy Sauce	12.00	23.50
羅漢扒大鴨 Braised Duck with Mix-Vegetable	13.50	26.00
紅棉扒大鴨 Braised Duck with Fish Maw	13.50	26.00
八珍扒大鴨 Braised Duck with Assorted Meat & Seafood	14.50	28.00
菜膽上湯雞 Steamed Chicken with Vegetable in Supreme Soup	11.00	22.00
紫蘿炒雞片 Sauteed Sliced Chicken with Ginger & Pineapple		9.50
蔥油脆炸雞 Braised Crispy Fried Chicken with Ginger & Green Onion		9.50
腰果炒雞丁 Stir Fried Diced Chicken with Cashew Nut		10.50
西檸煎軟雞 Deep Fried Boneless Chicken with Lemon Sauce		10.50
辣爆雞丁 Stir Fried Diced Chicken with Spicy Sauce		9.50

Golden Thai

105 Church Street
Toronto
416-868-6668

Southeast Asian
DOWNTOWN

V / MC / AmEx / DC

lunch

dinner

take out

beer/wine

cocktails

non-smoking

reservations
  recommended

dress informal

An antidote to endless winter, Thai restaurants lay claim to more corners than Starbucks in this town. Everyone has their darling, but a track record speaks for itself: Golden Thai has been packing the house for more than a dozen years. The original servers are still around, which speaks volumes, and Kiem and Hoeng Thung are still among the most gracious hosts on Toronto's restaurant scene. Tapestries shimmer under a zany collection of chandeliers, the jazz track urges you to loosen up, and the cooking, while breaking no new ground, never skimps on sweet basil, lemongrass, and chiles. Often-neglected vegetarians get respect here, too.

GOLDEN THAI

21. THAI MUSHROOM SOUP *   5.95
Fresh mushrooms, lemon grass, lime juice, and chilies.
(Vegetarian version also available.)

22. TOM YAM GOONG: LEMON SHRIMP*   6.95
A favorite! Shrimp in a lemon grass, mushroom, coriander, chili broth.

23. TOM YAM GAI: LEMON CHICKEN*   5.95
Tender chicken and mushrooms in a spicy lemon grass broth with lime juice and fresh chilies.

24. TOM KHA GAI: CHICKEN COCONUT   6.95
Chicken and mushrooms in a coconut broth with galangal.

25. THAI HOT AND SOUR SOUP *   5.95
Tofu, bamboo shoots, mushroom, and egg in a hot and sour chicken broth.

57. GAI YANG: GRILLED CHICKEN   7.95
Marinated grilled chicken served with Golden Thai sauce.

58. CASHEW CHICKEN*   9.95
Chicken breast stir-fried with roast cashews, peppers and tamarind sauce.

59. GAI PHAD KRAPHAO: BASIL CHICKEN**   8.95
Chicken stir-fried with spicy Thai basil sauce.

60. GAI PHAD KHING: GINGER CHICKEN*   7.95
Chicken tossed with shredded ginger, mushrooms, and onions.

61. GREEN CHICKEN CURRY**   8.95
Chicken in a coconut curry sauce spiked with Thai basil and chilies.

Goldfish

372 Bloor Street West
Toronto
416-513-0077
www.toronto.com/goldfish

Bistro
ANNEX

V / MC / AmEx / DC

Sunday brunch

lunch

dinner

late supper

take out

beer/wine

cocktails

private parties

non-smoking

reservations
   recommended

dress informal

menu changes
   seasonally

True story: A jazzy dude and his Drew Barrymore look-alike girlfriend are sashaying past Goldfish. The girlfriend stops and peruses the menu. The dude twitches with irritation, glances up at the restaurant logo, and growls, "C'mon, you know you don't like *seafood!*" The goldfish is a good luck symbol in the Iranian culture of proprietors Sandy and Hamid Lotfi. Goldfish is also the last word in Annex chic, a pale, smartly minimalist room serving California-style plates of layered flavors. Pizzas, grills, and rack of lamb crusted in nuts are always good bets. People still call to ask about goldfish on the menu: Will that be fried, grilled, or hmmmm, a nice tartare?

goldfish

PASTAS

SPINACH GNOCCHI, GRILLED CHICKEN, MUSHROOM FRICASSE, CUMIN CREAM SAUCE	15
ANGEL HAIR, GRILLED SHRIMP, LEEK, GALANGAL FLAVOURED TOMATO BROTH	17
PENNE, EGGPLANT, GARLIC, CAPER BERRIES, TOMATO, NICOISE OLIVE, EXTRA VIRGIN OLIVE OIL	12
TAGLIATELLE, BAY SCALLOPS, ARUGULA, FINE HERBS & OLIVE OIL	16
LINGUINE, BRAISED RABBIT, TARRAGON-MERLOT REDUCTION	14
BEET RAVIOLI, CRANBERRY JAM, CURRY CREAM SAUCE	13

PIZZAS

DUCK CONFIT, BRAISED ONION, CHEVRE	14
ARTICHOKE PUREE, ROASTED VEGETABLES, TALEGGIO	14
HERB PESTO, SMOKED SALMON, SHAVED RED ONION, NICOISE OLIVES, DICED TOMATO	13
ROASTED TOMATO SAUCE, CHICKEN, SHAVED ASIAGO, MUSHROOMS, BASIL	13

MAINS

GRILLED OSTRICH, ORZO, LOBSTER, CARROTS, RED PEPPER, CHRISTOPHINE, VANILLA-ORANGE CREAM SAUCE	27
DEBONED CORNISH HEN, PRESERVED LEMON & RAISIN ISRAELI COUS-COUS, CARROT REDUCTION	22
PAN SEARED BEEF TENDERLOIN, YUKON GOLD, SWEET POTATO & EGGPLANT GRATIN, RED CABBAGE, ASPARAGUS, SAGE JUS	27
ORANGE-POPPYSEED CRUSTED BAKED SALMON FILLET, SMOKED SALMON & WILD RICE SKILLET CAKE, MUSKMELON SALSA, SUNDRIED CHERRY COULIS	21
HERB ROASTED CAPON BREAST, POTATO & TALEGGIO CROQUETTE, PORTOBELLO MUSHROOM CAP, SAUTEED SPINACH, NATURAL PAN JUS	21
MACADAMIAN NUT CRUSTED AUSTRALIAN LAMB RACK, RUSSET MASH, HARICOTS VERTS, CARROT & ZUCCHINI TURNADE, SAUTEED CHANTERELLE MUSHROOMS, MARSALA JUS	28
STRIPED BASS, WARM SPINACH & LOBSTER SALAD, TOMATO CONFIT, ROASTED SWEET POTATO, BLACK BUTTER	24
WILD MUSHROOM RISOTTO, SWEET PEAS, TOMATO, FRESH SHAVED TRUFFLE	17

Grand Yatt

9019 Bayview Avenue
Richmond Hill
905-882-9388

Chinese
SUBURBAN NORTH

V / MC / AmEx
lunch
dinner
take out
beer/wine
cocktails
private parties
non-smoking
reservations
  recommended
dress informal
menu changes
  seasonally

The Big Abalone of Chinese palaces on Toronto's northern frontier, Grand Yatt has it all: lights so bright you're ready to confess to crimes you didn't know existed, servers who couldn't go faster on greased ice, and abundances of shark's fin, Peking duck, and suckling pig. To negotiate the Cantonese-language menu for snake soup, sea cucumber, and seasonal critters routinely deemed too foreign for timorous sensibilities, bring an omnivorous Chinese friend. In any event, you can't go wrong with deep-fried this, crispy-skinned that, or juicy-fleshed anything that swims. Dim sum and congee—silky rice porridge—comfort Hong Kong expats over lunch.

居悦魚翅酒家
GRAND YATT

Mixed Chinese Special Vegetarian $14.00
ミクス中華野菜炒め

Braised Fresh Mushroom with Crab Meat.. $14.80
キノコとカニ肉煮

Braised Vegetable with Bamboo Shoots & Mushroom $14.80
竹の子と椎茸炒め

Stir Fried Seasonal Vegetable $12.00
季節野菜炒め

Stir Fried Mixed Vegetable $12.00
季節野菜かき回す炒め

Braised Leaf Mustard with Chinese Ham... $15.50
野菜と中華ハム煮込

Spring Sprout with Garlic & Consume.. $13.00
ニンニクと豆苗スープ

Chinese Lettuce w/ Shredded Chili & Bean Curd Sauce $12.00
中華野菜とピーマン發酵した豆乳ソース

Fried Bean Curd w/ Fungus & Shrimp Roe... $13.00
豆腐と竹の髄ヽェビの卵煮もの

Grano

2035 Yonge Street
Toronto
416- 440-1986
www.grano.ca

Italian
MIDTOWN

V / MC / AmEx / DC
breakfast
lunch
dinner
late supper
take out
beer/wine
cocktails
high chairs
private parties
non-smoking
dress casual
menu changes
seasonally

Roberto Martella is a big, happy guy who likes to see people eating. His rambling Grano, part café, part restaurant, part piazza, part classroom (Italian "language and linguine" lessons Mondays) is, after all these years, a midtown institution. Shoppers scour the antipasto shelves for caponata and eggplant breaded Sicilian-style. In rooms run riot with home-mixed Mediterranean hues, vintage posters, and wine bottles, diners stuff their gaping maws with *bombolini* (giant raviolis), pan-fried Provimi veal liver, and such. Martella, his wife, and four children still live upstairs—enough to give family values a good name.

Antipasti

Insalata rosso, bianco & verde   8.95
arugola salad with goat cheese crostini & pear slices
in a fig, mustard & extra virgin olive oil dressing

Sapore di marE   9.95
sea scallops with grilled radicchio wrapped in
pancetta, caramelized onions and an arugola pesto

CAlaMari ai Ferri
grilled squid w chili & reduceda vinegar 10.95

Calamari   deep fried squid   10.95

Italia Mia   10.95
prosciutto di Parma, mozzarella di bufala & a shard
of grana padano topped with aged balsamic vinegar

Carpaccio di vitello   9.95
raw veal with cracked black pepper & extra
virgin olive oil with grana padano & cannellini beans

PaSta   full order 12.95 1/2 10.95

Spaghetti alla Chitarra agrodolce
Square cut spaghetti from the Abruzzo region
in a zucchini, peppers, celery & onion ragu with
infornate olives & provolone cheese

Linguine al nero di seppia
flat spaghetti with squid & octopus in a black
squid ink sauce with white wine, garlic & capers

Orecchiette della nonna
ear shaped pasta shells from Puglia with rapini &
speck (smoked prosciutto) in a sundried tomato
puree, garlic, extra virgin olive oil & white winesauce

Hemispheres

Metropolitan Hotel
108 Chestnut Street
Toronto
416-599-8000
www.metropolitan.com/hemis/

Global
DOWNTOWN

Wheelchair
  access

valet parking

V / MC / AmEx /
  D / DC

breakfast

lunch

dinner

beer/wine

cocktails

high chairs

private parties

non-smoking

reservations
  recommended

dress informal

menu changes
  daily

Deeply overshadowed by the stellar Lai Wah Heen in Henry Wu's swank Metropolitan Hotel, Hemispheres remains a perennial discovery. The room has looks to burn: undulating blond wood surfaces, smart contemporary art, and a glass wall allowing voyeurs to peer into the kitchen and watch a team of cooks in a flurry of action worthy of a John Woo movie. Quail glazed in Ontario ice wine and duo of duck—rare breast and crispy-skinned confit—set the style, with kaffir lime–blueberry tart to finish. Breakfast should be considered, too; not ham and eggs, but an elegant spin on Chinese congee—silken rice porridge studded with condiments and loads of ginger.

Hemispheres
RESTAURANT BISTRO

Grilled Sea Scallop and Ahi Tuna Tartare on Nori Green Tea Rice Cake $14
with Sesame Oil, Soy Glaze, Chili Oil and Wasabi Cream

Lobster Ravioli with Fine Vegetable Julienne and Herbed Lemon Grass Sauce $16

Hot and Sour Calamari Salad with Fine Beans, Avocado, Mango, Papaya $12
and Tomato Salsa, Taro and Lotus Root Crisps

Goat Cheese, Char-grilled Eggplant, Tomato and Zucchini Tian with $11
Arugula Lettuce, Basil and Tomato Oils

Cookstown Organic Baby Greens in Charred Zucchini Ribbon with $ 9
Roasted Bell Peppers, Lime Segments and Soft-herb Balsamic Vinaigrette

Warm Dungeness Crab Cake on Citrus Segments, Tomato, $13
Mango and Avocado Salsa

Chef's Selection of Vegetarian Bento Box: $20
Cookstown Baby Greens, Spaghetti with Asian Pesto, Steamed Baby Vegetables,
Cabbage and Mushroom Timbale

Halibut Fillet crusted with a Sea Scallop Mousse, Mussels and Clams, $27
with Fennel and Trio of Bell Peppers, Green Pea Nage and Chives

Crispy Sea Bass Fillet on Thai Shrimp Cake, Fine Vegetable Pearls and $29
Champagne Sauce

Veal Medallions wrapped with Double Smoked Veal Bacon with $30
Asparagus Risotto, Creamed Mushrooms and Green Peppercorn Jus

Roast Honey and Soy Marinated Duck Breastwith Portobello Mushroom $29
and Napa Cabbage Timbale, Caramelized Butternut Squash and Shiitake Jus

Herbs

3187 Yonge Street
Toronto
416-322-0847
www.herbsrestaurant.com

Bistro
UPTOWN

V / MC / AmEx / DC
lunch
dinner
late supper
take out
beer/wine
cocktails
high chairs
private parties
non-smoking
reservations
  recommended
dress casual
menu changes
  seasonally

Pastel hues, a tented ceiling, reprints of art from van Gogh, and lovingly racked wines provide the Mediterranean framework for Tony Nuth's flamboyantly contemporary cuisine. In its first decade, Herbs established a solid following, and into its second, the restaurant holds its own on a brutally competitive uptown strip. The menu changes frequently (calf's liver excepted because regulars can't bear to see it go). Just bring me crisped prosciutto and goat cheese to start and then duck confit in a sweet-and-sour raspberry glaze. How about osso buco in coffee and sambuca? Lemon tart is the dessert du jour—and every jour—in an eatery that rarely snoozes.

HERBS
Restaurant

LA SOUPE
The daily composed soup 6.

LES ESCARGOTS ET LES CHAMPIGNONS
Mushroom caps stuffed with escargot de Bourgogne gratinées with bacon herb brioche 12.

LA ROMAINE ET LES EPINARDS
Caesar salad with baby spinach, grana padano and herb croutons 7.

LES COQUILLES SAINT JACQUES ET LENTILLES
Jumbo sea scallops seared with tender leeks and du Puy lentil broth 14.

LA MACHE ET LE RADIS
V Leaf lettuce and mâche salad with organic valentine radish, sprouts and a red wine vinaigrette 8.

LE FOIE GRAS ET LA POIRE
Pan seared foie gras and rosemary- wine poached pear with toasted brioche 21.

LE CHEVRE ET LA BETTERAVE ROUGE
V French goat cheese baked in filo pastry with organic beet tartare and frisee salad 12.

LES CHAMPIGNONS ET LE XERES
V Cremini mushroom soup with sherry and white truffle essence 7.

LE GRAVLAX ET LES CALAMARS
Dill cured salmon gravlax with sautéed calamari and pineapple relish 13.

LE RISOTTO VERT ET LES CAILLES
Parsley risotto and de-boned quail with a bundle of white asparagus app 14. main 26.

LES RAVIOLIS ET LE RIS DE VEAU
Ravioli filled with sweetbreads served with Parma ham and sage cream sauce app 13. main 24.

Hiro Sushi

171 King Street East
Toronto
416-304-0550

**Japanese
DOWNTOWN**

V / MC / AmEx

lunch

dinner

take out

beer/wine

private parties

non-smoking

reservations
  recommended

dress casual

menu changes
  daily

If the service moves with the speed of escargot on Valium, it's no matter: Chef-owner Hiro Yoshida's fare comes renowned for its breadth and depth of miniature masterpieces, Toronto's most intricate sushi and sashimi. The ultimate spoiling is *omakase,* the Japanese version of "trust me," in which the ritual procession of dishes arrives at the chef's choice and pace (count on three hours)— a tour of Yoshida's harmonious little universe and his spin on the Zen-inspired *kaiseki,* each course a contrast to the senses, the delightful accents including wasabi root and shiso blossoms. Nine trips to Japan, and I've never experienced anything quite like it.

HIRO SUSHI

Karei No Kara Age   18.00

Tender deep fried flounder
meat and crispy bone, with
ponzu sauce

Gyu Tataki   10.00

Thin-sliced very rare beef on
sliced onion, served with ponzu
sauce, green onion and chili
radish on top

Tempura   12.00

Deep fried shrimp and vegetables
in our own special tempura batter
with home made tempura sauce

Edamame   4.00

Boiled green soy beans

Yakitori (2 pieces)   5.00

Skewered chicken, broiled with
home made Yakitori sauce

Age Dashi Tofu   6.00

Deep fried tofu in a light soup with
chili radish and green onions

Ika Sugata Yaki   9.00

Grilled, tender squid with Soy
sauce and chili pepper

Vegetable Tempura   8.00

Deep fried vegetables in our
special tempura batter

Ika Shio Kara   4.00

Home made salty marinated
squid (Excellent with sake)

Kinoko Foil Yaki   8.00

Several kinds of flavourful
mushrooms with butter and soy
sauce

The Host

14 Prince Arthur Avenue
Toronto
416-962-4678
www.welcometohost.com

Indian
YORKVILLE

V / MC / AmEx / DC

lunch

dinner

take out

beer/wine

cocktails

high chairs

private parties

non-smoking

reservations
   recommended

dress jacket/tie

menu changes
   weekly

Settled into the premises of the defunct Le Rendezvous on Prince Arthur, Host boasts unprecedented ambience for Toronto Indian: Other than a few subcontinental touches—check out the smirking Rajasthani camels—the five rooms are as sumptuous as ever. Chef-owner Sanjeev Sethi takes nothing for granted, turning out layered, powerhouse flavors on every front, infusing his curries with armloads of spices, baking fresh Indian Ocean pomfret in the tandoor and devising a clever menu for health-fixated diners. The weekday lunch buffet leaves you crawling out on all fours. Coveted atrium tables call for reservations. In summer, the patio emulates some spoiled maharajah's garden.

Also: 160 East Beaver Creek Road
        Richmond Hill
        905-709-7070

        33 City Centre Drive
        Mississauga
        905-566-4678

Sab-Se-Pehle
(Starters)

Vegetable Samosa ★★
Crisped patties stuffed with spiced potatoes and green peas
$3.50

Pakora Platter ★★
Platter of garden fresh vegetable fritters and onion bhajia
$4.99

Bhel Puri ★★
Chick pea flour twigs, puffy rice mixed with
onion, potatoes and tamarind sauce - served cold
$4.99

Vegetable Kebab ★★
Mixed vegetables finely minced and skewered in clay oven
$7.99

Paneer Tikka ★★
Homemade cottage cheese cubes, marinated
in yogurt and spices, B.B.Q. in Tandoor
$8.99

Fish Amritsari ★★
Fish fillet, in gram flour batter and deep fried
$7.99

Il Mulino

1060 Eglinton Avenue West
Toronto
416-780-1173

Italian
WEST TORONTO

V / MC / AmEx / DC

dinner

take out

beer/wine

cocktails

private parties

non-smoking

reservations
recommended

dress casual

menu changes
weekly

The room, with its arched ceiling, seventeenth-century hurricane lamps and smoked glass mirror for scribbling daily specials, steals thunder in a neighborhood so peppered with *ristorantes* that you might go Italian by osmosis. Michael and Margi Pagliaro defined their style—the warm welcome, the gust of olive oil, plates of designer greens, fish lovingly bedded on the grill—in the glory days of Barolo, but they've fine-tuned it at Il Mulino, surpassing themselves with stellar octopus carpaccio, basil-tomato ice cream bolstering *mozzarella di bufala,* and juicy quails—stuffed with salt-cured foie gras.

IL MULINO
RISTORANTE

PASTA & RISOTTO

Risotto Sapori Di Mare
Risotto with Mixed Seafood in a
Light Tomato White Wine Sauce $ 18.95

Risotto Romagnolo
Risotto with Wild Mushroom,
Truffle Oil and Shaved Parmigiano $ 18.95

Penne Del'Ortolano
Penne with Grilled
Vegetables Tomato Sauce $ 11.95

Linguine Verdi
Fresh Green Linguini with a
Julienne of Veal and Roasted Peppers
in a Garlic and Extra Virgin Olive Oil $ 14.95

Paglia E Fieno
Green and White Linguini with
Chicken in a Tomato Cream
Sauce, Topped with Arugola $ 14.95

Tagliolini Gorgonzola
Fresh Tagliolini, Broccoli,
Pinenuts & Sundried Tomato,
Gorgonzola Cheese Sauce $ 14.95

SECONDI

Lombata Di Vitello
Grilled Veal Chop, Caramelized
Shallot, Natural Jus Reduction $ 24.95

Vitello Alla Sorrentina
Veal Scaloppine with Eggplant
Tomato & Cheese $ 22.95

Galletto Al Mattone
Grilled Boneless Half Free Range
Chicken with Lemon Juice & Fresh Herbs $ 20.95

Vitello Alla Cece
Veal Scaloppine, with Wild Mushrooms
Topped with Melted Bocconcini Cheese $ 23.95

Bistecca Ai Ferri
New York Striploin Steak, served
with Marinated Red Peppers
and Roasted Potato $ 28.95

Agnello Del Fornaio
Roast Rack of Lamb, served
with Rosti Potatoes in a Honey
Mustard sauce $ 29.95

Quaglie Mulino
Boneless Quails Stuffed with Salt
Cured Foie Gras, Berries Compote,
Port Wine Reduction $ 27.95

Pesce Alla Griglia
Daily Fresh Fish   **(Market Price)**

Il Posto Nuovo

York Square
148 Yorkville Avenue
Toronto
416-968-0469

Italian
YORKVILLE

V / MC / AmEx / DC

lunch

dinner

late supper

take out

beer/wine

cocktails

private parties

non-smoking

reservations
 recommended

dress smart
 casual

menu changes
 twice yearly

An irresistibly Italianate *giardino* in summertime—tourist busloads actually pause to have snapshots taken here—Il Posto has reigned as doge of York Square in the heart of Yorkville for more than two decades. The word *Nuovo* in the name signals the proprietorship of veteran restaurateur Frank Agostino, who's both upgraded the surroundings (the collection of 1812 Rossini archaeological prints is an original from Sotheby's) and maintained the tradition of pampering expense-account regulars. Chilean sea bass and Provimi veal chop are predictable best-sellers, but the minced calf's liver sauced in balsamic vinegar says much about a serious kitchen.

IL POSTO
NUOVO

FETTUCINE ALL' UOVO CON CAPPESANTE
Egg Fettucine with Seared Sea Scallops and
Fresh Peashoots, Herbs, Light Butter Sauce ... 19.00

LINGUINE AI FRUTTI DI MARE
Fresh Seafood Tossed with Linguine
in a Spicy Tomato Sauce ... 18.00

GNOCCHI AI CARCIOFI E TIMO
Homemade Gnocchi with Fresh Artichokes,
Thyme and Reggiano Sauce ... 17.00

FEGATO ALLA VENEZIANA
Emincee of Provimi Calves' Liver, Glazed Onions
In a Balsamic Natural Jus ... 21.00

SALMONE ALLA GRIGLIA
Grilled Atlantic Salmon Filet with a Sushi Ginger,
Caper and Tomato Salsa, Minted Couscous and
Purple Cabbage Confit...24.00

BRANZINO AL FORNO
Roasted Seabass Topped with a Herb,
Parmigiano Crust – Lemon and Yellow Pepper
Coulis, Rice Vermicelli ... 28.00

Indian Rice Factory

414 Dupont Street
Toronto
416-961-3472

**Indian
ANNEX**

V / MC / DC

dinner

take out

beer/wine

cocktails

high chairs

non-smoking

reservations
  recommended

dress casual

menu changes
  seasonally

Three decades in the restaurant business means you must be doing something right: applause for the indefatigable Amar Patel and her Indian Rice Factory. Well established but never resting on its laurels, the IRF is a kitsch-free zone, easy on the eye, with burnished hardwood floors, suspended multicolored halogens, and smart Indian prints and fabrics on the walls. Mrs. Patel's kitchen is showing a fine measure of consistency these days, with its reach extending from feathery pakoras and samosas to the lush heights of Indian vegetarian cuisine: Give me *kofta*, softly textured grenades of minced, melded vegetables singing ever so sweetly in jackets of yogurt and spice.

Indian Rice Factory

À LA CARTE

JHINGA: Marinated shrimps, broiled, finished in a light tomato, coconut and ginger-garlic curry. $15.95
SHRIMP VINDALOO: Marinated, very **hot** and sour Goan curry. $15.95
HURRI MUCHI: Fresh Chilean sea bass, marinated, grilled, and finished in a green curry (spinach, green chillies, mint, coriander, green onions, ginger-garlic). $15.95

BUTTER CHICKEN: Boneless, marinated in yogurt and spices, broiled and finished in a tomato, cream and butter curry seasoned with green chillies, ginger, green pepper and fenugreek leaves. $15.95
CHICKEN KHASHABAD: Breast of chicken stuffed with almonds, cashew nuts, raisins and mild paneer cheese finished in cashew and coconut milk, yogurt, onion, cream. $15.95
CHICKEN VINDALOO: Boneless, simmered in a very **hot** and sour Goan curry. $13.95
CHICKEN CURRY: Simple, traditional, tomato, ginger and onion curry. $12.95

LAMB TORONTO: Slow-simmered lean lamb shank, finished in a smooth spinach curry. $14.95
LAMB ROGAN JOSH: Lean lamb shank, slow-cooked in a mild tomato and aromatic spices curry. $13.95
LAMB VINDALOO: Shank of lean lamb in a very **hot** and sour Goan curry. $14.95

BEEF CURRY: Tomato, green chilli, ginger, garlic and onion curry. $13.95
BEEF VINDALOO: Finished in a very **hot** and sour Goan curry. $14.95
BEEF BHUNA: Braised, in a thick tomato, green chilli, ginger and onion curry. $14.95

BHARTA: Roasted eggplant, puréed and seasoned with green chillies, onions, garlic and tomatoes. $9.95
CHANNA MASALA: Chick peas, ginger, green chillies, tomato and spices. $9.95
DAAL: Fresh lentils of the day, slow-cooked, traditionally seasoned. $7.95
VEGETABLE KOFTA: Balls of shredded fresh vegetables served in a yogurt and ginger-garlic curry. $9.95
AALOO METHI: Fresh fenugreek leaves steam-sautéed, lightly seasoned, potato. $9.95
AALOO GOBI: Steamed cauliflower finished with ginger, tomato, spices and potato. $9.95
MATAR PANEER: Mild paneer cheese, green peas simmered in a mild cream-tomato curry. $9.95

**SPECIAL REQUESTS**: Priced accordingly.

Irie

808 College Street
Toronto
416-531-1599
www.exclusive.com/irie.html

Caribbean
LITTLE ITALY

V / MC / AmEx /
  D / DC

dinner

late supper

take out

beer/wine

cocktails

high chairs

private parties

non-smoking

reservations
  recommended

dress casual

menu changes
  seasonally

Jamaica's fiery-fruity cuisine is the most distinct in the Caribbean, and Irie is the best place in Toronto to find it because Eglon Walker is probably the only professional chef in Toronto doing it. His Irie is as carefree as a sultry day by the turquoise sea, a beach hut without the beach and the *ganja*, festooned with Bob Marley memorabilia and aromatic with allspice. Pan-seared jerk pork, chicken, and snapper are better than I remember from numerous times in Mo' Bay or Ocho Rios. And Walker doesn't compromise on incendiary Scotch bonnet peppers: Timid palates are advised to invest in asbestos suits.

IRIE CARIBBEAN RESTAURANT

APPETIZERS

Irie Pepper Shrimp	8.50
Coconut Rum Batter Shrimp	8.50
(with Mango & Papaya Chutney)	
Jerk Shrimp On A Stick	8.50
(with Mango & Papaya Chutney)	
Irie Spicy Wings	6.50
Irie Pizza	6.50
Topped with Avocado, Jerk	
Chicken & Vegetables	
(Vegetarian available)	

SOUP

Irie Pepper Pot Soup	4.00
(Vegertarian Style)	
Soup of the Day	4.00
(Ask your server)	

SALAD

House Salad	4.50
(Exotic greens, Tomato,	
Cucumber & house dressing)	
Jerk Chicken Salad	8.00
(Assorted greens topped with	
tender Jerk Chicken , Mango,	
Papaya, Avocado & Jack Fruit)	
Jerk Shrimp Salad	12.00

ENTREE

Served with Rice & Peas and Vegetables

Jerk Chicken	9.00
Curry Chicken	9.00
Stewed Chicken	9.00
Island Style Fry Chicken	8.00
Braised Oxtail	11.00
Stir Fry Vegetables	8.50
Irie Jerk Steak	12.50
Jerk Red Snapper	12.00
(stuffed with vegetables)	
Steam Red Snapper	12.00
(with banana, dumpling, okra,	
carrot & calaloo)	
Escovitch Red Snapper	12.00
Stewed Fish	12.00
Jerk Salmon Fillet	12.95
(with eskellion & thyme jus)	
Stir Fry Shrimp	12.00
Shrimp Rundown	12.00
Rundown (Coconut Cream Sauce)	
Curry Shrimp	12.00
Jerk Shrimp on a Stick	12.00
Ackee and Cod Fish	12.00
Shrimp Creole	12.00
Fish of the Day	
(Market Price)	

Izba

648 The Queensway
Toronto
416-251-7177
www.ibza.on.ca

Polish
WEST TORONTO

V / MC / AmEx
lunch
dinner
take out
beer/wine
cocktails
high chairs
private parties
non-smoking
reservations
  recommended
dress casual

On a bleak stretch of the Queensway, Izba is a Polish restaurant merrily festooned with gingerbread trim, painted furniture, crockery, dolls, and fake flowers, more tchotchkes than the eye can register in a week. You expect owner Monica Sarsh to polka out of the kitchen juggling pork schnitzels the size of hovercraft—and she does. The food—simple, hearty, and unabashedly Old World; schnitzels the whole show—comes at prices you haven't seen in thirty years. Zywiec beer imported from Poland in half-liter bottles is awfully good, but watch out for the Polish coffee: Spiked with three fruit brandies, it can send you into the street cross-eyed.

IZBA RESTAURANT

Salads

Cucumber Salad.................$3.95
Lettuce Salad....................$3.95
Tomato Salad...................$3.95
Mixed Salad.....................$3.95

A La Carte

Vienna Schnitzel with potatoes
and fresh vegetables...$6.95

Chicken Breast Fillet with
potatoes and fresh vegetables................................$8.95

Fillet of Sole grilled or breaded with
potatoes and fresh vegetables................................$8.95

Broiled Salmon with
potatoes and fresh vegetables................................$8.95

Pork Tenderloin Shish Kabob with mushrooms, onions, potatoes
and fresh vegetables...$8.95

Pierogies with cheese and potato.......................$8.95

Jacques Bistro du Parc

126A Cumberland Street
Toronto
416-961-1893
www.toronto.com/jacquesbistro

French
YORKVILLE

V / MC / AmEx / DC

lunch

dinner

late supper

beer/wine

cocktails

non-smoking

reservations
  recommended

dress casual

Chef Jacques Sorin opened this pocket-sized, second-story room almost three decades ago as Jacques' Omelettes. Now, hung with Parisian street scenes and overlooking Cumberland Park (a circus in fair weather; book a window table for the view), the restaurant is more cheerful than ever. The fluffy omelettes (if they weren't perfect by now, we'd call for a guillotine) are still present, ten in all. The Bretonne lobster is my current favorite. But for an honest, old-fashioned cholesterol hit, I much prefer the sweetbreads, the nicely trimmed gland flamed in Calvados. That's when Jacques' starts to feel like a Rive Droite hideaway. *Salut.*

Jacques Bistro
du Parc

À la carte ce soir

Saumon frais de l'Atlantique au basilic $21.50
Fresh Atlantic salmon poached or grilled with basil butter sauce

Les filets de truites fraîches sautés avec crevettes et champignons $20.95
Fresh fillet sof rainbow trout sauteed with baby shrimp and mushrooms

Les escalopes de veau forestière $21.95
Tender slices of Provimi veal in Madeira sauce with wild mushrooms

Le carré d'agneau à la Provençale $27.95
Roasted rack of lamb with Dijon mustard, bread crumbs and garlic

L'entrecôte au poivre vert $27.95
New York sterling silver striploin 8-oz in a green peppercorn sauce

Filet de porc , sauce moutarde $20.95
Roasted pork tenderloin with Pommery mustard sauce

Jalapeño

725 King Street West
Toronto
416-216-6743
www.jalapeno.ca

Mexican
WEST TORONTO

Wheelchair
  access

V / MC / AmEx / DC

lunch

dinner

late supper

take out

beer/wine

cocktails

high chairs

live
  entertainment

private parties

non-smoking

reservations
  recommended

dress casual

No sombreros, no silver spurs, no leering Pancho Villas—Jalapeño is not your average south-of-the-Rio Grande beanery. Travel posters flavor the walls, and complexity rules the kitchen, a scholarly approach to Mexican states from Puebla to the Yucatán. Heaping corn chips with a trio of first-rate salsas arrive as soon as you do, rendering appetizers redundant. Stellar among pages of main dishes is mole poblano, chicken sauced in unsweetened chocolate, chiles, and twenty-six other ingredients, originally created for the hapless Austrian archduke and emperor of Mexico Maximilian in 1864—and a good thing, because revolutionaries executed him three years later.

Authentic Mexican Food

Jalapeño

RESTAURANT

GREEN TAMAL Corn dough wrapped and steamed in banana leaves. Topped with green tomatillo sauce, shredded chicken breast and mozzarella cheese. Served with rice. Traditional dish from Oaxaca 13.95

CHILE RELLENO Stuffed unique poblano chile covered with cooked egg batter, tomato basil sauce and sour cream. Garnished with rice Mexican style, black refried beans on a crispy tortilla basket and handmade tortillas.
Your choice of beef or cheese 15.95
Add cheese on beef 2.00

COCHINITA PIBIL Shredded pork marinated in Mayan condiments loaded with flavor. Baked with banana leaves. Pride of Yucatan. Served with red onion, refried beans, rice and handmade tortillas 15.95

TAMARIND CHICKEN "HOT CHOICE" Grilled chicken breast in tamarind sauce with smoked Morita pepper. Served with rice Mexican style, refried beans on a crispy tortilla basket and handmade tortillas 15.95

FAJITAS JALAPENO'S GENEROUS SERVING
Grilled chicken tender strips with a selection of bell peppers, red and white onion, bacon and our secret dressing. Served with rice, beans, sour cream, lettuce, Monterrey jack cheese, guacamole and corn tortillas 16.95
BEEF 18.95   VEGETARIAN 14.95

ENCHILADAS JALAPENO'S How can we be a Mexican restaurant without this TOP CHOICE! Soft tortilla filled with shredded chicken breast in green tomatillo salsa made from scratch. Topped with melted cheese and sour cream. Garnished with rice and refried beans 14.99

POZOLE After tequila, pozole is the tradition of Jalisco Mexico. Big soup with tender pork chunks, hominy, lettuce, radish, tostadas, oregano, lime and chili pepper on the side. Chicken choice also available 13.99

Jerusalem

955 Eglinton Avenue West
Toronto
416-783-6494

Middle Eastern
WEST TORONTO

Wheelchair
  access

V / MC / AmEx

Sunday brunch

lunch

dinner

take out

beer/wine

cocktails

high chairs

live
  entertainment

non-smoking

reservations
  recommended

dress casual

An enthralling cuisine of *Arabian Nights* sensibility, Middle Eastern comes and goes faster than a
genie's promise in this town. Only Jerusalem, its
faux honeyed stone recalling ancient walls in
Israel, Jordan, and Syria, holds fast, plying the
multitude with the same wonders (crisp falafels,
lemony tabbouleh, pungent hummus, velvety baba
ghanoush) that seemed exotica itself when the
restaurant opened more than thirty years ago.
Gluttons may even proceed to charred and herbed
kababs or fish pan-fried in tahini. If the place
needs a traffic cop, blame colossal portions,
consistent quality, sweetly retro prices, and the
appalling absence of such blessings elsewhere
in the mainstream.

JERUSALEM RESTAURANT

seafood dinners

Fresh Sea Bass
Fresh sea bass fried and topped with a splash of house dressing, served with middle east salad and your choice of taheena sauce or rice.
(Priced according to size and market. Please ask your server.)

Bourkan Shrimp **$13.95**
Delectable shrimp sauteed in tomato and garlic sauce, served on a bed of rice with house salad.

chicken dinners

Chicken Breast **$10.95**
Marinated charcoal-broiled chicken breast cooked to perfection, served with rice and middle east salad.

Shish Tawoo **$10.95**
Two skewers of tender chicken breast cubes marinated in garlic and spices, served with rice and middle east salad.

a taste of jerusalem dinner specials

combination for two

Any three skewers of your choice:

- *Shish Kabab (lamb or beef)*   • *Kabab (kafta)*
- *Shish Tawoo (chicken)*   • *Liver*

with baba ghanouje, hummos, falafel, tabbouleh salad, mixed pickles, fried tomatoes or eggplant
Served with rice, salad and pita bread.

For two people – only $32.00

Joso's

202 Davenport Road
Toronto
416-925-1903
www.josos.com

Seafood
MIDTOWN

V / MC / AmEx / DC

lunch

dinner

late supper

beer/wine

cocktails

private parties

non-smoking

reservations
   recommended

dress informal

menu changes
   weekly

The fleshpot art—bodice-ripping bosoms, billowing Rubensesque bums, rooms dusted in lust—distract wickedly, but when you reassemble your senses, you can see why Joso's has flourished for more than a quarter of a century. The nightly selection of eight to ten varieties of fish, some resembling sea monsters, is presented by mischievous servers who delight in shocking faint-hearted landlubbers. Gamer customers wind up with gleefully delivered instruction in eating skin, brains, and eyes. The celebrity crowd—Danny DeVito, Michael Douglas, Mark Wahlberg—can't keep away from the place. Even Anthony Hopkins has been seen here. Server, bring *him* a fish head. See if he orders a nice Chianti.

Spaghettini

Alla Siciliana Unique to Joso's, a rarely prepared sauce of sepia simmered in its ink.   10.17 -

Alla Leonardo A fresh lemon sauté of diced octopus, shrimp, garlic, capers and white wine.   10.17 -

Alla Marinara Mussels and clams sautéed in a mildly spicy tomato sauce.   10.17 -

Alla Joso A Mediterranean tomato sauce of octopus spiced with bay leaves, rosemary and peppercorns.   10.17 -

(also available pasta aglio-oglio and pasta with fresh tomato sauce)

Risotti *(please allow 20 minutes to prepare, serves 2-4 persons)*

Risotto Alla Milanese A sixteenth century delicacy of Arborio rice, porcini mushrooms, marsala and saffron.   39 -

Calamari alla Griglia Fresh whole squid grilled to tenderness with olive oil, garlic, parsley and lemon.   19 -

JOV Bistro

1701 Bayview Avenue
Toronto
416-322-0530

Global
MIDTOWN

V / MC / DC

dinner

beer/wine

cocktails

private parties

non-smoking

**reservations
recommended**

dress casual

**menu changes
regularly**

If JOV is a humble bistro, I'm the Marquis de Sade. Soft gray and ivory tones, perched candles, and an open kitchen (the place *has* you the moment you stick your nose in the door) speak of occasion, even if you have to invent one. JOV scored as one of Toronto's best high-end bistros from day one. Top-ranking CIA (Culinary Institute of America) alumnus Owen Steinberg mans the stoves, his take contemporary French with the usual Asian accents, while sister Jill manages the front of the house with seasoned business sense and an eye on long-run clientele. The fixed-price "trust me" menu is, well . . . trust it.

JOV
BISTRO

appetizers

Steamed shu mai dumplings $6.^{95}

Eggplant Carpionate – eggplant lightly fried tossed with
cherry tomatoes, garlic, anchovy, parsley, & lemon dressing $7.^{75}

Grilled lightly curried calamari, with vine-ripened tomatoes
crème fraiche and balsamic glaze $8.$ ^{50}$

Citrus crusted baked goat cheese with
house cured salmon, wasabi aioli & lemon basil oil $9. ^{95}$

meats

Roast free range chicken breast stuffed with
red peppers & brie, served with a shallot & sherry jus $24.^{00}

Duck confit with wilted bitter greens and grilled kumquat jus $24.^{00}

Braised lamb shank with mushroom jus $23.^{00}

Meat & potatoes du jour p/a

vegetarian

Provencale tart with artichokes, mushrooms, olives, asparagus
& a caponata sauce $19.^{95}

Napolean printemps-goat cheese, wild mushrooms, spinach, roasted
peppers & toasted almonds $18.^{95}

Jump

Commerce Court East
18 Wellington Street West
Toronto
416-363-3400
www.oliverbonacini.com

Global
FINANCIAL DISTRICT

Wheelchair
  access

V / MC / AmEx / DC

lunch

dinner

late supper

beer/wine

cocktails

live
  entertainment

private parties

non-smoking

reservations
  recommended

dress casual

menu changes
  seasonally

Too often taken for granted, Jump remains a bright spot among concrete corridors in which sustenance usually translates as steak with baked potato. With its palm trees, skylights, and energetic fare—there's no fear of flavor here—Jump's jump should be on foodie bankers and brokers who aren't over at Bymark chomping into $33 hamburgers. A special here might be *lobster* shepherd's pie, which contains more than a pound of crustacean flesh and makes the aforementioned burger look sedate by comparison.

Nor are the frites, with their sweet-and-seething dip any slouch in this first effort from the Midas-touch team of Peter Oliver and Michael Bonacini.

CAFÉ & BAR

Blackened Tiger Shrimps on a jicama, tomatillo and tortilla salad	11.95
Sun-Ripened Tomatoes with Goat Milk Feta, basil, Italian black olives and extra virgin olive oil	8.95
Air Dried Bresaola and Portobello Salad with arugula, Reggiano, extra virgin olive oil and lemon	9.75
Grilled Calamari with anchovies, capers, Gaeta olives, roasted garlic and lemon brown butter	10.25
A Pound of Steamed P.E.I. Mussels in a mild red curry, lime leaf, ginger and coconut milk broth	9.50
Linguine with Sautéed Calamari, fresh garden peas, extra virgin olive oil and white wine pan juices	19.95
The Veggie Plate with sweet corn and goat cheese soufflé, baked mushroom cutlet, jasmine rice and grilled vegetables	15.75
Mahogany Roasted Sea Bass with stir-fried vegetables, almond basmati rice and a mild aromatic red curry	27.50
Grilled 12 oz Provimi Veal Chop with eggplant mash, roasted artichokes and a gorgonzola butter	29.75
Crispy Lemon Rosemary Roasted Chicken with ricotta gnocchi, bacon, spinach and a light chicken jus	22.25
Grilled Fillet of Atlantic Salmon on a salad of fingerling potatoes, fine green beans, black olives, ripe tomato and lemon dressing	24.00
Sweet Potato Stuffed Agnolotti with smoked country ham, fava beans and a sage brown butter	16.95
Grilled 10 oz Sterling Silver Steak with creamy garlic mash **or** Jump fries, charred tomato salsa and a sticky mushroom gravy	28.50

Kaiseki Yu-Zen Hashimoto

6435 Dixie Road, Unit 10
Mississauga
905-670-5559

Japanese
SUBURBAN WEST

Wheelchair
  access
valet parking
V / MC / AmEx / DC
lunch
dinner
take out
beer/wine
private parties
non-smoking
reservations
  required
dress informal
menu changes
  daily

Taking its poetic dimension from Zen Buddhism, the tea ceremony, and Shinto reverence for the changing seasons, *kaiseki* dining is both Japan's last word on the beauty and harmony of food and an event for grand occasions. Tucked in a strip mall waaaay out on the northwest frontier is Toronto's first all-*kaiseki* Japanese restaurant. The trappings are homespun, but the fare is for real, a procession of many little courses landscaped on lacquerware and ceramics chosen for stunning visual effect. Japanese executives, an ocean and then some away from home, congregate to sate their yen and blow their expense accounts under chef Hashimoto's artificial moon, and why should we not join them?

Sakizuke:	goma doufu, wasabi, wari shouyu, Yomogi to yuzuan no sasamakifu
Sake:	Okunomatsu Sakura -Fukushimaken
Mukouzuke:	katsuo warayaki, myouga, sudachi shouyu
Sake:	Asabiraki Tezukuri Daiginjou - Iwateken
Wanmono:	hamo honegiri botanjitate
Yakimono:	kamogan yuwanyaki
Sake:	Tengumai Junmai Yamahaishikomi - Ishikawaken
Nimono:	takono oharagi maki
Sake:	Okunomatsu Sakusaku Dry - Fukushimaken
Shiizakana:	kamonasu agedashi, ebi soboroan
Susumezakana:	kunsei sake no asupara maki kamasu kara age, kimizuan
Gohanmono:	unagi no sasamushi
Shiru:	fukusa jitate, nankin umani, mushibuta
Kounomono:	kyuri asazuke, ikasumi takuan, yurine bainikuae
Mizugashi:	budou kanten yose

Kaji

860 The Queensway
Toronto
416-252-2166
www.kaji.ca

Japanese
WEST TORONTO

Partial wheel-
chair access

valet parking

V / MC / AmEx

dinner

beer/wine

private parties

non-smoking

reservations
required

dress casual

menu changes
daily

A strip mall on the Queensway seems a weird location for the in spot for expat Japanese, but the rents allow sushi master Mitsuhiro Kaji (formerly of Furasato, Shogun, Ematei, widely regarded as one of Canada's best) to do things his way: that means a tranquil room in silent celery and mauve hues, an eight-seat sushi bar where Kaji submits his art to a hushed congregation (among the faithful, stellar talents like Arpi Magyar) that's followed him for years. Eight-course menus change daily. Newcomers breathlessly encounter chrysanthemum leaf salad; grilled yellowtail neck; live shrimp; and monkfish liver that looks like foie gras, tastes of the sea, and lingers on the palate.

CHEF DINNER $65

Hors d'oeuvres
Sashimi
Today's chef's special
Sushi
Soup
Dessert

KAJI DINNER $85

Hors d'oeuvres
Sashimi
Today's kaji's special
Hassun(assorted grilled & fried dish)
Sushi
Soup
Dessert

OMAKASE DINNER $120

Hors d'oeuvres
Sashimi
Today's omakase specials
Hassun(assorted grilled & fried dish)
Sushi
Soup
Dessert

Katsura

Westin Prince Hotel
900 York Mills Road
Toronto
416-444-2511
www.toronto.com/katsura

Japanese
NORTHEAST TORONTO

Wheelchair
    access
V / MC / AmEx / DC
lunch
dinner
beer/wine
cocktails
high chairs
private parties
non-smoking
reservations
    recommended
dress informal
menu changes
    seasonally

After three decades of feeding Japanese road warriors and increaingly hooked *gai jin*, Katsura is
showing remarkable staying power. This has as
much to do with atmosphere as food, for the
sprawling, country-inn style premises do have the
welcome feel of stepping into another world. It's
also just about everything for everybody: More
than two hundred seats flank gleaming teppan
grills in the softly lit room. There stand a sushi
bar and robata counter, while mysteries unfold
behind the paper-thin walls of tatami rooms. Its
gastronomic heart is fresh fish, often flown in
from Japan—a nibble of uni (raw sea urchin)
prompts spasms of delirium, and grilled Alaska
cod has the consistency of butter. Privately
imported sakes may finish the job of sweeping
you off to volcanic Kyushu.

KATSURA 桂

SHOKADO BENTO   39.75

SALAD サラダ
Freshly tossed Vegetables from the Katsura Garden
with House Dressing

MISO SOUP 味噌椀
Classic Soy Bean Soup with Tofu, garnished with
Thinly Sliced Green Onions

BENTO BOX お弁当
Assorted Japanese Delicacies served in a traditional Lacquer Box
Shrimp Tempura. Grilled Salmon. Chicken Yakatori Skewer.
Beef Teriyaki Skewer. Cooked Seasonal Vegetables.
California Roll. Cucumber Roll Sushi

GREEN TEA ICE-CREAM 抹茶アイスクリーム

松花堂弁当

Kensington Kitchen

124 Harbord Street
Toronto
416-961-3404

Bistro
DOWNTOWN WEST

V / MC / AmEx /
  D / DC

Sunday brunch

lunch

dinner

late supper

take out

beer/wine

cocktails

high chairs

patio dining

private parties

non-smoking

reservations
  recommended

dress casual

menu changes
  weekly

Since 1981, Kensington Kitchen has evolved from hippi-dippie vegetarian to Middle Eastern to a broadly Mediterranean sweep—actually, the balding, bespectacled regulars may have been the hippies of yore—and must be doing something right to get by with such neighbors as Splendido and Messis. "Whimsies"—toys, purses, fabrics, exotic-looking Canadiana—festoon the room. We might argue fries slathered in cumin-infused harissa are KK's finest moment, but it's also fun playing Turks dining on mezes, the chorus line of appetizers from creamy baba ghanoush to pungent Armenian sausage, or Arabs digging into aromatic skewers of charred meat on beds of hummus.

Kensington Kitchen

Cafe • Restaurant • Bar • Patio

Farfalle w snow-peas, red peppers, onions & sun-dried tomatoes tossed in pesto   9.95
         w Chicken or Spicy Italian Sausage   add 3.50

Angel Hair & Seafood (Shrimp, Scallops and Mussels)
         w mushrooms, leeks, roasted garlic in a fresh Tomato Coriander sauce   15.50

Moroccan Cous Cous - Hearty stewed vegetables with chickpeas, tomatoes & spices   10.50
         w Chicken, Lamb , Merguez or Kofta   add 3.50
             w Seafood or 'Royale'   add 4.75

Seven Vegetable Stir-Fry on a bed of Hummus w Harissa or on brown rice topped w Feta   10.95
         w Spicy Italian Sausage   add 3.50

Eggplant Provençale with tomatoes, herbs, black olives & toasted pine nuts on brown rice   9.50
         w Kofta   add 3.50

Marinated Vegetable Brochette- grilled zucchini, sweet yams, onions, mushrooms,   12.50
         tomatoes & peppers served on a bed of Hummus w Harissa
         or on Romaine with tahini lemon dressing
         w Chicken or Lamb   add 3.50   w Tiger Shrimp   add 4.75

Meshwi - grilled brochettes of marinated Chicken, Lamb or Kofta   12.50
         served w Brown rice, Fries, or on a bed of Hummus w Harissa

Lamburger- our own 8oz. spiced burger grilled & topped w melted Feta   8.50
         served w Caesar salad or K.K. fries

Istanbul Braised Lamb w raisins, eggplants, apricots, figs, onions, tomatoes,   12.95
         red wine & herbs, served w brown rice and minted yogurt

Turkey Breast stuffed w spinach, chevre & sun-dried tomatoes on lemon-sage Farfalle   13.95

Saffron Paella   w Vegetables   9.95   w Chicken & Sausage   12.95   w Seafood   13.95

Grilled Lamb Chops, garlic mashed potatoes w black bean, sweet corn & red pepper salsa   14.50

Market Fish of the Day grilled w black olive tapenade served w potato pancake,   14.95
         steamed vegetables, Napa leaves and coriander-lime jus

King's Garden

214 King Street West
Toronto
416-585-2221

Chinese
ENTERTAINMENT
DISTRICT

V / MC / AmEx / DC

Sunday brunch

lunch

dinner

beer/wine

take out

beer/wine

cocktails

high chairs

private parties

non-smoking

reservations
  recommended

dress casual

menu changes
  seasonally

Steps from the Royal Alex and Roy Thompson Hall and dressed to impress, King's Garden is the only Chinese restaurant in the Entertainment District and the only downtown property capable of giving Lai Wah Heen a run for its money in the finesse department. Jasper and Thisby Wong are hands-on owners, and it pays off: Their dim sum shows ambition and refinement, with steamed lobster dumplings, and crisply fried pancake laced with shrimp and Chinese chives. Their deep-fried eggplant renders Japan's tempura almost indelicate by comparison. By night, the prince of the room is Peking duck, the plump, burnished bird carved at the table to richly deserved oohs and ahs.

雞鴨　　*Poultry*

Imperial Peking Duck (2 courses)	*$ 38.00*
Crispy Cantonese Roast Duck (half)	*$ 15.00*
Golden Fried Crispy Chicken (half)	*$ 13.50*
Smoked Chicken w/Soya Sauce & Tea (half)	*$ 13.50*
Kung Pao Chicken	*$ 13.00*
Chicken w/Lemon Sauce	*$ 13.00*
Deep Fried Diced Chicken w/ Shrimp Paste	*$ 15.00*
Poached Chicken in Clear Soup w/Vegetable (half)	*$ 16.00*

海鮮　　*Seafood*

Live Fish (Steamed, Deep Fried or Broiled)	*Market Price*
Sauteed Fillet of Grouper w/ Seasonal Greens	*$ 20.00*
Smoked Black Cod	*$ 18.00*
Braised Sea Bass w/ Vegetables in Clay Pot	*$ 20.00*
Sea Bass Fillet Roll w/ Asparagus with Spicy Salt	*$ 32.00*
Live Maine Lobster	*$ 38.00*

(Sashimi/ Black Bean Sauce/ Sauteed/ Steamed/ Garlic/ Ginger & Green
Onion; Deep Fried/ Spicy Salt/ Soya Sauce) *** sashimi add $12.00 ***

Live Crab	*$ 26.00*

(Steamed/ Sauteed/ Pan Fried w. Garlic Sauce or Hot Chilies)

Korea House

666 Bloor Street West
Toronto
416-536-8666

Korean
LITTLE KOREA

V / MC
lunch
dinner
late supper
take out
beer/wine
high chairs
private parties
non-smoking
  smoking
reservations
  recommended
dress casual

Most Korean chefs run vastly more profitable Japanese restaurants, so it's a treat to discover an eatery that might have been beamed over from Korea's ancient capital of Kyongju and that imparts some fine-tuning to this earthy, robust cuisine. In its penchant for offal and strange-sounding dishes—among them *juk, kuk, muk,* and *tuk-kuk*—Korean may be one of the least accessible Asian cuisines, but here it's easy to develop a taste for terrific kimchi (the national dish of fiery chile-garlic pickles), juicy *bulgogi* (barbecued beef), and a stew of beef, seafood, and tofu—Korean surf 'n' turf, growling with garlic and chiles.

KOREA HOUSE
코리아 하우스
KOREAN RESTAURANT

1. 스끼야끼 : SUKI YAKI $ 25.00
   -*Sliced beef stewed with beancurd, vegetables and noodle in a tasty sauce (2 person)*-

2. 불고기 정식 : BUL - GO - KI DINNER $ 25.00
   -*Sliced marinated beef. Single order : we grill it Two or more orders : grilled at your table*-

3. 갈비정식 : KALBI DINNER $ 13.50
   -*Barbequed marinated beef ribs*-

4. 해물전골 : HAE - MOOL CHONGOL $ 25.00
   -*Assorted seafood with vegetables and noodles in a hot broth. Cooked at your table*-

5. 곱창전골 : KOP-CHANG CHONGOL $ 25.00
   -*Beef chitterlings with vegetables, noodles in a hot broth. Cooked at your table*-

6. 순대전골 : SOON-DAE CHONGOL $ 25.00
   -*Pig intestine, vetables and korean style sausage in a hot broth. Cooked at your table*-

7. 생선찌개 : FISH STEW $ 12.00

La Fenice

319 King Street West
Toronto
416-585-2377

Italian
ENTERTAINMENT
DISTRICT

V / MC / AmEx / DC

lunch

dinner

take out

beer/wine

cocktails

private parties

non-smoking
  smoking

reservations
  recommended

dress business
  casual

menu changes
  seasonally

One of Toronto's top-rated Italian restaurants since 1984, La Fenice (named for the opera hall in Venice) in the Entertainment District will be hip as long as fresh flowers, gracious service, prime ingredients, and a dedicated kitchen remain fashionable. Customer loyalty speaks volumes: People who ate here in year one still visit regularly. Suits are known to lunch five times a week. Simplicity prevails, with fish from the daily platter slapped on the grill and drizzled with olive oil and herbs. The lovely watercolors are a legacy from late chef and founder Luigi Orgera, whose sense of beauty obviously journeyed far beyond the plate.

PESCE

SCELTA DAL VASSOIO
DAILY FRESH FISH   PRICE ACCORDING TO CHOICE

GRIGLIATO MISTO DI MARE
MIXED GRILLED SEAFOOD   28.00

GAMBERONI GRIGLIATI
GRILLED JUMBO TIGER SHRIMP WITH LA FENICE
EXTRA VIRGIN OLIVE OIL   PRICE ACCORDING TO SIZE

TRANCIA DI SALMONE
GRILLED OR POACHED SALMON FILLET   22.00

CARNE

SCALOPPINE DI VITELLO CON FUNGHI FRESCHI
VEAL SCALOPPINE WITH FRESH WILD MUSHROOMS   21.00

SCALOPPINE DI VITELLO ALL'ERBETTE
VEAL SCALOPPINE WITH FRESH HERBS   21.00

NODINO DI VITELLO AI FERRI
GRILLED EXTRA THICK, DOUBLE-CUT VEAL CHOP SEASONED WITH HERBS   30.00

MEDAGLIONI DI VITELLO AL TARTUFO NERO
GRILLED VEAL MEDALLIONS WITH BLACK TRUFFLE PASTE   24.00

FEGATO CON SALVIA
GRILLED PROVIMI LIVER WITH SAGE AND BRAISED PEARL ONIONS   17.50

SUPREMA DI POLLO ALL'ERBE DI STAGIONE
BREAST OF CHICKEN WITH FRESH HERBS AND DRY SHERRY   17.00

La Palette

256 Augusta Street
Toronto
416-929-4900

Bistro
KENSINGTON MARKET

V / MC / AmEx / DC

Saturday and
  Sunday brunch

dinner

late supper

take out

beer/wine

cocktails

private parties

non-smoking
  section

dress casual

reservations
  recommended

menu changes
  seasonally

The Portuguese-Caribbean bustle of Kensington Market seems an odd milieu for a hole-in-the-wall bistro with a Montmartre feel, but La Palette was born successful. Only twenty-six seats, a saucy wait staff, a hip throng huddled around the tiny bar, and Toulouse-Lautrec posters on the walls make for an amiable, casual atmosphere. The menu charges off in all directions at once, and quality zigzags, but you can't go wrong with the best steak frites Toronto's seen since much-lamented L'Entrecôte closed: Bring on chef Michael Harrington's prime Black Angus sirloin juicily grilled to order and those Yukon Gold frites, bless them, that have never seen a freezer.

La Palette
bistrot • bar • café

Les Entrées:

Soupe du Jour - Composed daily $5 *

Salade Verte - Field greens tossed in an aged red wine vinaigrette $4 *

Salade Basque - Port glazed chicken livers with wild mushrooms on a
mélange of mixed greens topped with a roasted red pepper relish $6 *

Escargots La Palette - Escargots baked in mushroom caps
and a garlic butter sauce $6 *

Grilled Calamari - Marinated calamari on a bed of sautéed
Chinese greens with a sesame soya jus and a dill aioli $9

Fromage Tiède - Crispy, fried camembert on julienned apples and
celeriac, served with a sweet fruit compôte $8

Rosette de Saumon Fumé - Smoked salmon rosette wrapped around
a zesty orange goat cheese on grilled portabello mushrooms
and a bed of watercress w/ lemon mint vinaigrette $9

Les Plats:

Gateau Végétarién - Roasted tomato, spinach & herb-feta-béchamel
layered in filo pastry served w/ a roasted red pepper
& tarragon coulis with daily vegetables $17 *

Pâtes Poulet Fumé - Fettucine with smoked chicken, fresh basil &
sundried tomato in a wild mushroom, white wine cream sauce $17 *

Poulet Bonne Maman - Juicy, french-cut chicken breast w/ roasted
potatoes, vegetables, zesty onion/red peppercorn compote
and a black currant raspberry jus $17 *

Moules / Frites - Sautéed mussels & julienned vegetables in a ginger,
saffron, tumeric cream sauce served with our famous frites $17 *

Lalot

200 Bathurst Street
Toronto
416-703-8222

Pan-Asian
DOWNTOWN WEST

V / MC
lunch
dinner
late supper
take out
beer/wine
cocktails
high chairs
private parties
non-smoking
reservations
  recommended
dress casual
menu changes
  seasonally

If Toronto lined up when Spring Rolls gallivanted through the kitchens of China, Singapore, Thailand, and Vietnam, the evolutionary next step was a bolder, vastly more refined approach to racy Southeast Asian cuisines. Enter Lalot, its finesse unmistakably Vietnamese—a double blessing when Toronto Vietnamese can't touch the buzz and finesse of Hanoi or Saigon—its handsome contemporary trappings transcending Chinatown grot. Signature *pho, com*, and *bun* sustain lunches. At dinner, I like baby squids stuffed with spiced minced duck and grilled to the cusp of tenderness, then lemongrass pork loin or peppered catfish in a clay pot, which leave me longing for sultry nights under Indochine stars.

lalot

fresh lychee with watercress, boston lettuce and pistachio nut salad   9
fresh chicken salad with medley of herbs and peanuts   9.5
spinach salad with golden crispy tofu and bean sprouts tossed with a soy vinaigrette   8
traditional vietnamese tamarind soup with black tiger prawns and chicken breast (to share)   11

crispy lobster and shrimp spring rolls   11
fresh jicama and shrimps salad roll with rau hue and sweet chinese sausage   5
grilled baby squid stuffed with dried shiitake mushrooms and duck meat   8
grilled ginger five-spice baby back ribs   9
grilled la lot beef (flank beef wrapped in a wild betel leaf)   9

pan seared chilean sea bass with summer fresh herbs and jalapeño peppers   24
caramelized catfish with fresh coconut juice, thai chili and song be black peppercorn in a clay pot   18
rich curried black tiger prawns with asparagus and yam   20
black tiger prawns sauté with spring onion, sweet garlic soy and organic baby spinach   20
steamed sea scallops in a ginger sesame soy broth with shiitake mushrooms and sweet chinese sausage   21

pan roasted duck breast with peanut sticky rice   18
drunken crispy chicken (grain fed) with gailan   15
caramelized fresh ginger chicken (grain fed) with a chardonnay reduction, served in a hot clay pot   15
cognac luc lac filet mignon with oxtail stock   24
grilled lemongrass pork loin with vermicelli   15

soft noodles with spring onions and enoki mushrooms   11
lemongrass crispy tofu with roasted bell peppers and shiitake mushrooms   9

spicy green beans with pickled radish   8
asparagus with oyster mushrooms garnished with toasted sesame seeds   9
grilled asian eggplant with green onions in spicy coconut sauce   8
garlic sautéed pea pod greens   9
fresh cut corn with oyster mushrooms   9
sweet sugar snap peas with enoki mushrooms   9
grilled fresh tomatoes with sweet garlic vinaigrette   6

Lai Wah Heen

Metropolitan Hotel
108 Chestnut Street
Toronto
416-977-9899
www.metropolitan.com/lwh/

Chinese
DOWNTOWN

Wheelchair
  access

valet parking

V / MC / AmEx /
  D / DC

lunch

dinner

beer/wine

cocktails

high chairs

private parties

non-smoking

reservations
  recommended

dress informal

menu changes
  seasonally

The darling of Chinese society out on the town, Lai Wah Heen is hotelier Henry Wu's seamless meld of classic Cantonese and Pacific Rim in an opulent downtown setting. Dance with us, Henry: Four-meter-high ceilings, subtle black-and-beige hues, and Narumi bone china banish notions of chinoiserie (no dragons need apply); servers ladle and spoon near invisibly; and the inventive Chinese kitchen ensures a menu that, although twenty pages long, rarely stands still. Fish and seafood elicit proper reverence, spring rolls stuffed with lobster and peaches set high style, and perfectly pink foie gras atop deep-fried eggplant epitomizes Wu's way with wooing and wowing.

極品包翅鮑魚餐 (兩位用)
Premium dinner for two $188.00

1) 紅燒大包翅
   Braised premium shark's fin in a thick chicken broth
2) 蠔皇乾鮑
   Dried abalone slowly cooked and seasoned with oyster sauce
3) 薑汁米酒蒸開邊龍蝦
   Steamed butterfly-cut lobster in ginger wine sauce
4) 瑤柱蛋白炒飯
   Shredded conpoy egg white fired rice
5) 精美甜品
   Dessert

金裝包翅乳鴿餐 (四位用)
Premium dinner for four $288.00

1) 紅燒大包翅
   Braised premium shark's fin in a thick chicken broth
2) 麗華脆燒乳鴿皇
   Roast marinated squab
3) 蠔皇花膠扣鮑脯
   Abalone, fish maw and vegetables braised in oyster sauce
4) 花雕蒸龍蝦
   Steamed lobster in Chinese aged wine sauce
5) 薑茸帶子蛋白炒飯
   Diced scallops fried rice flavored with ginger
6) 精美甜品
   Dessert

Le Continental

Westin Prince Hotel
900 York Mills Road
Toronto
416-444-2511
www.toronto.com/lecontinental

Global
NORTHEAST TORONTO

Wheelchair
 access
valet parking
V / MC / AmEx / DC
lunch
dinner
beer/wine
cocktails
high chairs
private parties
non-smoking
reservations
 recommended
dress jacket/tie
menu changes
 seasonally

Le Continental is an out-of-the way hotel dining room catering to Japanese corporate employees and tourists. The room is grand and spacious, with suspended halogen spots highlighting tables and a wine list that peaks with Margaux '82 at a mere $860. The kitchen balances first-rate steaks with such contemporary French touches as Beluga lentils (ringers for caviar) and foie gras. The tray of thirty cheeses, nowadays such a rarity, harks back to a leisurely, civilized era of dining that has almost disappeared from the Toronto scene. But we'd appreciate also a little more subtlety here: Suits blathering on cell phones make Willy Loman look like a sweetheart.

Le Continental

Fish & Shellfish

Filet of Arctic Char on Light White Wine Sauce with Chive   19.75
Slices of Potatoes & Asparagus

Escalope of Salmon on Citrus-Coriander Sauce with   19.50
Stir-Fried Vegetables

Panfried Pacific Tilapia on Noilly Prat Flavoured Fish-fumé with   19.75
Filets of Oranges & Slices of Vegetables

Risotto with Shrimp, Scallop, Lobster,   23.00
Mussels and Asparagus

Meat & Fowl

Coq au Vin "Bourguignonne"   18.50
Braised Spring Chicken in Red Wine Sauce with
Pearl Onions & Mushrooms

Lamb Chops Provençale with   22.50
Galette Potatoes & Green Beans

Mignons of Pork with Chanterelles   19.00
Fried Polenta & Braised Nappa Cabbage

Alberta Beef Sirloin Steak (6 oz. / 170 gr.) with Sautéed Field Mushrooms   23.50
Fried Potatoes & Vegetable Pot-Pourri

Grilled Mignon of Beef with Olive Oil-Herb Juice   27.00
Combination of Forest Fruit, Vegetables and Potatoes

Le Sélect Bistro

328 Queen Street West
Toronto
416-595-6405

French
QUEEN WEST VILLAGE

Wheelchair
  access

V / MC / AmEx / DC

Sunday brunch

lunch

dinner

late supper

beer/wine

cocktails

private parties

non-smoking

reservations
  recommended

dress casual

menu changes
  weekly

An institution, Le Sélect opened in 1977—before the Queen Street West Village emerged as Toronto's SoHo—a Parisian bistro picked up by a tornado and plunked down on the shores of Lake Ontario. It survived the journey: the zinc bar; ochre hues; signature French posters; playfully suspended breadbaskets; and on the menu, escargots, cassoulet, and confit de canard. The kitchen covers the territory amiably if less than spectacularly (this, too, is authentically Parisian) but generally pleases those with starry memories of the City of Light and a yearning for a little something French or else. The frites aren't bad, either.

BISTRO

SPÉCIALITÉS

using only the freshest products selected daily with care

ROUGET DE L'ATLANTIQUE AUX LENTILLES
roasted herb-crusted red snapper with lentils
and a caper coriander *beurre blanc* 21.95

CONFIT DE CANARD
confit of free range duck legs, moist with crispy skin,
served with an orange sauce & cranberry relish 19.95

CUISSOT DE LAPIN AU CABERNET
roasted rabbit leg with a shitake, Cabernet, bacon and
shallot sauce, served on spinach and mashed potatoes 19.95

BAVETTE AUX ÉCHALOTES
traditional Parisian steak with sautéed
shallots and frites 17.95

PAVÉ DE BOEUF DE L'ALBERTA
Alberta 8oz center cut Filet, flambéed in Brandy, and
served with a green peppercorn cream sauce 26.95

CARRÉ D'AGNEAU GRILLÉ
grilled rack of lamb with a basil and sun-dried
tomato dressing 24.95

---

*All entrées are served with vegetables unless specified.
Substitutions for our home made fresh frites are welcome.*

PRIX FIXE DINNER *

your choice of starter, entrée and dessert $23.95

soupe du jour	mussels marinières	chocolate mousse
salade maison	grilled salmon	crème brûlée
Caesar salad	chicken pasta	ice creams
pâté maison	bavette frites	sorbets
spring rolls	duck confit	parfait praliné

* Substitutions are not possible. When ordering, please specify
that you are choosing from this selection. Later adjustments
cannot be made. Thank you

Lee Garden

331 Spadina Avenue
Toronto
416-593-4408

Chinese
SPADINA CHINATOWN

Wheelchair
access

V / MC / AmEx

dinner

late supper

take out

beer/wine

high chairs

non-smoking

reservations not
taken

dress casual

menu changes
weekly

Restaurants in China-on-Spadina are all flashing neon, blaring interiors, and grotty appointments compared to the swank Cantonese emporia of the northeast burbs. But this area is also the most lively of Toronto's Chinatowns, returning me to the backstreets of Kowloon or Guangzhou in a way that polished suburban glitz can never do. Lee Garden remains the emperor of the street, year in, year out, pleasing the faithful with the guilty, greasy pleasure of deep-fry every which way, respect for fresh fish, and rib-sticking Cantonese comfort food such as grandfather smoked chicken. Seasonal, off-menu specialties include snake soup (but are prices writhing?).

Lee Garden Restaurant (Spadina)

CHICKEN

Grandfather Smoked Chicken • Honey • Sesame Seeds	*Half*	14.00
Chicken • Baby Ginger • Fresh Pineapple In Hot Pot		14.00
Deep-Fried Crispy Skin Chicken	*Half*	12.00
Steamed Chicken • Ginger • Green Onion	*Half*	12.00
Steamed Chicken • Chinese Vegetables	*Half*	12.00
Pan-Fried Two Styles Chicken • Vegetables		12.00
Stir-Fried Sliced Chicken • Snowpeas • Black Bean Sauce		12.00
Diced Chicken • Vegetables • Cashew Nuts		12.00
Stir-Fried Sliced Chicken • Choy Sum		12.00
Boneless Chicken • Black Bean Sauce On Hot Plate		14.00
Stir-Fried Sliced Chicken • Fresh Pineapple		14.00
Deep Fried Boneless Chicken • Veg. In Szechuan Sauce		12.00
Sweet & Sour Chicken • Fresh Pineapple		12.00
Pan-Fried Tenderized Chicken • Lemon Sauce		12.00

DUCK

Braised Duck • Tiensin Cabbage	*Half*	12.00
Braised Duck • Mixed Seafood • Meat • Vegetables	*Half*	16.00
Braised Duck • Lo-Hon Vegetables	*Half*	14.00

PORK

Honey Garlic Orange Back Ribs	14.00
Porkloin • Sweet & Sour Garlic Sauce	12.00
Deep Fried Porkloin • Garlic Pepper	12.00
Sweet & Sour Pork • Fresh Pineapple	11.00
Sweet & Sour Spare Ribs • Fresh Pineapple	11.00

Lemon Meringue

2390 Bloor Street West
Toronto
416-769-5757
www.toronto.com/lemonmeringue

Bistro
BLOOR WEST VILLAGE

V / MC / AmEx

lunch

dinner

take out

beer/wine

cocktails

private parties

non-smoking

reservations
  recommended

dress informal

menu changes
  seasonally

The owners of this Bloor West Village hottie are sisters Slava Iwasykiw and Sonia Potichnyj, but don't come looking for borscht and pierogies: With chef Derek Strachan manning the stoves, they've sourced top-of-the-line ingredients—for instance, smoked salmon from legendary Willy Krauch of Tangier, Nova Scotia, purveyor to the Queen of England—and set their sights on solid middle-range fare with world-wise flourishes. Thus you'll find beef carpaccio drizzled with truffle oil, salmon with sweet miso paste, and scallops atop velvety risotto. Reservations are a must at this thirty-seat bauble on the neck of the city's Eastern European zone.

LEMON MERINGUE

APPETIZERS

soup
7,00

seared calamari
nut butter sauce, lemon zest,
capers, anchovies, tomatoes & olives
9,00

roasted tomato salad
goat cheese, tomato jam, crispy potatoes
balsamic shallot vinaigrette
9,00

cured beef carpaccio
arugula, reggiano & truffle oil
10,00

roasted pear salad
bitter greens with stilton &
carmalized pecans
8,00

escargot, hazelnuts & white asparagus
mushroom reduction
11,00

MAIN COURSES

pistachio roasted pork tenderloin
ricotta gnocchi and goat cheese cream
fresh beans & apple compote
23,00

beef tenderloin
truffle mashed potatoes
rappini and roasted shitake mushrooms
sweet garlic sauce
27,00

miso glazed salmon
warm salad of wilted greens
bean sprouts & ginger
21,00

jumbo sea scallop risotto
balsamic roasted radicco & leeks with
double smoked bacon
24,00

margaret of duck
wild rice & wheatberry pilaf
kumquat, cilantro & basil
28,00

seared sea bass
roasted potato, caperberry, black olives
cherry tomato, roasted shallots, grapes
black olive broth
28,00

Lily

786 Broadview Avenue
Toronto
416-465-9991

Japanese
DANFORTH

V / MC / AmEx
dinner
late supper
beer/wine
cocktails
high chairs
non-smoking
dress jacket/tie
menu changes
    weekly

Talk about gilding the Lily: Lily's off-Danforth location marries Japanese lanterns and prints to European sophistication (the premises used to be Café Brussel) of leather banquettes and mahogany trim. It's the perfect room for chef Aoki Mokoto's teasing spin on tradition. Sushi and sashimi take a backseat as diners jump at fancies such as a seaweed-wrapped roll in which three kinds of raw fish and two flying fish roes dally in perfect harmony. And the uni brings huge bites of Pacific sea urchin—think foie gras of the sea—tucked into a hollowed lime. Regulars are the people smartly abandoning caution and taking the amused chef up on his *omakase* ("trust me") menu.

LiLy
Japanese Restaurant

Assort Vegetable Teriyaki :
snow peas, carrot.

Onion.cabbage.sweet pepper.baby corn
Dinner   22.75

Chicken Vegetbles Teriyaki : "Teri" means luster and "Yaki" means grill or boil.
Chicken Vegetbles with homemade Teriyaki sauce,The sauce gives the food a shiny
look and its wonderful taste   **Dinner   26.75**

Salmon Onion Teriyaki: **Dinner   26.75**

Japanese Curry Chicken: Japanese curry is usually thicker than curry found in.
in other cuisines. Its sweet but can be made spicy as well Ingredients includes
potato, onions and tender chicken.   **Dinner   26.75**

Tempura :   Shrimps and Vegetable covered by a thick batter and immediatley
deep fried to give it a crispy and crunchy texture. Eaten with " te tu yu "
                                              Dinner   26.75

Grilled Cod w/Miso Sauce: The cod is merinated in miso sauce for
two to three days and than lightly grilled. The sweet miso sauce gives it extra
flavour.   **Dinner   27.75**

Beef Teriyaki : Grilled sliced tender beef with teriyaki sauce and vegetables
                                              Dinner   27.75

Sukiyaki For Two   "Suki" in Japanese means to like. "Yaki",means grill
or boil. So Sukiyaki is cooking what you like to eat. Imes inclued sliced beef ,U-don
shiitake mushroom,spinach, to fo etc.

                                              Dinner for 2 48.00

Little Tibet

712 Queen Street West
Toronto
416-306-1896

Himalayan
WEST TORONTO

V / MC / AmEx

lunch

dinner

high chairs

private parties

non-smoking

reservations
  recommended

dress casual

My food memory of Tibet is yak—roasted, grilled, stewed, baked, boiled, and most successfully, as yak burger—but don't expect this pretty and inviting room to be that faithful to its origins. Smartly, owners Namgyal and Lhamo Gongya embrace a broad Himalayan palette of *momos*—the vegetarian or beef, crisp or soft, dumplings that are ubiquitous among the peaks of Tibet, Nepal, Sikkim, and Bhutan—plus rice and noodle dishes with legitimate Indian and Chinese accents. The chanting of Tibetan monks remains a thankfully subtle effect, but along with photographs of life among the *ghompas,* it carries journeyers toward the *Lost Horizon* of the imagination.

little tibet restaurant

---

12. PHING-SHETS... $ 7.75
Lightly sauteed bean thread with dried mushrooms
and red peppers.

13. POTSE... $ 7.85
Fresh spinach and tofu lightly sauteed in a ginger and
garlic sauce.

14. TSE NANZOM... $ 7.85
Seasonal mixed vegetables sauteed with ginger, garlic
and herbs.

16. POTSE... $ 8.50
Fresh spinach lightly sauteed with choice of beef or
chicken.

17. SE-SHA TSE... $ 8.75
Sauteed fresh mushrooms with zucchini and herbs with
choice of beef or chicken.

18. TSE TOFU.. $ 8.95
Sauteed organic tofu, snow peas, green beans, red and
green peppers with sliced beef.

LVIV

2469 Bloor Street West
Toronto
416-604-9688

Ukrainian
BLOOR WEST VILLAGE

V / MC / AmEx

Sunday brunch

lunch

dinner

take out

beer/wine

cocktails

high chairs

live
   entertainment

private parties

non-smoking

reservations
   recommended

dress casual

No sun-dried tomatoes, no goat cheese, no truffle oil—you can't get much more unfashionable than this warm and welcoming Ukrainian restaurant in which I like nothing better than noshing on a two-buck salmon caviar sandwich—waiter, make that a double and hold the bread—while tossing back a silky-smooth, freezer-chilled Ukrainian vodka. LVIV embraces Toronto's broader Eastern European communities with a phalanx of faves from the lightest veal-stuffed dumplings in town to out-standing breaded chicken breast, all at prices to make the customers jump up and dance. A piano player infuses the cozily retro rooms with great old world charm; the tendency is to linger.

LVIV RESTAURANT-CLUB

Borsch	$3.00
Meat solyanka	$7.00
Assorted varenyky	$7.00
Crepes with vegetables; chicken; cabbage; ricotta cheese & spinach filling	$7.00
Cabbage rolls served with mushroom sauce	$7.00
Grilled chicken breast in "Dijon" sauce	$9.00
Grilled chicken kebab in yogurt-dill	$9.00
Sautéed pork cutlet	$9.00
Veal cutlet with "parmesan" cheese	$10.00
Trout roasted with almonds	$12.00
Grilled salmon with mango sauce	$15.00
Mashed potatoes; home fries; rice; buckwheat; corn meal; pasta	$1.50
Sautéed vegetables; fresh vegetable salad/beet horseradish, carrots, cabbage	$2.50

Magic Wok

4331 14th Avenue
Toronto
905-305-6088

Chinese
SUBURBAN NORTHEAST

Wheelchair
   access
valet parking
V / MC
dinner
late supper
take out
beer
high chairs
non-smoking
reservations
   recommended
dress casual
menu changes
   weekly

As the address implies, it's *waaaaaaaay* out there, where Markham and its tedious industrial parks gaze hungrily into endangered horse pastures. Magic Wok's big family clientele, however, prefers to be gazing into the fish tanks, where healthy grouper, snapper, eel, lobster, and Dungeness crab hit the high notes for a repast of unblemished freshness. Be sure to ask about off-menu house specialties, maybe fat Pacific oysters in black bean sauce, Alaska black cod, and soft-shell crab sizzling from the deep fryer. Moderately priced and consistent (one of its owners is a Lee Garden partner), this place is a godsend if you're in the neighborhood.

Magic Wok Restaurant

Dinner Good for Ten

#5
1 Shrimps Toast
2 Scallops with Vegetables
3 Bean Curb with Seafood Soup (L)
4 Sea-Cumber Black Mushroom with Duck Feet
5 Special Chicken Top with Green Onions & Ginger (Whole)
6 Steam Fish
7 Honey Orange Back Ribs
8 Lobster with Ginger and Onion
9 E-Fu Noodle
10 Chicken Fried Rice

$ 178.00

Dinner Good for Eight

1 Shredded Duck Meat Soup
2 Lobsters with Ginger and Green Onion
3 Vegetable Top with Conpoy
4 Sweet & Sour Pork
5 Grandfather Smoke Chicken (Half)
6 Deep Fried Duck Stuffed with Taro (half)
7 Scallops with Vegetable
8 Steamed Fresh Fish

$118.00

Mammina's

6 Wellesley Street West
Toronto
416-967-7199

Italian
DOWNTOWN

V / MC / AmEx

lunch

dinner

beer/wine

cocktails

non-smoking

reservations
recommended

dress casual

menu changes
weekly

Compact, stylish, and run by the dashing Valentini brothers, Mammina's is better known in Hollywood than Toronto: It's a hangout for visiting movie stars, including Al Pacino, Paul Newman, Goldie Hawn, and the Bridges clan. On my last visit, I saw Bryan Brown slipping out the door. It seduces Torontonians with a flat wine markup of $5 per bottle—as opposed to the 200 and 300 percent markups elsewhere—so an Amarone going for $120 up the street is less than $50 here. Oh, and the food: I'll have mussels with capers and chiles and a lovely sage-seasoned saltimbocca alla Romana, *per favore.*

Mammina's

Italian Restaurant

Zuppa Del Giorno	*Soup of the Day*	$6.50
Insalata	*Boston & Radicchio Lettuce Salad*	$6.50
Insalata Cesare	*Caesar Salad, Creamy House Dressing*	$7.00
Funghi	*Braised Oyster Mushrooms*	$7.50
Antipasto Di Mare	*Marinated Shrimps & Squid*	$8.50
Cozze	*Steamed Mussels, Garlic, Tomato*	$9.00
Fusilli Primavera	*Pasta, Vegetables, Tomato, Cream*	$14.50
Gnocchi Bolognese	*Potato Dumplings, Ground Beef, Tomato*	$15.00
Penne Calabrese	*Pasta, Italian Sausage, Spicy Tomato*	$15.50
Spaghettini Mammina	*Pasta, Grilled Chicken, Olive Oil, Garlic, Basil*	$16.00
Linguine Pescatore	*Pasta, Shrimps, Scallops, Mussels & Squid*	$19.50
Dentice	*Red Snapper Fillet, Tomato, Onions, Capers*	$17.00
Pollo Al Timone	*Chicken Breast, Shrimps, Brandy, Cream*	$18.50
Manzo Ai Ferri	*Char-Grilled N.Y. Striploin (10 oz.)*	$20.00
Gamberi Al Diavolo	*Sauteed Shrimps, Garlic, Onion, Spicy Tomato*	$21.00
Vitello Saltimbocca	*Provimi Veal, Prosciuto Ham, Sage*	$22.00
Cafe Latte		$4.50
Cappuccino		$3.00
Espresso, Coffee/Tea		$2.50

Mata Hari Grill

39 Baldwin Street
Toronto
www.mataharigrill.com
416-596-2832

Pan-Asian
DOWNTOWN WEST

Wheelchair
 access

V / MC / AmEx / DC

lunch

dinner

take out

beer/wine

cocktails

high chairs

private parties

non-smoking

reservations
 recommended

dress casual

menu changes
 seasonally

Malaysian cuisine is a hard sell simply because its racy fusion of Chinese, Malay, and Indian—Asian multiculturalism—eludes the ordinary grasp. Zenn and Tricia Soo persist spiritedly at the defiantly hip Mata Hari Grill, their painstakingly authentic Malaysian including even the cooking of the Nyonyas, the Chinese-Malay Creole class who gave us the world's first fusion cuisine. Exotica flies through the air. Curries roar in on clouds of galangal, lemongrass, and chiles. Not on the menu but available on request is my cherished *nasi lemak* (in Southeast Asia, the Malay breakfast) of rice fragrantly steamed in coconut milk and studded with fiery *sambal,* cooling cucumber, crunchy peanuts, and pungent little anchovies.

MATA HARI GRILL

Appetizers

Soto Ayam spiced soup with shredded chicken and bean sprout topped with shallots	**$5.25**
Assam Udang prawn in a spicy sour tamarind soup	**$5.50**
Whole Shrimp Wonton Soup made fresh everyday	**$5.50**
Eggplant Malay brushed with belachan and grilled	**$6.95**
Calamari Matahari marinated in tamarind and grilled, with peanut sauce	**$7.50**

Satay Grilled served with Matahari's Own Peanut Sauce, marinated in our secret mix of spices

chicken	**$6.95**	beef	**$6.95**
sea scallop	**$8.95**	shrimp	**$7.50**

Spring Rolls with Matahari Sauce, stuffed with shrimp and julienned jicama	**$6.95**

Chicken Kapitan marinated chicken breast with fresh lemongrass, galanga, lime leaf, lime juice and coconut milk	**$11.95**
Red Chili Chicken marinated chicken breast with a blend of spices, stir-fried with red onions and tomato in a sweet, hot sauce	**$11.95**
Matahari Curry the ultimate chicken curry with potatoes	**$11.95**
Mango Chicken fresh mangoes stirfry with chicken breast, red and green peppers, red onions and hot peppers	**$11.95**
Casbah Cashew Chicken stir-fry with hot peppers, onions, mushrooms and cashews, of course	**$11.95**
Rendang Beef short ribs simmered with Matahari's secret blend of spices and coconut milk	**$12.95**
Nyonya Lamb simmered in a special blend of fresh galanga, lemongrass, dried chili, eggplant, tofu and soya sauce	**$12.95**
Sambal Green Beans with Prawns sambal is a blend of sundried baby shrimp, shallots, garlic and dried chili	**$14.95**
Sarawak Pepper Prawns stir-fry with red and green peppers, red and green onions, mushrooms, garlic and black pepper	**$14.95**
Hot Pepper Cashew Prawns stir-fry with onions, mushrooms, garlic and soya sauce	**$14.95**
Sambal Udang marinated prawns grilled with a sour and spicy tamarind shallots sauce	**$14.95**

Messis

97 Harbord Street
Toronto
416-920-2186

Bistro
DOWNTOWN WEST

V / MC / AmEx

lunch

dinner

beer/wine

cocktails

high chairs

private parties

non-smoking

reservations
  recommended

dress casual

menu changes
  daily specials

Messis is Latin for "harvest." Some harvest; you want everything. You may require a therapist to consult on a decision. Blame the conflicts on chef Eugene Shewchuk: The man can cook like nobody's business. His food, like the mostly California wine list, is about largesse, with mouth-filling flavors in perfect harmony and glorious flights of fancy with Med-Asian fusion. I'd cross town for his charcoaled calamari served in a Japanese mushroom broth, sesame-crusted salmon, and any slab of fish Shewchuk cares to toss on the grill. Solicit your wine-savvy server for a Chardonnay or Cabernet that blows you clear out of your socks.

M E S S I S

salads:
    Caesar
    5⁷⁵

    Grilled shrimp with pineapple & mango salsa, mango coulis and
    a green onion drizzle
    8⁵⁰

    Baby spinach with bermuda onion, goat cheese, cherry tomatoes with
    a red wine vinaigrette
    7⁵⁰

    Belgian endive with avocado, baby greens, shaved asiago, crispy shallots in a
    sweet lemon & pepper vinaigrette
    7⁵⁰

pizza:
    Roasted red pepper sauce, black olives, roma tomatoes, red peppers, mozzarella
    and parmesan cheese with fresh herbs
    13⁰⁰

pasta:
    Penne with grilled beef, zucchini, eggplant, red peppers and tomatoes in a
    mushroom cream sauce
    14⁰⁰

vegetarian:
    Mushroom, spinach and sweet potato phyllo flan served with a
    wehini rice, red pepper, walnut and cranberry salad, grilled vegetables
    and mixed greens
    14⁰⁰

fish:
    Pan-seared tikka marinated seabass with apple pickled ginger risotto sauteed
    with red peppers, fennel, spinach and bok choy, with a fish veloute and
    a citrus, red plum drizzle
    19⁵⁰

Mildred Pierce

99 Sudbury Street
Toronto
416-588-5695
www.mildredpierce.com

Global
WEST TORONTO

Wheelchair
  access

V / MC / AmEx / DC

Sunday brunch

lunch

dinner

beer/wine

cocktails

high chairs

private parties

non-smoking

reservations
  recommended

dress casual

Mildred Pierce? Owner Donna Dooher named her restuarant after her favorite movie (Why not, the superlative Scaramouche is named after mine), a 1945 weepie with Joan Crawford essaying the unlikely role of restaurateur. By coincidence, the restaurant opened on March 8, the date Crawford copped her best actress Oscar as Millie. A former warehouse in an obscure neighborhood, the joint belongs in a movie, a Fellini movie, with its sur-real, high-ceilinged space, chandeliers suspended from ductwork, and giant murals inhabited by medieval foodies. The cooking, however, has never been more down-to-earth; nor have the desserts, including the signature warm tarte tatin, been more enticing.

RESTAURANT

DINNER

Appetizers

Shrimp and roasted red pepper bisque
with curried coconut cream
$7

Mesclun salad
with sherry Dijon vinaigrette
$7

Warm chevre in vine leaves
with marinated sweet peppers,
parchment flat bread and garlic herb oil
$8

Salad of fennel, pear, celeriac
and watercress with orange vinaigrette,
cambozola and spiced nuts
$8

Vietnamese grilled calamari
with spicy green mango
and papaya salad
$9

Entrées

Handmade tagliatelle
with roasted tomatoes, onion confit,
asiago and crispy leeks
$17

Grilled calves' liver
with crispy potato thyme gnocchi,
rapini and bacon & shallot jus
$18

Roast chicken biryani
clove scented basmati pilaf
with cashews, apricots
and date & fig chutney
$19

Grilled salmon
with steamed mussels,
tomato and kaffir lime fumet,
jicama and Asian greens
$20

Roast pork tenderloin
with tamarind ginger glaze,
sweet potato hash and baby bok choy,
$21

Roast rack of lamb
with buttermilk mashed potatoes
glazed cipollini, carrots and French beans
$25

Millie's

1980 Avenue Road
Toronto
416-481-1247
www.toronto.com/milliesbistro

Bistro
UPTOWN

V / MC / AmEx / DC

Sunday brunch

lunch

dinner

late supper

take out

beer/wine

cocktails

high chair

private parties

catering

non-smoking

reservations
  recommended

dress casual

menu changes
  daily

It's only possible to adore Millie's, Gary Hoyer's sunnily dispositioned restaurant dispensing pan-Mediterranean (much from the neglected Eastern Mediterranean) cuisine rife with olives, saffron, sesame, preserved lemon, pistachios, and pine nuts. How can you not love a kitchen that makes everything from chorizo to goat cheese from scratch? Or gives vegetarians respect with fantasias presented in beautiful Moroccan tagines? Or offers the opportunity to orchestrate your own tapas symphony? Or landscapes main dishes to share on beautiful painted ceramic platters? Or shows a generosity that has patrons groaning "too much, too much" even as they tuck into more? Neighborhood bistro, yes, but also one of a kind.

Millie's
Bistro & Gourmet Market

Appetizers:
Moroccan Legume and Vegetable Soup with Harrisa $5.95
Organic Greens with Lemon, Mint and Sumac $7.95
Fresh Grilled Calamari with Red Rice and Ginger in a Spicy Lemon & Fresh Herb Marinade $9.95
Grilled Pear and Fennel Salad with Roasted Sweet Peppers, Walnuts and Pomagranate Vinaigrette $8.95

Vegetarian:
No-Pasta Lasagna with Yukon Gold Potatoes, Portabella Mushrooms,
    Sweet Peppers, Goat Cheese and Melted Leeks $16.95
Spaghettini with Marinated Fresh Artichokes, Parsley and Boconcini
    in a Trebbiano and Chive Broth $14.95
Canneloni with Roasted Organic Squash, Fresh Shitake and Rapini with a Lemon Celeriac Puree and
    Fresh Basil Beurre Noisette $15.95
Cocas...a Spanish Pizza with Almond Tarator, Roasted Portabella Mushrooms and Sweet Peppers with
    Roasted Garlic and Scallions $13.95

Fish:
Fresh Grilled Tuna Steak with a Wild Mushroom, Pearl Onion and Carrot Ragout,
    Potato Tian and Coconut Chutney $27.95
Paella with Saffron, Shrimps, Clams, Quail and Chorizo Sausage with Garlic Sauce $25.95
Fresh Fish of the Day ...priced accordingly

Meat:
Dry Aged Prime New York Striploin Steak with a Gateau of Yams, Celery Root and Swiss Chard,
    Roasted Shallot And Fresh Thyme Jus $27.95
Tagine of Free Range Chicken with Braised Greens, Carrots, Zucchini and Turnips
    in an Aromatic Sauce with Almonds & Couscous $18.95
Fresh Lamb Both Ways (Braised Shoulder with Fennel, Tomato, Parsley and Nicoise Olives
    and a Grilled Chop) with Egg Noodles $25.95

Let us know if you are in a hurry, as our food is made to order. We can recommend
dishes that will fit your schedule.
Ask for our children's menu & try our gourmet market & catering service for your next occasion.
At Millie's we use as much local organic food as possible!

Mistura

265 Davenport Road
Toronto
416-515-0009

Italian
MIDTOWN WEST

Wheelchair
  access

V / MC / AmEx /
  D / DC

dinner

take out

beer/wine

private parties

non-smoking

reservations
  recommended

dress smart
  casual

menu changes
  seasonally

A nymph curled in an oyster shell sets a sensual
tone for lushly draped, candlelit rooms tailored for
romance (or more) at the Ave-and-Dav. Mistura
claims more than its share of corporate bigwigs,
fretting post-Napster music industry types, and
insufferable yuppies, but it's much more fun to
embrace the foodie throng seduced by deft Italian
fare from chef Massimo Capra, who ran the
kitchen at Prego della Piazza for close to a decade.
Among starters, seared foie gras with white
asparagus and roasted figs is a seducer. Just don't
succumb to the monumental veal chop if you're
verging on a tryst.

Mistura

Atlantic Salmon filet, lemon-thyme sautéed cherry tomatoes and a vegetable Mistura.

24½

Roasted Cornish Hen with preserved lemon, green olives, chick pea polenta nuggets and garlic rapini.

Veal Sweetbreads with grilled radicchio, onions, buttery mashed potatoes and white "Balsamico" reduction.

28

Braised Australian Lamb Shank, green onions, mashed potatoes and black eyed pea ragout.

Grilled Deep Sea Scallop and Shrimps in a spiced carrot broth, julienne vegetables and fresh spinach.

33

Grilled Sea Bass with caramelized squash, sautéed winter greens and chestnut infused beurre blanc.

Mizzen

Westin Harbour Castle
One Harbour Square
Toronto
416-869-7454

Global
WATERFRONT

Wheelchair
access

valet parking

V / MC / AmEx /
D / DC

Sunday brunch

breakfast

lunch

dinner

beer/wine

cocktails

high chairs

private parties

non-smoking

reservations
recommended

A mizzen may sound like an appetizer from the
Middle East, but it's acutally a mast on a sailboat,
an appropriate name for the lakefront location of
the off-lobby, all-day, second (the first being the
glam rooftop Toula) restaurant at the Westin Harbour Castle Hotel. The absence of a view disap-
points, but Mizzen's pastels do their best to evoke
a September sunset on the harbor. Executive chef
Raymond Taylor plays exuberantly on the grill,
juggling infusions, glazes, crusts, and balsamic
drizzles, most effectively with juicy slabs of fish
(sea bass, salmon, swordfish). Duck breast in a
crust of coriander is a standout, and rosemary ice
cream with ginger syrup is the dessert of choice.

THE **MiZ/ZEN**

SIMPLE, CREATIVE | WITH BOLD FLAVOURS

Pannini & Pasta Specialties

Maple Roasted Ham on Ciabatti   12
*Swiss Cheese, Roasted Peppers, Red Onions & Wilted Greens
Dijon Aioli*

Grilled Vegetable foccacia   12
Squash, Roasted Peppers, Melted Provolone, Basil Pesto

Roast Beef on Sourdough   14
*Swiss Cheese, Charred Peppers, Caramelized Onions on Sourdough
Arugula*

Entrées

Balsamic-Brined Free Range Chicken Breast   22
Garlic Whipped Potatoes, Filet Beans, Port Wine Fig Sauce

Grilled Pork Rack   24
Sweet Potato Corn Pudding, Swiss Chard, Apple & Rosemary Sauce

Honey-Glazed Lamb Shanks   24
Confit of Vegetables, Pommes Carlos, Spicy Marsala Glaze

Citrus Barbecued Atlantic Salmon   24
Leek & Taro Root Crisp, Blackberry Essence and Broccoli Sprigadello

Monsoon

100 Simcoe Street
Toronto
416-979-7172
www.monsoonrestaurant.ca

**Pan-Asian
ENTERTAINMENT
DISTRICT**

V / MC / AmEx / DC

lunch

dinner

late supper

beer/wine

cocktails

private parties

non-smoking
 section

reservations
 recommended

dress casual

menu changes
 seasonally

Templelike Monsoon was designed by Yabu
Pushelberg, the powerhouse Toronto firm whose
portfolio includes the Princess of Wales Theatre
and the Tiffany renovation in Manhattan. But
cooking's no second fiddle: Design is squarely on
the plate, and the thrust is Asian fusion, with chef
Robert Craig in control of his flurry of Cantonese,
Thai, Japanese, and Indian accents. Cantonese
roast pork tenderloin showcases superlative
Ontario pork. Atlantic salmon dances out dredged
in tandoori spices, with swatches of miso, sesame,
and wasabi-tangerine "paint." It all looks glorious.
The Asian-friendly list of sakes and big, fruity
wines boasts an award of excellence from the
Wine Spectator.

monsoon

small

dim sum. har-kau shrimp, ginger chicken, bamboo with bok choy, beef and water chestnuts   9
wok steamed mussels in pineapple yellow curry with grilled naan   10
monsoon cold rolls with mint, asian pear, and vermicelli with hoisin sweet chili sauce   6
bahme bound black tiger prawns with tamarind soy   12
thai ginger carrot soup with coconut cream   7
sweet yam fries with soy chili sambai dip   6
thai green mango salad with asian pear and seared tuna in white sake dressing   12
tsunami tempura roll. atlantic salmon and bluefin tuna in nori   14
mushroom spring roll with black and white coral mushrooms, sweet and sour carrot dip   6
tandoori salmon in rice paper with miso sesame and wasabi tangerine paint   9
baby greens, grilled shiitake mushrooms, in toasted sesame, champagne dressing   9
shiro miso soup. with togarashi seaweed, bean curd and scallions   7

large

seared burmese prawns on soba noodles with golden peanut sauce   32
mint chili chicken with crispy taro frites and wok fried spinach   26
grilled arctic char (whole) in banana leaf. with green chili paste and asparagus in lime coriander   3
seared bluefin tuna in toasted nori wrap, with miso tamarind and curried lentil mash   34
tikka masala rack of lamb. with black sticky rice and gooseberry chutney   39
oolong steamed atlantic salmon with thai chili and blood orange curry   26
beef tenderloin (organic). in cabernet teriyaki reduction with wasabi mashed potatoes   39
sake sea bass with oyster and shiitake mushrooms, on bahme noodle pancake   28
cantonese roasted pork tenderloin (organic) with sticky rice and shiitake mushroom parcel   26
(V) seared tofu with shiitake mushrooms, on tomato curry with sesame grilled asparagus   19
(V) bento box. with green tea soba noodles, hijiki tofu rolls and tempura vegetables   23
(V) pikadilyo vegetable hot pot in filipino curried broth with jasmine rice   22

Myth

417 Danforth Avenue
Toronto
416-461-8383
www.myth.to

**Greek
DANFORTH**

Wheelchair
 access

V / MC / AmEx / DC

dinner

late supper

beer/wine

cocktails

high chairs

live
 entertainment

private parties

non-smoking
 section

reservations
 recommended

dress casual

Myth had an epic quality even when a big chunk of the Homeric room was devoted to billiards tables (happily down to two at this writing). It remains the Danforth siren, offering up finessed Greek fare from calamari to lamb chops, but also journeying to Lebanon (grilled haloumi cheese), Italy (tagliatelle with grilled scallops), France (truffled sweetbreads), and Japan (tuna sashimi). It's hip, globe-hopping approach makes Myth the essential Toronto bistro, but on summer nights when the glass front rolls up and happiness spills out on to the street, it's a bacchanal of un-Toronto proportions.

myth

Pasta

Penne with Ricotta
Tomato Sauce, Spiced Eggplant

11

Taglietelle with Grilled Scallops
Cauliflower, Walnuts, Olive Oil

13

Linguini Vongole
Steamed Clams, White Wine, Chili Flakes, Ollive Oil

13

Main

Lamb Burger with Kaseri Cheese
Toasted Kaiser, Mint Aioli, Shoestring Potato

14

Brown Rice, Sweet Potato & Spinich Roll
Walnut Crust, Bean & Watercress Salad

16

Seared Crispy Skinned Salmon & Pancetta
Lentils & Baby Spinach Tossed in Spiced Yoghurt

18

Rabbit Braised in Port & Cinnamon
Parsnip & Potato Puree, Root Vegetables

18

Roasted Lemon Chicken
Sauteed Rapini, French Fried Potato

18

Nami

55 Adelaide Street East
Toronto
416-362-7373

Japanese
DOWNTOWN

V / MC / AmEx / DC
lunch
dinner
take out
beer/wine
cocktails
private parties
non-smoking
reservations
  recommended
dress informal

As blue-and-black Nami assumes the comfortable patina of an old silk slipper, excellence from the sushi bar and robata grill is something we've come to take for granted. Seafood is the name of the game, *yose nobe* the reigning blowout hot pot, the bento box a treasure chest of treats. The kitchen plays fast and loose with beef sashimi, which comes seared and sauced with ponzu, and sushi pizza, which is neither sushi nor pizza, but you have to love it anyway. Romantically inclined customers understand the intimacy of the tatami room, and the steam emitting therein may have little to do with cooking.

NAMI

APPETIZERS

Appetizer Sushi	Chef's daily assortment of three pieces of *sushi* and three pieces of cucumber roll	8.95
Appetizer Sashimi	A selection of tuna, salmon and octopus *sashimi*	13.00
Sushi Pizza	A NAMI original, this is marinated salmon *sashimi* topped with onions and flying fish roe, garnished with spicy sauce, and served on a deep fried *sushi* rice cake	10.50
Hirame Usuzukuri	Fluke *sashimi* sliced paper thin	10.50
Maguro Natto	Tuna with fermented soy bean	8.95
Ika Natto	Squid with fermented soy bean	7.25
Ikura Oroshi	Salmon roe with radish	6.75
Spicy Tuna Sashimi	Tuna *sashimi* marinated in spicy sauce	9.95

MAIN SUSHI AND SASHIMI DINNER

Sushi Moriawase	Tuna roll, tuna, salmon, yellowtail, snapper, mackerel, surf clam, flying fish roe, and shrimp *sushi*. Includes *miso* soup	20.95
Sashimi Moriawase	Tuna, salmon, yellowtail, snapper, mackerel, surf clam and octopus *sashimi*. Served with steamed rice and includes *miso* soup	20.95
Chirashi Sushi	Tuna, salmon, snapper, mackerel, surf clam and salmon roe, shrimp, octopus, crab cake and fried egg *sashimi* served on a bed of *sushi* rice with Japanese style pickles. Includes *miso* soup	18.95
Premium Sushi	Half of a cucumber roll, half of a green onion and yellowtail roll, tuna, salmon, yellowtail, snapper, mackerel, scallop, salmon roe, barbeque eel, and shrimp	22.50
Chef's Selection	The chef can prepare a personalized selection of *sushi* and *sashimi* based on specific tastes and number of guests	**Chef Price**

Natarãj

394 Bloor Street West
Toronto
416-928-2925
www.nataraj.ca

Indian
ANNEX

Wheelchair
  access
V / MC / AmEx / DC
lunch
dinner
take out
beer/wine
cocktails
non-smoking
reservations
  recommended
dress casual

An Annex fave packed like a Bombay bazaar, the
Naturãj is more than just the crowded University
of Toronto student hangout it often seems to be.
Chalk this up to the Chinese-Indian sensibility of
owner Michael Lee, whose family journeyed from
Calcutta twenty-five years ago. The din of Bollywood pop aside, the room sets itself apart from
the crowd by taking fish and seafood seriously.
The array of shrimp dishes alone ranges from
crisp pakoras to coconut-scented Goan shrimp
curry. Atlantic salmon, roasted in the tandoor or
groaning under pillows of cumin and coriander,
does well with the symphony of spices. Start with
onion bhajia, a bulging thicket of deep-fried onion
and the best of its kind in town.

NaTaRaj
Indian Cuisine

Naurattan Korma .... $ 7.50
(Mixed vegetables cooked in fresh Indian spices,
with dry fruits & fresh cream)

Subzi Makhani .... $ 7.50
(Mixed Vegetables cooked in a tomato,
onion cream gravy & butter)

Saag Paneer .... $ 7.95
(Homemade cottage cheese cooked in onion & spinach)

Kebab Labadar .... $ 9.50
(Pieces of marinated chicken baked in a tandoor & saute
with green peppers)

Murgh Makhani (Butter Chicken) $10.50
(Tandoori chicken cooked in a tomato, onion,
cream gravy & butter)

Kadai Murgh .... $ 8.95
(Chicken pieces cooked in a cashew paste with fried onions,
spices & garnished with fried potatoes & red peppers)

Madras Murgh .... $ 8.95
(Chicken cooked in special spices, dry red pepper & lemon juice)

New Orleans Desire

2050 Avenue Road
Toronto
416-488-5947
www.desirecajun.com

Bistro
UPTOWN

Wheelchair
  access
V / MC / AmEx / DC
dinner
take out
beer/wine
cocktails
high chairs
private parties
non-smoking
reservations
  recommended
dress casual
menu changes
  seasonally

No streetcar, not even Desire, comes this far, but who's to spurn N'Awlins French Quarter tourist fare—the gamut from seafood gumbo to blackened everything—in unpretentious uptown digs? Owner Voya Funduk pays respects to Paul Prudhomme, makes all his seasonings from scratch, and knows enough to stew (not grill or deep-fry) the formidable 'gator. From a kitchen leaning toward seafood, Cajun mussels swim in a zesty tomato-based sauce, Emeril's shrimp etouffée capitalizes on TV foodiedom, and jambalaya for two delivers a hurricane of sultry flavors. Bananas Foster may not equal Brennan's, but you don't need a ticket from Air Canada, either.

NEW ORLEANS DESIRE CAJUN RESTAURANT

APPETIZERS

COCONUT BEER SHRIMPS
COCONUT COATED, SERVED
WITH DIJON MUSTARD, ORANGE
AND FRESH HORSERADISH SAUCE $6.95

SHRIMP COCKTAIL
SPICE, WARM, WITH
TOMATO COCKTAIL SAUCE   6.95

CAJUN CALAMARI
FLASH DEEP FRIED
SERVED WITH COCKTAIL
TOMATO SAUCE, SPICE   5.95

CAJUN MUSSELS
SERVED IN OUR TRADITIONAL
NEW ORLEANS HERBED TOMATO
SAUCE, SPICE $5.95

STEAMED MUSSELS
GARLIC, BUTTER, WINE,
AND FRESH GREENS   4.95

SMOKED SALMON
CAPERS, DILL AND ONION   6.95

MARINATED HERRING
SERVED WITH SOUR CREAM,
ONION AND CLOVE   4.95

PASTA

RED HOT
ROTINI, CREOLE SAUCE
CRISP VEGGIES, CAJUN SPICE
AND PARMESAN $6.95

YES, SPAGHETTI
SPAGHETTI, OLIVE OIL, GARLIC
FRESH PARSLEY, BASIL AND PARMESAN   6.95

MR. ZEE'S SEAFOOD SPAGHETTI
SPAGHETTI, CREOLE SAUCE
MUSSELS, SHRIMPS, CRISP VEGGIES
FRESH PARSLEY AND PARMESAN $10.95

PASTA "NEW ORLEANS"
ROTINI, CREAM SAUCE
CHICKEN, CRISP VEGGIES AND PARMESAN   9.95

ENTREES OF NEW ORLEANS

PRUDHOMME'S B.B.Q. SHRIMPS
SPICE SHRIMPS WITH GARLIC,
BUTTER, FRESH GREENS, SERVED
WITH RICE AND ROSEMARY SAUCE $12.95

SHRIMPS IN CREOLE SAUCE
SPICE SHRIMPS WITH GARLIC,
BUTTER, FRESH GREENS, SERVED WITH
RICE AND CREOLE SAUCE   12.95

EMERIL'S SHRIMPS ETOUFFÉE
NOT SPICY, GARLIC, BUTTER
MUSHROOMS, FRESH GREENS,
35% CREAM, HERBS SERVED ON RICE   14.95

ALLIGATOR MISSISSIPPIENSAS STEW
ASK YOUR SERVER FOR DETAILS   PRICED
                                     ACCORDINGLY

FROG LEGS SAUCE PIQUANTE
SPICE, SAUTEED, SERVED WITH
RICE AND SEASONAL VEGETABLES $19.95

LOUISIANA PORK TENDERLOIN
SPICE , BLACKENED, GRILLED
MUSHROOMS, RICE AND
GREEN PEPPERCORN SAUCE   15.95

CRAWFISH BOIL-"MUDBUG"
CAJUN SPICE, BOILED, SERVED
WITH GARLIC-BUTTER SAUCE,
SERVED WITH CHOICE OF
DAILY VEGETABLES   16.95

Noce

875 Queen Street West
Toronto
416-504-3463

Italian
WEST TORONTO

V / MC / AmEx / DC

lunch

dinner

late supper

beer/wine

cocktails

private parties

catering

non-smoking
section

reservations
required

dress informal

menu changes
seasonally

On a recently galleried and Starbucked stretch of Queen Street West, restaurateurs Elena Morelli and Guido Saldini have carved out their niche with intensely renovated Italian tradition. *Noce* translates as "walnut" (for the Walnut Avenue entrance), and the kitchen kicks in with walnut, pear, and asiago salad and walnut-and-leek-stuffed pork tenderloin. Gnocchi, made on the premises every day, comes feather light, not at all the anticipated lead pellets. Pastas change daily: Pray for puttanesca, the racy "whore's sauce" from Naples. Game from venison to musk ox elicits inspiration in the kitchen. And in the blue air of summer dusk, look to the flower-filled patio for beguilement.

I NOSTRI PRIMI

Daily homemade gnocchi	*$ p/a*
Risotto of the day	*$ p/a*
House made fresh pasta of the day	*$ p/a*
Seafood pasta of the day	*$ p/a*

(Appetizer portion of "I Nostri Primi" also available)

LE NOSTRE PIETANZE

Roasted pork tenderloin stuffed with walnuts, leeks and currants in a pommery mustard cream sauce	*$ 22*
Osso Buco - Braised Provimi veal shank with garlic, lemon rind & fresh parsley, served on "polenta"	*$ 25*
Oven roasted rabbit in a white wine & rosemary sauce with cherry tomatoes and green olives	*$ 26*
Breast of pheasant stuffed with a truffle liver pate' in a juniper and natural reduction	*$ 28*
Grilled sterling silver striploin with a three peppercorn sauce & shaved black truffles	*$ 29*
Roasted Delft Blue veal chop with roast garlic, thyme and a natural jus	*$ 32*
Oven roasted rack of Australian lamb served in a natural jus reduction with fresh rosemary and a puree of potatoes with caramelized shallots	*$ 35*
Grilled certified Angus beef tenderloin with savoury brioche & a porcini sauce	*$ 35*
Grilled whole Mediterranean sea bream with lemon and extra virgin olive oil	*Priced Accordingly*

North 44

2537 Yonge Street
Toronto
416-487-4897

Global
UPTOWN

Wheelchair
  access
valet parking
V / MC / AmEx / DC
dinner
late supper
take out
beer/wine
cocktails
private parties
non-smoking
  section
reservations
  required
dress informal
menu changes
  seasonally

The restaurant's logo—a chef standing by a vintage aircraft in takeoff—provokes chatter and epitomizes Toronto cool. *Gourmet* magazine anointed North 44 the city's top restaurant with good reason: The Yabu Pushelberg design is a knockout of hushed monochromatic elegance and textural richness, templelike in its ability to stroke the psyche. Over a dozen years, Mark McEwan's cuisine has evolved from Cal-Ital to classical French with studied Asian flourishes. Foie gras—both truffled terrine and pan-seared duck liver sharing the plate—does it for me, but here, what doesn't? A *Wine Spectator* award of excellence salutes 800 carefully chosen labels. North 44 isn't cheap, but it's definitely grand.

NORTH 44)°

Giant prawns with citrus garlic sauce, Shittake mushrooms,   39.95
water chestnuts and greens
Suggested Wine: Kistler Chardonnay '99, Carneros

Seared seabass baked in banana leaf with leek hearts,   38.95
coconut and coriander served with scented basmati rice
Suggested Wine: Mason Cellars Sauvignon Blanc 99, Napa

Lobster in natural broth with lemon grass, ginger, sweet onion   Market Price
and coriander
Suggested Wine: Chardonnay "Rossj-Bass" '96 Gaja

Soy lacquered "Sterling" salmon with crisp skin, sweet onion   30.95
infused potatoes and scallion fritters
Suggested Wine: Mer et Soleil Chardonnay '98, Monterey

Roasted Yellow Tail snapper with seasonal squash, spinach, tahini   37.95
and citrus garlic sauce
Suggested Wine: Vouvray "Le Sec" '99 Chateau Gaudrelle

Seared swordfish baked in parchment with braised potatoes,   37.95
sweet onion, oven cured tomatoes and aromatics
Suggested Wine: Xanadu - Lagan Estate Semillon '98, Margaret River (AUS)

Whole roasted Dover sole in brown butter with capers, lemon,   Market Price
chive spun potatoes and organic sweet beets
Suggested Wine: Pouilly Fuisse '90 J.J. Vincent

Olive & Lemon

119 Harbord Street
Toronto
416-923-3188

Italian
DOWNTOWN WEST

V / MC / DC
dinner
late supper
take out
beer/wine
cocktails
private parties
non-smoking
reservations
   required
dress informal

With Trattoria Giancarlo and the College Street Bar and Grill to their credit, Giancarlo and Marlene Carnevale almost single-handedly resurrected Little Italy, now one of the city's most sizzling—boiling over, actually—restaurant strips. Now the Carnevales are playing Mom and Pop on Harbord, in the same neighborhood as Splendido and Messis. Giancarlo cooks Sicilian with lauded pastas, wild salmon from Alaska, grilled jumbo quails, and—selling out in two seconds flat—spaghetti with meatballs. Meatballs? The meatballs are made with minced veal and basil, but they are still meatballs. Stellar lawyer Eddie Greenspan once showed up to eat them for his birthday. Case closed.

OLIVE & LEMON

Bucatini all' Amatriciana
Bucatini with tomato sauce, pancetta and hot peppers 16.00

Linguine con Frutti di Mare
Linguine with shrimps, mussels, caviar and hot peppers 19.00

Rigatoni al Limone
Rigatoni with lemon, cream and saffron 16.00

Penne d'Estate
Penne with greens, raddichio, endive, romano and hot peppers 14.00

Farfalle ai Fegatini
Farfalle with chicken liver, sage and white wine 16.00

Fusilli ai Funghi
Fusilli with shiitake mushrooms and black peppercorns 17.00

Risotto alla Pescatora
Seafood risotto with clams, mussels, shrimp and saffron 21.00

Risotto con Indivia e Olio Tartufato   18.50
Risotto with grilled endive and truffle oil 18.50

Risotto Nero
Risotto with cuttlefish ink, squid and shrimp 21.00

Omi

451 Church Street
Toronto
416-920-8991

Japanese
DOWNTOWN

V / MC / AmEx / DC

lunch

dinner

late supper

take out

beer/wine

cocktails

private parties

non-smoking

reservations
   required

dress casual

menu changes
   seasonally

Here the hitherto unchallenged sushi supremacy of Hiro Yoshida gets a shaking from former disciple John Lee, who gives substance to the Korean claim of inventing sushi and sashimi in the first place. Lee reveres his fish and seafood, and he knows precisely where and how to play, with Atlantic salmon turning up with nuggets of deep-fried soft-shell crab secreted like diamonds in rolls of sticky rice, and Miles Davis on the sound system. Take the plunge and order live shrimp, the critter beheaded and deveined with quick strokes, the tail flesh raw and sweet, the head fried to crispy perfection.

OMI RESTAURANT

MAIN DISHES

TEMPURA	Light & crispy shrimps with seasonal vegetables	$16.95
CHICKEN TERIYAKI	Grilled chicken with teriyaki sauce	$12.95
SAKANA BUTTERYAKI	Today's fresh catch pan-fried with lemon butter sauce	$15.95
BEEF TERIYAKI	Grilled AAA Black Angus beef with teriyaki sauce	$15.95
EBI-FRY	Pan-Ko breaded shrimps with tangy sauce	$15.95
TONKATSU	Pan-Ko breaded pork with tangy sauce	$12.95
OMI SUSHI	Daily sushi combination including seven sushi pieces and sushi roll	$16.95
OMI SASHIMI	Daily sashimi combination of assorted fresh fish	$16.95
CHIRASHI	Daily selection of fresh fish on a bed of sushi rice	$20.00

Opus

37 Prince Arthur Avenue
Toronto
416-921-3105
www.opusrestaurant.com

Global
YORKVILLE

V / MC / AmEx / DC

dinner

late supper

take out

beer/wine

cocktails

private room

non-smoking

reservations
  recommended

dress informal

menu changes
  seasonally

Opus's picture window gazes on the floodlit gal-
leries and cafés of chic Prince Arthur, and the
snazzy bar and softly lit dining room glimmer
with understated opulence. Owners Tony and
Mario Amaro respect ritual and the faithful
include Sir Peter Ustinov (who famously called
Toronto "New York run by the Swiss"), Samuel L.
Jackson, and Jennifer Lopez. Chef Jason Cox covers the bases from rare ahi tuna to salt-meadow
lamb. He was on to foie gras years before the
bandwagon rolled. The *Wine Spectator* Best of
Award of Excellence salutes an ever-expanding cellar of 1,800 labels and 15,000 bottles dear to the
expense-account set.

Appetizers

White leek and potato soup with crème fraîche and
ocietra caviar 14.

Feuillatine of dungeness crab with a tomato gelée and orange
anise reduction 18.

Smoked duck breast risotto with fresh herbs and
parmigiano-reggiano shavings   16./32.

Seared Quebec foie gras with maple glazed apples
and black currant purée 22.

Main courses

Roast 'Peking' duck on salsify purée with a red wine duck jus
34.

Pan seared **"rare"** black pepper crusted tuna with a shoyu
sake green onion beurre blanc on a crispy rice cake 32.

Grilled beef tenderloin on pomme purée with a truffled
sweetbread ravioli and Merlot thyme reduction 37.

Champagne butter poached Nova Scotia lobster
with a lobster essence 39.

Oro

45 Elm Street
Toronto
416-597-0155
www.ororestaurant.com

Global
DOWNTOWN

Wheelchair
  access

V / MC / AmEx / DC

lunch

dinner

beer/wine

cocktails

private parties

non-smoking

reservations
  recommended

dress jacket/tie

menu changes
  weekly

Indefatigable restaurateurs Dominic and Connie
Ciccocioppo transformed Old Angelo's—a legendary lasagna house since 1922—into a miracle
of modernity and finesse. Three stylish rooms
have long replaced a cavernous interior, stained-
glass lingering from the old days, the fireplace
crackling on winter nights. Firebrand chef Daria
Tumaselli, who jilted the fashion world for the
kitchen, aims for nothing short of a "life experience" and delivers with seared monkfish liver, tea-
smoked sea bass, and a heady combo of venison
rack, foie gras, and truffled potato. Chronically
and unjustly omitted in lists of Toronto's best
(where it belongs), Oro maintains a big following
in New York and Chicago.

Hand-cut Stratford greens in a balsamic-citrus vinaigrette
with rosemary-toasted pumpkin seeds 12

Pastilla of goat cheese, aged in-house with
oven-dried tomato, peperoncino, baby arugula,
pickled salsify and beets gastric 14

Marinated octopus and grilled calamari
with gaeta olives, jicama salad and lemon confit 15

Seared diver scallop and wakame salad
on a sea urchin beurre blanc with tart apple purée 18

Roasted Atlantic salmon triangle with charred artichoke
and fine beans in chili oil on a sauce gribiche 24

Tea-smoked Chilean sea bass with Thai curry-mashed potato
and baby bok choy sprouts, in a carrot-sake emulsion 28

Maple and miso-crusted white tuna with smoked salmon
and potato gallette on preserved lemon-tarragon emulsion 29

Skillet-roasted Cornish hen with savoury bread gnocchi,
charred cabbage, blood orange marmalade and pan juices 24

Hoisin and tamarind-roasted pork tenderloin
with cumin-scented red onion purée on a corn fondue 24

Ouzeri

500A Danforth Avenue
Toronto
416-778-0500
www.ouzeri.com;
www.toronto.com/ouzeri

Greek
DANFORTH

Wheelchair
  access

V / MC / AmEx / DC

lunch

dinner

late supper on
  weekends

take out

beer/wine

cocktails

high chairs

live
  entertainment

private parties

non-smoking

reservations
  recommended

dress casual

menu changes
  weekly

If the Danforth is a Greek chorus of authentically bad restaurants, the Ouzeri, on a good night, can seem like a revelry transported from some carefree Cycladean island, its raucous celebration shaking the roof as clouds of oregano and rosemary blow through the room. The selection of meze draws from Greece and the vast recipe books of Istanbul sultans, cracking phyllo pastry footballs stuffed with rabbit, chicken, and herbs the high points on the menu. Tuesday, the customary off day, gets a boost from Greek Night in summer, when traditionally conservative Torontonians can be heard *opahhhing* into the wee, small hours.

Seafood Chowder
A rich, flavourful soup that consists of shrimps, scallops, crabmeat and diced vegetables. **$5.50**

Bean Fasolada
A unique presentation of a Greek favourite. **$4.25**
With olives, feta and onions. **$5.50**

Classic Mousaka
Eggplant, zucchini and spiced ground beef layered and covered with a béchamel cream. **$10.95**

Vegetarian Mousaka
Chickpeas and green beans are the substitute for the meat. **$9.95**

Seafood Pasta
Mussels, prawns and scallops served on a bed of linguini with your choice of tomato or cream sauce. **$13.95**

Pastichio
Pasta and spiced ground beef layered and topped with béchamel cream. **$9.95**

Chicken Rosemary Pie
An oven baked dish that consists of pieces of chicken breast and mushrooms in a rosemary sauce wrapped in layered filo. **$9.95**

Lamb Rosemary Pie
Lamb, feta, mushrooms and rosemary sauce wrapped in layered filo. **$10.95**

Oyster Boy

872 Queen Street West
Toronto
416-534-3432
www.oysterboy.com

Seafood
WEST TORONTO

V / MC / AmEx / DC

Sunday brunch

dinner

late supper

take out

beer/wine

cocktails

non-smoking

reservations
    not taken

dress informal

menu changes
    daily

A neighborhood oyster bar on a mostly bleak stretch of Queen Street West, this cheery, raucous slice of Atlantic Canada proffers first-rate bivalves (a limited variety, with Malpeques omnipresent) on the half shell and warmed through in a dozen ways, from Rockefeller to Imperial, the last with caviar and Cognac. People who like their seafood dead, like Woody Allen, tuck into hearty Down Home specialties including P.E.I. lobster roll and seafood pie practically bursting with salmon, scallops, and shrimp. There's no meat on the menu, which is fine with me, and the fries are fresh, not frozen, which is finer still.

OYSTER BOY

RETAIL · WHOLESALE · CATERING

Baked oysters *6 for $11.50, 12 for $22.00*

Oyster Boy chowder *$4.95*

Fresh green salad *$4.25*
with a blue poppyseed dressing or house vinaigrette

Caesar salad *$6.95*
with smoked trout, add $4

Shrimp Louie salad *$9.95*

Crab Louie salad *$10.95*

Warm salt cod spread *$7.95*
with warm garlic and fennel toasts

Deep fried oysters *$8.95*
with Oyster Boy slaw

Spicy grilled shrimp cocktail *$8.95*
with Oyster Boy slaw and classic cocktail sauce

Fresh P.E.I. mussels *(seasonally available) small $6.00, large $9.00*
steamed in white wine with roast garlic and served with fries

Fresh steamed clams *small or large plate - market price*
steamed in white wine with roast garlic and fresh herbs

Beer battered fish'n'chips *$11.95*
with spicy tartar sauce, served with Oyster Boy slaw and fries

Oyster stew *$10.95*

Fresh seafood pot pie *$12.95*
served with green salad

Seafood linguine of the day *market price*

Pan on the Danforth

516 Danforth Avenue
Toronto
416-466-8158
www.toronto.com/panondanforth

Greek
DANFORTH

V / MC / AmEx
dinner
late supper
take out
beer/wine
cocktails
non-smoking
reservations
   recommended
dress casual

In spite of impinging gentrification, Toronto's Greektown unfurls along the Danforth, a gauntlet of squid and souvlaki houses. The competition is as fierce as it is on Mykonos or Santorini, only the food can be better. Pan stakes its claim to Greek chic by transcending the hackneyed with prime ingredients and attention to robustly orchestrated flavors. Atlantic salmon with feta pine-nut pesto and char-grilled lamb with black olive mash leave the competition in the ruins. The ambience is strictly taverna, but revelers, quaffing ouzo and fantasizing about Aegean escapes—the island of Naxos for me, thank you—aren't complaining.

PAN ON THE DANFORTH

entrees.

moussaka - casserole of chopped beef, potato and eggplant served with a green salad.	$13.95
vegetable moussaka - casserole of zucchini, eggplant and potato served with a green salad.	$12.95
half rack of lamb with roasted baby beets, walnut oil and feta scalloped potatoes.	$19.95
char-grilled loin of lamb with fresh fig and orange glaze, served with black olive mash and seared baby spinach. *Figs are seasonal.*	$17.95
in house smoked double pork chop, baked and served with a smoked pepper grilled zucchini relish and feta scalloped potatoes.	$16.95
braised lamb shank with sage, mushroom, tomato and leeks - served over orso pasta.	$14.95
santorini chicken, stuffed with spinach and feta served with new mini potatoes and seared rapini.	$16.95
lemon roasted chicken breast, with fried onion and feta scalloped potatoes.	$16.95
pan seared grouper in a white wine cream reduction with new mini potatoes and seared baby spinach.	$16.95
atlantic salmon - filled with mushrooms and baby spinach, wrapped in a thin layer of phyllo pastry, served with garlic mash potateos and a vegetable medley.	$17.95
grilled seabass with tomato, onion, capers and roasted garlic salsa, served with new mini potatoes and seared baby spinach.	$19.95
kakavia - a traditional seafood dish of shrimp, mussels, sea bass, calamari, onion, tomato white wine and garlic crostini.	$15.95
seared fillet of beef tenderloin with a balsamic red wine reduction, roast vegetable and new mini potatoes. 8 oz	$22.95
shrimp with onion and feta, served with a spinach orso pasta.	$18.95
jumbo quail - stuffed with sausage, mushroom and schallots, served with new mini potatoes a vegetable medley, finished with pearl onion and a dark roast chicken and red wine reduction.	$17.95
pan seared rainbow trout with a white wine dill butter, served with wild greens and new mini potatoes.	$15.95
ioli sparkling mineral water/ greece 750ml	$5.95
ioli sparkling mineral water/ greece 333ml	$3.25
ioli flat mineral water/ greece 1000ml	$5.95

No substitutions allowed. Side orders available for $3.95.

Pangaea

1221 Bay Street
Toronto
416-920-2323
www.pangaearestaurant.com

Global
MIDTOWN

Wheelchair
access

V / MC / AmEx /
D / DC

lunch

dinner

late supper

beer/wine

cocktails

live
entertainment

non-smoking

reservations
recommended

dress casual

menu changes
weekly

People waste infuriating amounts of time trying to pronounce the name. Translating from the Greek word meaning "all the lands," it's pronounced "*Pan-jee-a*." Chef-owner Martin Kouprie forges his cuisine from the multicultural food basket and draws a crowd of sophisticates—hip ad agency types mentally dressing voluptuous bronze nudes (statues, not customers) at the post-modern bar, politicians and rock stars claiming generously spaced tables under the panoply of halogen stars. Kouprie's cooking is not so much flash and dash as precision in the Swiss cuckoo clock mode, from grilled fish sauced in anchovies, olives, and capers to Canadian cuisine standard-bearers Arctic char and caribou chops.

main course   dinner

sterling salmon: 25.95
mahogany glazed, on wilted bok choy, water chestnuts,
shiitake mushrooms, preserved ginger, lime-caramel sauce

roasted sea bass: 27.95
with braised beets, mussels, chanterelles, lemon broth

bouillabaisse Venus: 29.95
lobster, scallop, shrimp, calamari,
salmon, new potatoes, shrimp velouté

caribou: 32.95
on braised napa cabbage with onions, speck, smoked apple,
wild grape reduction

new york steak: 33.95
12 ounces, grilled, pearl pasta, creamed oyster mushrooms

lamb rack: 31.95
roasted with sunflower-lemon crust, horseradish-whipped turnips,
rosemary-lamb reduction

squab: 29.95
pan-seared, with sweet potato rosti, Chinese cabbage,
sweet and sour five-spice sauce

liver: 21.95
grilled, on fried onion whipped potatoes, market vegetables,
plums stewed in port

duck: 28.95
pan-roasted, sautéed chanterelles with duck offals,
yukon gold potato-caraway rosti , lingonberry sauce

rabbit: 28.00
ballottine wrapped with fine vegetables and spinach,
truffled potato hash, foie gras sauce

Pastis

1158 Yonge Street
Toronto
416-928-2212

**French
MIDTOWN**

Wheelchair
access

V / MC / AmEx / DC

lunch

dinner

beer/wine

cocktails

private parties

non-smoking

reservations
recommended

dress casual

menu changes
seasonally

Veteran restaurateur George Gurnon traded his Pastis raspberry for sunny bistro hues, making privileged Rosedalers groan, but then they all ran to join the plebes in the queue. Gurnon's instincts have always been sharp as a guillotine, and Toronto loves a bistro. Who needs more than Gallic comfort food—ravioli stuffed with snails, proper soupe de poissons with croutons and rouille, melting beef cheeks à la Bourguignonne, and hand-cut frites, not to mention the addictive salty-sweet potato crisps at the bar—in happy surroundings? It's also food that has never stopped making sense, and it pleases inexpressibly on a night when you'd rather be strolling in the Marais than shuffling through slush in Toronto.

LES ENTREES:
Le potage du jour 7
Pastis fish soup, croûtons, rouille , grated cheese 9
Frogs legs with a chipotle aioli, caramelized onions 9
Goat cheese soufflé on caramelized Vidalia onion 10
Green salad with olive oil dressing 7
Tomato salad, fresh tarragon dressing 10
Steamed mussels with tomato, white wine, leeks 10
Our own ravioli with snails, garlic and herb butter 11

LE FOIE GRAS:
Terrine of duck foie gras with toats 16
Duo of foie gras and duck confit, sweet Balsamic dressing 19

LES PLATS:
Steamed mussels with tomato, leeks, white wine and frites 13
Pastis fish and chips, tartar sauce 15
Grilled salmon, lemon thyme vinaigrette, Basmati rice 17
Herbed crusted chicken breast, sauce Diable, Yukon frites 17
Barbequed baby ribs, Yukon frites, barbecue sauce 20
Brochette of shrimps with fettucine, pesto butter 19
Pan-seared calf's liver, shallots, lardons, Yukon frites 21
Rabbit Provencale, polenta gnocchi 21
Fresh cod "en papillote", beurre rouge 22
Veal scallopini, light lemon sauce, house-made tagliatelli 21
French style grilled lamb chops, roasted potatoes, mixed greens 22
Steak frites 8 oz, beurre maître d'hôtel 22

L'ASSIETTE DE FROMAGES: Bleu d'Auvergne and chèvre fermier 10

Pearl Court

633 Gerrard Street East
Toronto
416-463-8778

Chinese
CHINATOWN EAST

V / MC
Sunday brunch
lunch
dinner
late supper
take out
beer/wine
cocktails
high chairs
private parties
non-smoking
dress casual

In Chinatown East, at Gerrard and Broadview—more like a Beijing *hutong* (back street)—Pearl Court bewilders diners with main menu, supplementary menu, and posted and blackboard specials that can total 300 choices (and more, depending on your Cantonese). Smart money ignores the numbers and charges upstairs to join the lunchtime queue for dim sum that shames the palaces of the megacity's northeast frontier. Carts jump out of the kitchen like crouching tigers, laden with Toronto's best shrimp dumplings: one wrapped in seaweed and deep-fried to crunchy perfection; another, impeccably steamed, pairing plump crustaceans with Chinese chives. Also of note are soft rice rolls secreting silken scallops and dollar plates of deliciously fried noodles.

小杭公海鮮酒家
Pearl Court Restaurant

時蔬豆腐類 VEGETABLE & BEAN CURD

35.	清炒油菜心	Pan Fried Seasonal Vegetable	7.50
36.	清炒唐芥蘭	Pan Fried Chinese Broccoli	7.95
37.	蠔油西生菜	Fresh Lettuce with Oyster Sauce	6.75
38.	羅漢會上景	Braised Mixed Vegetable	7.95
39.	紅燒炆豆腐	Braised Bean Curd with Vegetable	7.95
40.	蠔皇會雙菇	Braised Two Kinds of Mushrooms	7.95
41.	蠔油扒北菇	Chinese Mushroom with Vegetable	8.75
42.	羅漢扒豆腐	Braised Bean Curd with Mixed Vegetables	7.95
43.	八珍燒豆腐	Bean Curd with Assorted Meat & Vegetable	8.50
44.	琵琶煎豆腐	Deep Fried Mashed Bean Curd & Vegetable	8.50
45.	炸釀豆腐	Deep Fried Stuffed Bean Curd	7.25

鐵板燒 HOT PLATE

50.	鐵板醬爆雞片	Spicy Chicken with Green Pepper And Onion on Hot Plate	8.95
51.	鐵板豉汁帶子	Scallops with Black Bean Sauce on Hot Plate	13.95
52.	鐵板海上鮮	Sea Food on Sizzling Hot Plate	10.50
53.	鐵板京燒骨	Pork Chop on Sizzling Hot Plate	8.95
54.	鐵板豆豉鷄	Chicken (Bone in) with Black Bean Sauce on Sizzling Hot Plate	8.95
55.	鐵板沙爹牛肉	Sliced Beef with Satay Sauce on Sizzling Hot Plate	8.95
56.	鐵板牛柳	Fillet Mignon on Sizzling Hot Plate	9.95

Pho Hung

350 Spadina Avenue
Toronto
416-593-4274

Southeast Asian
SPADINA CHINATOWN

Wheelchair
  access

V / MC

lunch

dinner

take out

beer/wine

high chairs

private parties

non-smoking

reservations
  recommended

dress casual

What a pity Vietnamese, the greatest of Southeast Asian cuisines, hasn't kept up with immigration in establishing its Toronto beachhead. Pho Hung, one of the busiest addresses on the Spadina strip, is by far our best. The lines don't quit from ten to ten, and the heated streetside patio fills up even in January. Start with pho, the national dish, a deeply reduced homemade beef broth (the kitchen boils 1,500 pounds of beef bones a week) spiked with sweet basil and piled high with noodles and beef, offal, or seafood. Vietnamese fried rice, laced with shrimp, minced pork, and half a dozen finely diced vegetables, could be the best five-buck lunch in town.

Also: **200 Bloor Street West**
       Toronto
       416-963-5080

PHỞ HƯNG
VIETNAMESE RESTAURANT

01. **PHỞ HƯNG ĐẶC BIỆT**
Hung's Special Beef Rice Noodle Soup
(Rare, well done, tripe and tendon) - - - - - - - - - - - - - - - - - - 5.50   4.50
金牌特別牛肉粉

02. **PHỞ TÁI**
Beef Rice Noodle Soup (Rare) - 5.50   4.50
上湯生牛肉粉

03. **PHỞ TÁI NẠM**
Beef Rice Noodle Soup (Rare & Brisket)) - - - - - - - - - - - - - 5.50   4.50
上湯生肉熟腩粉

04. **PHỞ TÁI GÂN SÁCH**
Beef Rice Noodle Soup (Rare with Fresh Tripe & Tendon) - - - - 5.50   4.50
上湯生肉片筋粉

05. **PHỞ CHÍN NẠC**
Lean Beef Rice Noodle Soup (Well done) - - - - - - - - - - - - - - 5.50   4.50
上湯熟牛腿肉粉

06. **PHỞ TÁI CHÍN NẠC**
Lean Beef Rice Noodle Soup (Rare & Well done) - - - - - - - - - - 5.50   4.50
生肉片、熟瘦肉湯粉

07. **PHỞ TÁI BÒ VIÊN**
Beef Rice Noodle Soup (Rare & Balls) - - - - - - - - - - - - - 5.50   4.50
生肉牛丸粉

08. **SÚP BÒ VIÊN**
Beef Balls Soup only - 3.75   2.75
上湯牛肉丸

09. **SÚP BÒ TÁI**
Rare Beef Soup only - 3.75   2.75
上湯生牛肉片

Piatto

1646 Dundas Street West
Mississauga
905-896-9111

Italian
SUBURBAN WEST

Wheelchair
   access

V / MC / AmEx / DC

lunch

dinner

beer/wine

cocktails

private parties

non-smoking

reservations
   recommended

dress casual

menu changes
   daily

The Pain Clinic in the same Mississauga manse is
not an omen. Piatto is a pleasure clinic. Savvy
restaurateur and intrepid mushroom hunter San-
dro Julita imbues his rooms with warmth and
grace, and chef Fernando Garcia mans the stoves
and sends out flavors of astounding largesse.
Eighty percent of regulars order from the dozen
daily specials on the blackboard. Anyone familiar
with Julita's expertise (he unearths chanterelles,
morels, and porcinis in the area, which calls for
genius) will jump at *funghi* every which way.
Julita's scaloppini in a truffle haze can induce
instant delirium. Piatto is simply the best in the
'burbs. If Julita were downtown, he'd be mobbed.

APPETIZERS

TEQUILA CURED FRESH SALMON with horseradish cream	$ 8.75
SEARED BEEF CARPACCIO with parmigiano and marinated mushrooms	$ 8.75
PROSCIUTTO with melon	$ 8.75
BOCCONCINI CHEESE, fresh tomato, basil and extra virgin olive oil	$ 7.75
INSALATA MISTA with a fresh basil vinaigrette	$ 5.50
BABY SPINACH SALAD with pecans, sliced apple and a honey sherry vinaigrette	$ 6.50
CAESAR SALAD with a creamy dressing and garlic croutons	$ 5.75
CALAMARI FRITTI with a garlic hot pepper aioli	$ 8.75
GRILLED CALAMARI with black olives, capers, onion and tomatoes	$ 9.25
FRESH MUSSELS in a piquante tomato sauce with julienne of vegetables	$ 8.75
SHRIMP sautéed with oyster mushrooms and sambuca cream	$10.75
OPEN FACE RAVIOLI with assorted mushrooms	$10.75
SPRING ROLLS filled with chicken and vegetables with a peanut sauce	$ 8.25
BROILED GOAT CHEESE on greens with a roasted pepper vinaigrette	$ 8.75

MAIN COURSES

PENNE with roasted peppers, sundried tomatoes and a spicy tomato sauce	$14.50
PORCINI PENNE with assorted mushrooms, pine nuts, fresh herbs and cream	$14.50
PENNE with Italian sausage, leek and garlic tomato sauce	$14.50
FETTUCCINE with smoked salmon, dill, absolut and tomato cream	$14.50
LINGUINE with assorted seafood and marinara sauce	$15.75
LINGUINE with white truffle oil, shiitake and oyster mushrooms	$15.00
MUSHROOM AGNOLOTTI with portobello, italian parsley, chives, rose sauce	$15.00
CANNELLONI stuffed with veal and fresh herbs and baked in a tomato cream sauce	$14.50
RISOTTO del giorno	priced daily

Prego della Piazza

150 Bloor Street West
Toronto
416-920-9900
www.pregodellapiazza.ca

Italian
YORKVILLE

Wheelchair
    access
V / MC / AmEx / DC
lunch
dinner
late supper
beer/wine
cocktails
high chairs
live
    entertainment
private parties
non-smoking
    section
reservations
    recommended
dress casual

At Bloor and Avenue Road (outsiders reel at the redundancy), Prego della Piazza proffers pizzazz to a crowd thick with celebrities (it's the unofficial headquarters of the Toronto Film Festival) and CEOs. Restaurateur Michael Carlevale, one of the city's great survivors (think Boston Tavern), is back on top in two opulent rooms, one the former Black and Blue, the planet's most gorgeous beefery. Prego, as the Reidel stemware on every table suggests, is for serious dining—for casual, go next door to Carlevale's—and the fare herein includes carpaccio of USDA prime as a main and tournedos Rossini cuddling sensuously under a duvet of foie gras.

PREGO
DELLA PIAZZA

New England Clam Chowder
9

Insalata Caprese ~yellow tomato and Buffala
Mozzarella with balsamic dressing
14

Truffled Asparagus spears and foie gras, with
balsamic reduction and blackberry jus
18

Baked Whole Red Snapper with lemon caper
sauce
32

Seared Seabass with a citrus salsa
29

Baked Salmon with sun-dried tomato, caper
and black olive tapenade
26

Rack of Lamb with a balsamic jus
39

12oz Delmonico steak with bearnaise sauce
40

Mafaldine with Prosciutto, pearl onions, sweet
peas, vodka, tomato and cream
21

Provence

12 Amelia Street
Toronto
416-924-9901
www.provencerestaurant.com

**French
CABBAGETOWN**

V / MC / AmEx / DC

Saturday and
  Sunday brunch

lunch

dinner

beer/wine

cocktails

private parties

non-smoking

reservations
  recommended

dress smart
  casual

A Cabbagetown house (the cabbages long given way to summer patios bedecked in flowers) evolved over more than two decades to a weathered Provence cottage, with two dining rooms and a copper-topped bar. Owner Elie Benchitrit and his youthful brigade aren't afraid to play—*soupe de poisson* arrives richly textured with emulsified fish and redolent of lemon and coriander rather than garlic and saffron—but salute tradition with the best *bavette frites* in town and duck confit. The enterprising Benchitrit tins the confit and exports as far as the Land of the Rising Sun (where I've seen throngs of Japanese puzzling over it).

FIRST COURSES

Salade de lentilles du Puy sur lit de cresson, noix et vinaigre de sherry 9.95
Salad of du Puy lentils on a bed of watercress, walnut and sherry vinegar 9.95

Tomates raisin, rémoulade de fenouils, vinaigrette citron et estragon 9.95
Grape tomato, fennel rémoulade, lemon tarragon vinaigrette 9.95

Terrine de foie gras de canard frais du Québec, gelée de muscat de Beaumes de Venise, toasts 16.95
Terrine of fresh duck foie gras from Québec, muscat de Beaumes de Venise aspic, toasts 16.95

Soupe de poisson, croûtons aillés et rouille 9.95
Fish soup, garlic croûtons, rouille 9.95

Omelette d'oeuf de cane truffée sur blinis 22.50
One duck egg truffled omelet on a blinis 22.50

Longe de thon frais sur julienne de radis acidulés, concassée d'avocats 15.95
Fresh tuna loin, slightly tartened radish, avocado concassée 15.95

MAIN COURSES

Vegetarian

Risotto aux chitaques sautés et petits légumes 19.95
Sauteed shitake mushroom risotto with assorted vegetables 19.95

Haricots verts français sautés à l'ail 7.00
Side order of fine French green beans sauteed with garlic 7.00

Pommes frites 7.00
Side order of frites 7.00

Quartier

2112 Yonge Street
Toronto
416-545-0505

Bistro
MIDTOWN

V / MC / AmEx / DC

lunch

dinner

take out

beer/wine

cocktails

booster seats

non-smoking

reservations
recommended

dress casual

menu changes
seasonally

A real, Parisian thing, the uptown Quartier, with Brittany-born Marcel Rethore sticking to his bistro guns in spite of turbulent staffing. It's all here: crusty baguettes, silken house pâté, Provençal fish soup with *rouille*, croutons, and steak frites, the whole Gallic works that sustains the ordinary Frenchman through the everydays. Cozy it is, with candles flickering, chanteuses breaking hearts on the sound system, and regulars who've followed le patron through three decades of Toronto restauranting. In summer, the patio is a charmer. The crispy-skinned confit with patates fried in duck fat is a guilty treat and individual tarte tatin is the siren dessert.

QUARTIER

Salade de Betteraves Rouges et Fromage de Chèvre Frais $ 9.50
Red Beet Salad with Fresh Goat Cheese

Strudel de Champignons et Petite Salade de Mesclun $ 10.00
Hot Mushroom Strudel and Mixed Baby Green

Tranche de Saumon Mariné, Pommes à l'Huile et petite Frisée $ 13.50
Fresh Atlantic Salmon Marinated (in Herring Style) with Fingerling Potatoes & Frisée Salad

Terrine Pressée de Poulet de Grain et Champignons $ 9.50
Pressed Grain fed Chicken and Field Mushroom Terrine

Six Huitres Malpèque Sauce Mignonette $13.00
Rodney's Choice Malpeque Oysters, Mignonette Sauce

Terrine de Foie Gras de Canard et sa Compote de Figues Sèches $17.00
Duck Liver Terrine with Dried Fig Compote

Moules Marinière $ 11.00   Avec Frites $ 14.00

Saumon Grillé, Petits Légumes, Vinaigrette au Saffran et Huile d'Olive Vierge $ 18.00
Grilled Salmon, Vegetable, Virgin Olive Oil and Saffron Dressing

Cotriade Bretonne $ 24.00
Brittany Style Bouillabaisse (Fresh Fish & Shellfish with Saffron)

Pot au Feu de Confit de Canard et ses Légumes, Vinaigrette à la Moutarde de Maux $ 20.00
Duck Confit Pot au Feu served with Vegetables and a Maux Mustard Vinaigrette

Foie de Veau Grillé accompagné de Légumes, Frites et d' une Sauce Diable $ 18.00
Calf's Liver with vegetables, Fries and Home Made Barbecue Sauce

Assiette Végétarienne $ 17.00

Bavette de Venaison Poelée, Légumes, Far de Blé Noir et Sauce Poivrade $ 21.00
Flank Steak of Venison, Vegetables, Buckwheat & Raisin Cake

Aile de Poulet de Grain Rôtie avec Purée, Légumes et un Jus de Truffes et Ail Rôti $18.50
Roasted Chicken Breast, Home Made Potato Purée, Vegetables and a Roasted Garlic & Truffle Jus

Gibelotte de Lapin, Vin Blanc, Petits Oignons et Champignons $23.00
Gibelotte of Rabbit in White Wine, Baby Onions & Mushrooms

Contre Filet de Bœuf (Alberta AAA Sterling Silver) Grillé, Beurre Vigneron $ 34.00
Grilled Rib-eye Steak with Vegetables, Home Made French Fries and a Red Wine & Shallots Butter

Navarin d'Agneau de l'Ile Verte, Petits Légumes et sa Côte Grillée $ 28.00
Lamb Navarin, Vegetables and a Grilled Lamb Chop

Rain

19 Mercer Street
Toronto
416-599-7246

Fusion
DOWNTOWN WEST

Wheelchair
access

V / MC / AmEx /
D / DC

dinner

late supper

beer/wine

cocktails

non-smoking

reservations
required

dress smart
casual

menu changes
seasonally

Another daring entry in the avant-garde oeuvre of designers II BY IV (Tundra) and sibling restaurateurs Michael and Guy Rubino, Rain comes on like a monsoon. When Robin Williams, Danny De Vito, and Michael Douglas marched in after it opened, Rain was anointed the hottest ticket in town. The $2 million design (black waterfalls, black leather banquettes, black tablecloths) is as cool as a vampire on roller blades, appropriate for the address that was Toronto's first women's prison. Smallish plates intended for sharing (and horrors, maybe with *strangers*), score heavily with artful Asian accents and presentation on rocks and such.

rain

Rain Hot Pot (for 2)
prepared daily

p.a.

Wok-seared Tofu
marinated miso vegetables, soy-dried tomato, sesame rice cracker

fifteen

Sugarcane Prawn Yakitori
fermented black beans, arame seaweed, persimmon jam

thirty-two

Rack of Lamb
peanut, green tea & sansho crust, chinese red date reduction

thirty eight

Fire-roasted Japanese Sirloin
ponzu dip, mango birds'-eye-chile jam

thirty three

"Peking" Muscovy Duck Breast
slow roasted sugar plum, umeboshi jus

thirty two

Chinese B.B.Q. Pork Tenderloin
shoa sing baked apple, water chestnut & ginger chile reduction

twenty seven

Rhapsody

10152 Yonge Street
Richmond Hill
905-884-0305

Hungarian
SUBURBAN NORTH

V / MC

Sunday brunch

lunch

dinner

take out

beer/wine

cocktails

high chairs

live
  entertainment

private parties

non-smoking

reservations
  recommended

dress casual

Toronto's once-abundant Hungarian eateries have succumbed to heavy competition, soaring rents, and the cooking-lite juggernaut. So we journey north to Richmond Hill, to Eva Kako's warm and homey Rhapsody, for a nostalgic fix of Magyar cuisine to the squeal of Gypsy violins. Rhapsody reminds downtowners how much we've lost: billowing cabbage rolls, chunky beef goulash, and schnitzels the size of stretch limos sprawling across red cabbage and crisp potatoes, not to mention a meat platter that might intimidate Jabba the Hut. Sweet *palacsintas*—crepes to you—get the dessert nod, but only certifiable gourmands get so far.

RHAPSODY

Schnitzel Dinners:

All of the following are served with your choice of potatoes or rice and vegetables or red cabbage:

Wiener schnitzel [becsi szelet] $11.95
    Breaded cutlet

Holstein schnitzel $12.95
    Cutlet Topped with fried egg and anchovies

Parisean schnitzel [parizsi szelet] $11.95
    Cutlet dipped in flour & eggs and pan-fried

House schnitzel [lecsos becsi szelet sajtal] $13.95
    Topped with stewed peppers, tomatoes & onions
    with melted swiss cheese

Veal Cordon Bleu $13.95
    Breaded veal stuffed with ham and cheese

House Platter [hazi tal]
    Wiener schnitzel, parisean schnitzel, naturel schnitzel,

debreszeni sausage & cabbage roll	for one	$22.00
	for two	$36.00

Hungarian Specialties

Cabbage rolls [toltot kaposzta] $10.95
    Eva's special home creation from the old country!
    Served with potatoes and sour cream

Beef Goulash [marha porkolt] $10.95
    Served with home-made noodles or rice

Chicken paprikas [paprikas csirke] $10.95
    Served with home-made noodles

Rich Congee Chinese Restaurant

7077 Kennedy Road
Markham
905-947-1880

Chinese
SUBURBAN
NORTHEAST

Lunch
dinner
late supper
take out
beer/wine
high chairs
non-smoking
reservations
  recommended
dress casual

Adjacent to the massive Pacific Mall in Markham, nosebleed territory for downtowners like me, this unassuming eatery turns out to be the Baskin-Robbins of congee—China's answer to risotto and the comfort food of millions of Asians from Hong Kong south to Bangkok and Singapore. Count 'em: The restaurant serves fifty different congees, from shrimp and scallop to "blood Jell-o" (congealed pig's blood) in steaming bowls large enough to feed the Peoples' Army. I love this place and make the trek happily for the silken porridge laced with ginger and green onion and loaded with juicy chunks of Atlantic salmon. And the deep-fried shrimp dumplings are no slouch, either.

Rich Congee Chinese Restaurant

生滾粥品　FRESH CONGEE

1	招牌大粥 House Congee in Super Bowl	$9.00
2	龍蝦大粥 Lobster Congee in Super Bowl	$13.99
3	溫哥華蟹大粥 Vancouver Crap Congee in Super Bowl	$16.99
4	蝦球帶子大粥 Shrimp & Scallop Congee in Super Bowl	$10.99
5	翅群三絲大粥 Mixed Shredded Congee in Super Bowl	$8.50
6	海鮮大粥 Seafood Congee in Super Bowl	$7.00
7	海皇冬蓉大粥 Seafood withWintermelon Congee in Super Bowl	$6.50
8	鳳凰雞鴨絲大粥 Shredded Chicken & Duck with Egg Congee in Super Bowl	$6.50

Richlee's

1959 Avenue Road
Toronto
416-483-9818
www.richlees.com

Bistro
UPTOWN

Wheelchair
  access

V / MC / AmEx / DC

lunch

dinner

beer/wine

cocktails

private parties

non-smoking

reservations
  recommended

dress fine casual

A justifiably popular North Toronto restaurant with exacting standards and a following of 98 percent regulars, which must be a record for fidelity in these fickle environs. Manuel Concalves, with more than forty years in the business, manages a room vaguely reminiscent of a European hunting lodge, gadding about like a firefly with advice on the big international wine list. Fresh fish and seafood dance out of the kitchen, almost everything grilled over live charcoal, and in jumbo portions. Regulars urge you to order signature hazelnut crème brûlée as an appetizer, because you'll never get there otherwise.

RESTAURANT

Pastas

Spaghettini with fresh diver scallops, Italian parsley and palm tomatoes tossed in a lemon créme fráiche.... *$17.00*

Penne with fresh shrimps and hearts of palm tossed in a extra virgin olive oil fresh herbs pesto sauce *$17.00*

fettuccine with bocconcini cheese and spinach in Vodka, fresh basil tomato sauce............................ *$15.00*

Main Courses

fresh rainbow trout, seared with fine Acadian spices and fresh lime *$18.00*

french-cut of fresh Ontario pork tenderloin, charcoal-grilled with Muskoka BBQ sauce,
and a touch of Quebec maple syrup *$19.00*

roasted spineless Meech Lake duckling with fresh raspberry cointreau coulis..................................... *$24.00*

fresh diver scallops, flash sautéed with olive oil served in a lobster fresh dill sauce............................ *$27.00*

shrimp á la Singh: fresh Louisiana jumbo shrimp sautéed Punjabi style in a richly flavoured sauce
seasoned with exotic Indian spices and fresh herbs, served with imported Major Grey chutney *$26.00*
        (specialty of the Chef-please specify mild, medium or hot)

an exotic assortment of grilled fresh market vegetables,
served with a fresh herb and aged balsamic vinaigrette *$18.00*

Mediterranean seafood casserole with shrimps, mussels,
fresh fish, clams, sea scallops, calamari and lobster
in a delicate Chablis and tomato broth seasoned with saffron *$35.00*

Portuguese style churrasco, grilled breast of free-range chicken,
marinated with olive oil, lemon, garlic and a touch of chili pepper *$18.00*

Provimi veal chop grilled over live charcoal, with chanterelle mushrooms
glazed with a vintage Madeira sauce *$38.00*

veal piccata al' limone: tender veal scaloppine, sautéed with fresh lemon and a touch of butter
served with pasta in a fresh tomato and basil sauce *$23.00*

Washington State rack of lamb, grilled over live charcoal
glazed with Oregon pinot noir, and seasoned with fresh rosemary and garlic *$38.00*

carefully aged, 10 oz. select U.S. prime New York steak, grilled over live charcoal
glazed with Cabernet Sauvignon and served with sautéed oyster mushrooms *$33.00*
        (Your steak can also be prepared as a pepper steak, or blackened Cajun style)

Rodney's
Oyster House

469 King Street West
Toronto
416-363-8105
www.rodneysoysterhouse.com

Seafood
DOWNTOWN WEST

V / MC / AmEx / DC

lunch

dinner

late supper

take out

beer/wine

high chairs

private parties

non-smoking

reservations
  recommended

dress informal

menu changes
  daily

Rodney's is no longer Toronto's only serious oyster bar, but it remains the one to beat: The sexy bivalve mollusk appears to outperform Viagra among the hip couples who patronize the basement grotto. In fact, you could probably have sex by osmosis at Rodney's. But it's the raucous shucking and sucking of up to twenty-six varieties of oysters—from addictive little British Columbia Sinkus to sweet, buttery Island Creeks from New England and others from as far afield as Chile—that gives the joint its soul. Even the unflappable owner, Rodney Clark, is taken aback by the ebullience of it all.

HOT

CHOWDER

	CUP	BOWL
NEW ENGLAND CLAM	5.55	7.65
MANHATTAN CLAM	4.90	7.10
OYSTER SLAPJACK	5.55	7.65
ANN MARIE'S CORN CHOWDER	4.10	6.65
STRING-CULTURED MUSSELS	9.85	
BRONZED SHRIMPS	22.95	
SHRIMP IN COCONUT & CURRY	22.95	
NICE FUNDY SCALLOPS	17.95	
PASTA WITH SCALLOPS	15.90	

SEASONAL

PERIWINKLES BY THE BOWL	6.12	
SOFT SHELL STEAMERS	11.90	
STEAMED QUAHOGS	10.50	

Rogues

1900 Dundas Street West
Mississauga
905-8222670

Italian
SUBURBAN WEST

Wheelchair
    access
V / MC / AmEx / DC
lunch
dinner
take out
beer/wine
cocktails
private parties
non-smoking
dress casual
menu changes
    daily

The scent of fresh herbs wafting from the open kitchen, a staff with its fingers on the pulse of its clientele, a room afloat with garlic—who says there's no cuisine in the burbs? For two decades, Tony Pereira's Rogues has been feeding increasingly affluent and food-smart Mississauga. Off-menu specials are almost the equal of what's on the menu, combinations (monkfish and crab legs over black Thai rice, veal chop with mashed purple spuds) flirting with exotica. Seafood elicits maximum respect, whether fat shrimp flamed with brandy or scallops barely warmed-through over noodles. Châteaus Petrus and Margaux, ahem, are available on request.

Vitello
Veal scaloppini sautéed and served with a lemon basil white wine sauce
$17.95

Filetto di Vitello
Grilled veal tenderloin medallions and grilled shrimp in a red wine sauce
with mixed peppers and extra virgin olive oil
$25.95

Vitello Fortunato
Veal scaloppini lightly breaded with herbed parmesan cheese and sautéed in olive oil
with a rosemary, shiitake-button mushrooms, pearl onion red wine sauce
$18.95

Pollo alla Boscaiola
Boneless chicken breasts, lightly dipped in egg with wild mushrooms
and ham in a white wine cream sauce
$17.95

Gamberi and Scallops
Sautéed shrimp, scallops and mushrooms with tomatoes, garlic, green
onions in a brandy cream sauce served with rice
$24.95

Fegato
Calves liver sautéed with black peppercorn, oyster
mushrooms, shallots and raspberry vinegar
$16.95

Romagna Mia

106 Front Street East
Toronto
416-363-8370
www.romagna-mia.com

Italian
DOWNTOWN

Wheelchair
    access

V / MC / AmEx / DC

lunch

dinner

late supper

take out

beer/wine

cocktails

high chairs

live
    entertainment

private parties

non-smoking

reservations
    recommended

dress casual

A stone's throw from the St. Lawrence Market, chef Gabriele Pagnelli's buzzing osteria-pizzeria the only restaurant in town to serve donkey, a specialty of his native Emilia-Romagna region, two or three times a year. Pagnelli's great triumph over Italian chefs clear across Canada was winning the Golden Spoon for Canada's finest risotto; it consists of creamy rice poured into a hollowed wheel of Parmigiano-Reggiano, spiked with flaming booze, and stirred with black truffle. Fish is what the chef does best now that pizza is deemed beneath him.

Ostriche Fresche con Salsa Piccante   **7**
6 fresh New Brunswick oysters served with assorted spicy sauce.

La Ribollita Tradizionale Toscana   **9**
Soup of bread, canellini beans and winter vegetables drizzled with extra virgin olive oil.

Timballo di Parmigiano-Reggiano con Julienne di Procsiutto e Salsa ai Funghi   **11**
Parmigiano-Reggiano flan served with mushroom sauce and julienne of Parma prosciutto.

Pappardelle al Ragu di Coniglio e Spinaci   **12**
Wide homemade fettuccine set in rabbit ragout with spinach and Parmigiano-Reggiano.

Chitarrine alla Gradisca con Scampi e Vongole   **17**
Egg homemade linguine in a tomato-vermouth sauce, with scampi and fresh clams.

Risotto al Ragù di Fagiano con Tartufo   **19**
Italian risotto set in a pheasant ragout, with truffle paste and Parmigiano-Reggiano.

Spiedini di Scampi e Seppie alla Griglia   **19**
3 grilled scampi and cuttlefish kebabs, served with mixed greens tossed in a balsamic dressing.

Brodetto di Pesce alla Romagnola con Fagiolini   **25**
Stew of sea bass, swordfish, cuttlefish, scampi and clams in a tomato and green peas sauce.

Branzino in Mantello di Patate con Salsa al Timo   **23**
Chilean sea bass wrapped in potatoes with thyme sauce served with Prosecco risotto.

Pesce Spada alla Messinese con Timballo di Patate   **22**
Grilled medallion of swordfish served with vegetables sauce and timballo of potatoes.

Pesce in Graticola Condito con Erbe Fresche   **pa**
A daily selection of whole fish, grilled with fresh herbs, extra virgin olive oil and lemon.

Petto di Faraona con Funghi Trifolati   **20**
Pan seared Guinea fowl breast served with sautéed mushrooms and potatoes.

Stufato di Cinghiale alla Grevigiana con Polenta   **21**
Stew of wild boar "Grevigiana" style (Greve in Chianti) served atop creamy polenta.

Rosedale Diner

1164 Yonge Street
Toronto
416-923-3122
www.rosedalediner.com

Fusion
MIDTOWN

V / MC / AmEx / DC
Sunday brunch
lunch
dinner
take out
late supper
beer/wine
cocktails
private parties
non-smoking
reservations
    recommended
dress informal

An impertinent eatery—local boy Keanu Reeves's favorite Toronto restaurant—opposite Thieves' Row in Rosedale. What else do you expect from a guy who once ran a vegetarian eatery named Lickin' Chicken? Dubi Filar and wife Esti have been operating the "diner" for more than two decades. The 1920s tin ceiling came with the joint. The collection of busts—Napoleon alongside Elvis, Groucho, Harpo, Laurel, Hardy, and other clowns—is Esti's. Fusion is the name of the game, with dishes like duck confit with Chinese five-spice and fish stew with lemongrass and Thai basil—Dubi was fusing before fusion came along.

the Rosedale Diner

Grilled USDA Certified Black Angus Striploin $24 / $36 (10 or 16 oz.)
With black olive butter, mashed Yukon Gold potato and sautéed spinach

Confit Of Muscovy Duck $22
W/ Chinese five spice, soy & ginger marinade, candied sweet potato, roast garlic, swiss chard,
brandy & blackcurrant demi glace

Sticky Asian BBQ Ribs $16.95
With hoi sin glaze and sesame seeds

Pan Roasted Atlantic Salmon $19.95
With black sesame crust, baby bok choy & shitake mushroom risotto, orange & wasabi butter sauce

Chicken Dijonaise $16.95
Slow roasted half chicken with creamy Dijon mustard sauce
and our famous frites.

Mediterranean Boneless, Roasted Chicken $17.95
W/ smoked sausage, porcini and sage stuffing, served w/ pan fried potato gnocchi & asparagus.
finished w/ demiglace and cream

Sweet Corn & Gorgonzola Polenta $14.95
With oven roasted tomato coulis, grilled oyster mushrooms

Herb Crusted Rack of Lamb • Available Fridays Only

The Rosedale Burger $9.95
Seasoned fresh ground prime beef, lettuce, tomato & onions,
in a pita with frites or salad.

•blue, cheddar, swiss, bacon, mushrooms, jalapeños
hot sauce, grilled onions, fresh roasted garlic: each: $1.25

•back bacon, brie, goat cheese, gruyere, roasted peppers
and substitute Caesar salad: each: $2.50

Rosewater
Supper Club

19 Toronto Street
Toronto
416-214-5888
www.libertygroup.com

French
DOWNTOWN

Valet parking

V / MC / AmEx / DC

lunch

dinner

late supper

beer/wine

cocktails

live
 entertainment

private parties

non-smoking
 section

cigar lounge

reservations
 recommended

dress informal

menu changes
 seasonally

The entrepreneurial Liberty Entertainment Group (Courthouse Market Grille, Left Bank, Liberty Grand) flaunts the jewel in its architectural crown with this transformation of the 1852 Consumer's Gas Building into one of downtown's most opulent spaces. Shimmering marble and hardwood floors, a three-story waterfall, and glowing upper rooms anticipate grandeur. The quality of its fare has been known to gallivant, but with Richard Andino, former exec chef at Mark McEwan's perfectionist North 44, at the pots, a refined and imaginative adventure is practically a sure thing.

Sautee of Quebec Foie Gras
Toasted Brioche, Baby Sorrel Preserved Sour Cherries and Marsala Figs $21

Warm Dungeness Crab Cakes
Served with Hollandaise, Caperberries and Heart of Leek Salad $18

Sweet Bufala Mozzarella Accompanied by Late Summer
Heirloom Tomatoes, Vidalia Onions and Roasted Garlic $16

Spaghettini with Grilled Jumbo Prawns, Scallops
Capers, in a Lemon Garlic and Olive Oil Reduction $21

Penne Pasta with Sicilian Eggplant
Wilted Greens, Leeks, Spicy Nero Sausage And Homemade Tomato Sauce $18

Porcini Gnocchi
Lightly Browned on Grilled Treviso, Prosciutto, Reduced Cream $20

Asian Noodles with Tossed Roasted Peking Duck
Julienne of Vegetables and Caramelized Oyster Sauce $18

14oz Provimi Veal Chop $42

14oz New York Cut Striploin (certified Angus) $44

Pandan Wrapped Black Cod Steamed Long Bean, Dashi Flavoured Potatoes
And Scotch Bonnet Coconut Broth $39

Grill kissed Ahi Tuna
Torched Japanese Eggplant, Green Mango Salad, and Waterchessnut Wraps $41

Crackling Cornish Hen On Jasmine Scented Rice, Garlic Fried Rapini,
Hand Picked Pine Mushrooms and Adobo Flavoured Jus $31

Rouge

467 Bloor Street West
Toronto
416-413-0713

Bistro
ANNEX

V / MC / AmEx / DC

Sunday brunch

lunch

dinner

beer/wine

cocktails

private parties

non-smoking

reservations
   recommended

dress casual

menu changes
   weekly

Restaurateur Leyla Kashani comes by the biz via DNA: Her family was instrumental in opening Annex rivals Serra and Goldfish, and her uncle owns Bellini and Verona. Rouge seems a riff on Goldfish's chic minimalist design—a compact, off-white room with a glowing, rouge four-seat bar at the back. Happily, Kashani is smart enough to know that good looks alone won't do it in this town. Although too many changes under the chef's hat have caused the execution to flag after a powerful opening, Kashani clings to her original vision of cuisine in the order of Atlantic salmon marinated in orange and big-league ravioli plated with oh-so-sweet lobster and creamy leeks.

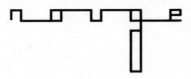

PASTA & RISOTTO

OPEN-FACED LOBSTER RAVIOLI WITH CHIVE LOBSTER
BISQUE SAUCE   18

OLD FASHIONED MACARONI AND CHEESE   11

SMOKED CHICKEN RISOTTO   13

VEGETARIAN RISOTTO   11

MAIN COURSES

GRILLED CALF LIVER WITH ONION, POTATO AND APPLE
SESAME SAUCE   18

CASSOULET OF CORNISH HEN   17

ROASTED LEG OF LAMB FROM QUEBEC WITH SEASONAL
VEGETABLES, GRATIN DAUPHINOIS
AND ROASTED SHALLOT SAUCE   20

SEARED BEEF TENDERLOIN WITH "POMMES DARPHIN"
AND WILD MUSHROOM SAUCE   23

SEARED ATLANTIC SALMON WITH COUSCOUS AND OYSTER
CREAM SAUCE   18

Ruby

1571 Sandhurst Circle
Toronto
416-298-1638

Chinese
EAST TORONTO

Wheelchair
    access
V / MC / AmEx
Sunday brunch
lunch
dinner
late supper
take out
beer/wine
cocktails
high chairs
private parties
non-smoking
reservations
    recommended
dress casual
menu changes
    seasonally

I don't mind trekking northeast for Ruby: The room, decorated in lanterns and dragons, a tad smaller (it has 800 seats) than the Forbidden City and always packed, is as close to Hong Kong as I'll get without a ticket from Air Canada. Everything comes on a grand scale: The menu is so dense, it comes with an index. The tanks stock fourteen varieties of live fish. At lunch, the dim sum trolleys roll with countless delicacies, from unrecognizable innards to cleaver-chopped quails and irresistible shrimp dumplings. At night, Cantonese icons—abalone, shark's fin, suckling pig—sustain Middle Kingdom gourmands. Just bring earplugs.

紅寶石大酒樓
Ruby Chinese Restaurant

Jumbo Shrimps, Boneless Chicken & Mixed Vegetable in Casserole	13.80
Diced Seafood with Bean Curd	12.80
Jumbo Shrimps in Taro Bird's Nest	18.00
Sliced Fresh Scallops with Hot Sauce	14.80
Szechuan Shrimps	12.80
Shrimps with Chilli, Pepper & Vinegar Sauce	12.80
Ma Po Bean Curd	9.75
Sliced Pork with Vegetable & Hot Sauce	9.75
Beef with Orange Flavour	9.50
Diced Chicken with Chilli	9.50
Eggplant with Chilli, Pepper & Vinegar Sauce	9.50
Mixed Vegetable with Hot Sauce	9.50

Ruth's Chris Steak House

Toronto Hilton Hotel
145 Richmond Street West
Toronto
416-955-1455
www.ruthschris-toronto.com

Steakhouse
DOWNTOWN

Wheelchair
  access

V / MC / AmEx / DC

dinner

take out

beer/wine

cocktails

high chairs

private parties

reservations
  recommended

dress casual

When the brick of beef staged its countercoup across a continent in open revolt against healthy eating, the venerable Ruth's Chris (launched in New Orleans in 1965) was the first of the big American steakhouses (Morton's of Chicago fast on its heels) to strike gold in Toronto. The urban barn seats 200, and everything's on a surreal scale, starting with Jurassic-style cuts of USDA prime seared at 1800 degrees Fahrenheit and served in sizzling butter on 500-degree plates. Seafood gourmands, not overlooked, can dig into lobsters up to five pounds apiece. RC's resounding achievement is a guilt-free environment, cholesterol be damned.

FILET
The tenderest cut of corn-fed Midwestern beef. Broiled expertly to a melt-in-your-mouth tenderness.

$43.95

PETIT FILET
A smaller, but equally tender filet.

$35.95

RIBEYE
An outstanding example of USDA Prime at it's best. Well marbled for peak flavour, deliciously juicy.

$39.95

NEW YORK STRIP
A favourite of many steak connoisseurs. This USDA Prime cut has a full-bodied texture that is slightly firmer than a ribeye.

$45.95

PORTERHOUSE FOR TWO
This USDA Prime cut combines the rich flavour of a strip with the tenderness of a filet.

$99.95

T-BONE
A full-flavoured classic cut of USDA Prime.

$55.95

SEARED TUNA
Fresh Yellowfin tuna steak seared or blackened to your order, served medium rare with lemon and butter.

$32.95

SIZZLIN' BLUE CRAB CAKES
Three jumbo lump crab cakes with sizzling lemon butter.

$35.95

LAMB CHOPS
Three chops cut extra thick. They are naturally tender and flavourful.

$45.95

FRESH LOBSTER
Flown in daily, ranging from 2.5 to 5 pounds.

MARKET PRICE

SALMON FILET
Moist and tender Atlantic Salmon, poached under the broiler.

$27.95

MARINATED CHICKEN
Double breast of chicken, flavoured with our own marinade. Also available blackened.

$26.95

Sam Woo Seafood

325 Bamburgh Circle
Toronto
416-502-2888

Chinese
SUBURBAN NORTHEAST

Wheelchair
  access

V / MC

breakfast

lunch

dinner

beer/wine

high chairs

private parties

non-smoking

reservations
  recommended

dress casual

menu changes
  seasonally

Sam Woo is archetypal Hong Kong transplanted to the city's northeastern burbs—a megaroom in a megaplaza lit up with Chinese characters, bright, blaring, and perpetually packed. The double-standard menu—one menu for Chinese, one in English for timid diners presumed to consume sweet-and-sour chicken balls—is the usual pain, compelling you to interrogate servers in order to lay your chopsticks on still-flapping fish from the tank steamed to utmost delicacy, fresh lobster, or even the phallic oddity of geoduck (pronounced "gooey-duck"). Crispy-skinned roast suckling pig sates landlubbers. Either way, play it again, Sam.

三和 ®
SAM WOO

	全隻 Whole	半隻 Half	例 Reg.
Steamed boneless chicken with Chinese ham & vegetable	38.00	19.00	—
Steamed chicken with supreme soup & vegetable	24.00	12.00	—
Deep fried chicken	24.00	12.00	—
Steamed chicken with ginger & green onion	24.00	12.00	—
Pan fried chicken black bean sauce			12.00
Pan fried boneless chicken lemon sauce			12.00
Sauteed shredded chicken with celery			12.00
Diced chicken & cashewnuts			12.00
Shredded fried chicken			14.00

	Reg. 例
Beef tenderloin black pepper sauce (hot & spicy)	15.00
Pan fried beef tenderloin sweet & sour sauce	15.00
Sauteed beef & vegetable	12.00
Sauteed beef oyster sauce	12.00
Sauteed beef with green pepper & black bean sauce	12.00
Sauteed beef 'Satay' sauce (hot & spicy)	12.00
Sweet & sour pork with pineapple	11.00
Pan fried porkloin in special sweet & sour sauce	12.00
Deep fried porkloin in spicy salt (spicy)	12.00

Sassafraz

100 Cumberland Street
Toronto
416-964-2222

Global
YORKVILLE

V / MC / AmEx / DC

Sunday brunch

lunch dinner

late supper

take out

beer/wine

cocktails

high chairs

live
  entertainment

private parties

reservations
  recommended

dress casual

menu changes
  seasonally

Sassafraz glitters brightly on the Toronto International Film Festival circuits. One wall is devoted to celebrity worship—Dennis Hopper's scary mug may be enough to put you off the mussels. The premises are handsome, especially the airy, skylit atrium planted with ficus trees, the way they grow in the Caribbean. Preppy servers dispense Technicolor fantasias such as Atlantic salmon with purple rice to a multitude of publicity agents, entertainment flacks, and hangers-on. To its credit, the kitchen turns out one of the better Caesar salads in a town where chefs are notorious for cheating on oomph, notably garlic and anchovies.

SASSAFRAZ

Market Soup	7
Tian of Wild Mushrooms Onion Confit and Baked Woolwich Goat Cheese, Oven Dried Tomato, Bouquet of Organic Greens	19
Smoked Salmon Vodka Cured Sterling Salmon, Herbed Cream Cheese, Red Onion, Capers, and Crostini	16
Organic Greens Fennel Julienne, Belgian Endive and Assorted Greens tossed with a Pomegranate Vinaigrette	13
Romaine Hearts Caesar style Asiago and Parmigiano Dressing. Crisp Pancetta and Roasted Garlic Crostini	13
Chilled Tiger Shrimp Fresh Horseradish Cocktail Sauce, Tarot Root Chips, Caviar Crème Fraiche	21
Foie Gras Du Jour Prepared Daily by our Chef	priced accordingly
Seared Sea Scallops Wilted Fennel, Baby Lettuces, Champagne Beurre Blanc, and Pomme Gaufrettes	19
Beef Carpaccio Shaved Marinated Angus Beef, Baby Arugula Salad in a Honey, Citrus Vinaigrette	18

MAIN COURSES

Red Pepper Fettucine Assorted Wild Mushrooms in a Light Cream Sauce and fresh Chives	20
Seafood Linguine Mussels, Clams, Tiger Shrimps, Assorted Fresh Fish, Tomato Cream Sauce	27
Seared Chilean Seabass, Roasted Fennel and Spinach, Tomato and Black Eyed Pea Fricassé. Caper, Sun Dried Tomato Antiboise	35
Sassafraz Signature Salmon Purple Rice Crusted Atlantic Salmon Filet, Minted Couscous, Champagne Beurre Blanc	26
Marinated Chicken Supreme, Roasted Free Range Chicken, Swiss Chard and Emmenthal Cheese Strudel, Natural Jus	28
Longbone Veal Chop Provimi Veal Chop, Yukon Gold Mash, Wild Mushroom Sautée, and a Creamy Four Peppercorn Sauce	35
Grilled Black Angus Steak, 12 Oz. USDA Certified, Lyonnaise Potato, Seasonal Vegetables and Truffle Butter	37
Australian Lamb Rack Mint Essence, Baked Acorn Squash Ring, Vegetable Caponata, with Natural Jus	39
Provimi Calves Liver Seared with Roasted Garlic, Green Olives, Capers and Duo of Onion Confit, Yukon Gold Mash, Buttery Natural Jus	25
Vegetable Papillotte Seasonal Vegetables baked in a Light Phyllo Crust with Organic Greens and Pepper Coulis	21
Cheese Plate Fresh Seasonal Fruits, and Assorted Imported Cheeses	19

Scaramouche

1 Benvenuto Place
Toronto
416-961-8011

French
MIDTOWN

Wheelchair
  access
valet parking
V / MC / AmEx / DC
dinner
beer/wine
cocktails
non-smoking
reservations
  recommended
dress jacket
menu changes
  weekly

The restaurant with the clown-cavalier as signature—few patrons remember the rollicking 1952 film Scaramouche—has been a Toronto superstar for more than twenty years. The floor-to-ceiling skyline view at dusk remains a stunning urban postcard. Customer stroking is second nature, and the service is seamless, from menu insights to wine stewardry. Chef Keith Froggett's take on French seamlessly melds classic and contemporary. A skate wing, ever so delicate, sauced in seafood, draped atop creamy risotto, emerges from the kitchen as a tower of pleasure. So much about Scaramouche is a high: Little wonder young men arrive to spring engagements on suspecting womenfolk, the diamond stashed under a silver cloche or in an oyster shell.

Scaramouche

RESTAURANT PASTA BAR & GRILL

Fresh Venison Loin   39.75
wrapped and roasted in double smoked bacon with potato and chestnut flour gnocchi, wild mushrooms, escarole and sage. Red wine glaze laced with melted gorgonzola.

Grilled Filet Mignon of Canadian Triple 'A' Beef   39.75
with mushroom and white truffle oil-whipped potatoes. Sauce Bordelaise.

Roasted Breast of Quebec Free Range Chicken   26.75
with caramelized vegetables, hummus and pea vine shoots. Sweet garlic jus.

Medley of Grilled Lobster, Scallops and Calamari   39.75
in a Mediterranean style lobster and tomato nage with grilled vegetables and fine olive oil.

Fresh Tuna 'Filet Mignon' (grilled rare)   39.75
with organic Italian lentils, cippolini onions, black olives, capers, parsley and tomato confit. White wine veal jus reduction with lemon gremolata.

Roasted Rack of Fresh Australian Lamb   39.75
with Provençal-style vegetables, rosemary and roasted garlic-whipped potatoes. Natural juices with chèvre cream.

Pan-roasted Thornback Skate   29.75
on a lobster, shrimp and saffron risotto. Roasted pepper sauce with basil essence and aged balsamic vinegar.

Scaramouche
Pasta Bar

1 Benvenuto Place
Toronto
416-961-8011

Global
MIDTOWN

Wheelchair
access

valet parking

V / MC / AmEx / DC

dinner

beer/wine

cocktails

non-smoking

reservations
recommended

dress jacket

menu changes
weekly

Not so much a pasta fix as a fiscally merciful taste of the legendary main restaurant—with the same romantic skyline view—this second restaurant salutes the swash and buckle of the Sabatini novel and movie *Scaramouche* with the opening lines: "He was born with the gift of laughter and a sense the world was mad." What a perfect attitude for anyone trying to survive in the restaurant business. The kitchen follows through with impeccable fare from pizzas studded with sunny Mediterranean flavors to pastas in lively sauces, crispy-skinned hunks of fish, succulent meats, and spuds whipped to velvet with infusions of olive oil.

Scaramouche

RESTAURANT PASTA BAR & GRILL

Lasagna Verdi
16.75

in the traditional Bolognese style.

Roasted half-chicken
19.75

with Tuscan-style bread dressing and natural juices.

Fresh peppercorn fettucine
18.75

with sautéed beef tenderloin, oyster mushrooms, toasted pine nuts, Madeira cream sauce and Gruyère herb crust.

Farfalle rigate
21.75

with sautéed shrimp, scallops, mussels and grilled calamari in a tomato, parsley, garlic and caper sauce.

Steak frites
24.75

Grilled 10 oz. rib steak with pommes frites and a red wine, tarragon and shallot butter.

Fresh hand-made ravioli
17.75

filled with shredded beef slow-braised with five spices on garlic-sautéed greens and shiitake mushrooms with Asian gravy.

Yukon Gold potato gnocchi
15.75

with fresh plum tomato stew, wilted spinach and Gorgonzola cream.

Grilled Provimi calf's liver
19.75

with parmesan whipped potatoes, crispy buttermilk onion rings and a thyme jus.

Medley of fresh fish and shellfish
24.75

with grilled vegetables in a lobster, white wine and herb bouillon enriched with aïoli.

Segovia

5 Street Nicholas Street
Toronto
416-960-1010

Spanish
DOWNTOWN

Wheelchair
  access

V / MC / AmEx

lunch

dinner

take out

beer/wine

cocktails

private parties

non-smoking

reservations
  recommended

dress casual

menu changes
  weekly

Even in the medieval quarters of Madrid, it's difficult to find a restaurant as nostalgic as Segovia. Kitschy, courtly, boisterous, and big hearted, Segovia stirs vivid memories in people like me who developed our travel legs journeying Spain on the cheap decades ago. Look for no *nueva cocina* here, no cunningly minced squids huddled in a swell of ink black as tar. Instead, settle for transport to a time when infatuation was as sweet and simple as a few threads of saffron and a whiff of olive oil. Shrimp swooning in garlic and bounteous seafood paella resonate like old travel snapshots, and that's worth an *olé!*

Appetizers

SPRING MIXED SALAD - $6.00
with sherry vinaigrette
ALI-OLI SALAD GREENS - $6.00
GAZPACHO ANDALUZ - $6.00
cold soup with tomatoes & cumin
SEAFOOD SOUP - $7.50
perfumed with anisette
GARLIC SOUP - $6.00
paprika & sherry flavoured

Tapas

STEAMED MUSSELS - $6.50
with white wine, herbs & saffron
GARLIC SHRIMP - $7.50
sauteed, deglaced with amontillado
CASSEROLE OF SNAILS - $6.50
with chorizo sausage & cumin
DEEP FRIED SQUID - $6.50
served with ali-oli dressing
GARLIC MUSHROOM - $7.00
TORTILLA - $6.00

Entrees

GRILLED FRESH SALMON - $16.00
marinated in herbs
ZARZUELA - $17.00
seafood casserole flavoured with brandy & saffron
FRESH FISH of the DAY - ask server
FILET MIGNON - $19.00
with mustard sauce
ROASTED LOIN of LAMB - $18.00
with herbs & pine nut stuffing
SIRLOIN STEAK - $17.00
with reduction of garlic vinegar
GRILLED CHICKEN - $14.00

Paella

AN ORIGINAL SEGOVIA FAVOURITE
PAELLA MARINERA - $35.00 (for two)
saffron rice cooked with fish of the day, scallops, squid,
shrimp and mussels
PAELLA VALENCIANA - $32.00 (for two)
saffron rice cooked with chicken and chorizo garnished
with shrimp and mussels

Sen5es

Soho Metropolitan Hotel
328 Wellington Street
Toronto
416-935-0400
www.senses.ca

**Fusion
DOWNTOWN WEST**

V / MC / AmEx /
  D / DC

dinner

beer/wine

cocktails

high chairs

private parties

non-smoking

reservations
  recommended

dress business
  casual

menu changes
  weekly

Transplanting the luxe Sen5es from the beige heart of midtown to the lobby level of his ultramodern Soho Metropolitan Hotel, Henry Wu (Hemispheres, Lai Wah Heen) actually improves on his ménage of fine dining, bakery, and charcuterie. Sen5es—the most cleverly named restaurant in town—glows in high-ceilinged glory and soars with the imagination of chef Claudio Aprile. Aprile's ebullient grasp of how food works manifests itself in such alchemies as foie gras with barbecued eel tart and triple-seared duck. His tasting menu is a romp on the cutting edge: stop, stop, you beg. After shiso cress and black truffles, it can't get any better. But it does, and Steven Song's extraordinary pastries provide the harmonious finish.

sen5es

seviche of prawns, sudachi lime, tobiko, avocado tempura 17

hot foie gras, regianno, corn cake, quince & marinated grapes 23

salad of tuna tataki, cucumber, nashi pear, crispy oyster, spices & seeds,
juice from yuzu 18

seared scallops, citrus fruit, cherry leaf, galangal dressing, spiced yogurt 17

sliced duck breast, cookstown beet roots, pineapple pulp, caramelized peanut sauce 16

rocket & fig salad, saffron onions, ricotta fritters, raspberries, white balsamic,
Kangaroo Island olive oil 11

3 tartares, spicy mayonnaise, mixed seedlings, mango, crab crisp 15

venison loin, lobster & golden squash cabbage roll,
shallot marmalade, chanterelle & XO sauces 44

triple-seared USDA prime beef tenderloin, salsify-stilton & miso tart,
foie gras sauce 46

roast arctic char, soy beans & shimeji, turnip, hijiki salad, casava-prawn gyoza,
chorizo-dashi broth 34

tea smoked squab breasts, crispy leg, confit ginger, cachapa, chocolate-pat chun sauce 44

Spanish rice cake, wilted greens, garroxta cheese, romesca sauce 29

braised black beef rib, black truffle noodle, pearl onions,
cookstown carrots, caramelized wild leeks 35

steamed west coast halibut, roast sunchokes & fingerlings,
warm "putanesca" vinaigrette, aromatic ocean bouillon 35

Serra

378 Bloor Street West
Toronto
416-922-6999
www.serrarestaurant.com

**Bistro
ANNEX**

Wheelchair
  access

V / MC / AmEx / DC

lunch

dinner

take out

beer/wine

cocktails

non-smoking
  section

reservations not
  taken for lunch

dress casual

menu changes
  seasonally

Window seats at Serra are the best in the house: Bloor Street's passing parade qualifies the Annex fave as dinner theater. In the throng of ravenous students, bespectacled professors, and food-smart locals, we also don't mind gawking at the procession of colorfully landscaped plates flying across the room. Serra's dishes are light, diverse, and high on flavor, with salads—a snappy Caesar arrives with whole pickled garlics—pastas, and pizzas from the wood-fire oven as house mainstays. The turnover is always brisk, maybe because hard-bottomed chairs torment soft human posteriors so relentlessly. Watch out for a kitchen that likes to pack it up and go home early.

PASTA

Angel hair with grilled chicken, sundried tomatoes, red onions, roasted garlic & olive oil in a light tomato sauce   12.45

Penne with smoked jalapeno, kalamata olives, & field mushrooms in a fresh basil roma tomato sauce   11.45

Spagettini with grilled eggplant, mixed sweet peppers, zucchini, leeks, & roasted garlic in a black olive paste   12.45

Linguine with black tiger shrimps, scallops, mussels, garlic, scallions, fresh tomatoes & white wine olive oil   14.45

Rigatoni with lamb sausage, fennel, spinach, feta cheese in a tomato sauce   12.95

Ravioli stuffed with chicken, spinach, leeks, & parmigiano in a roasted red pepper cream sauce   13.45

Fusilli with smoked chicken, woodland mushrooms, artichoke hearts & baked garlic in a rose sauce   12.75

Goat cheese filled Angolotti with grilled portobello mushrooms in a basil pesto cream sauce   13.45

Risotto of the day   P/A

WOOD BURNING OVEN PIZZAS

1. Spicy Italian sausage, charred onions, mixed sweet peppers, basil tomato sauce & mozzarella cheese   11.45

2. Ground lamb sausage, caramelized onions, roasted garlic, Fontina cheese & mozzarella   12.95

3. Sundried tomato paste, grilled chicken, roasted red peppers, baked garlic & goat cheese   12.95

4. Grilled beef tenderloin, smoked jalapeno, roma tomatoes, field mushrooms, mozzarella & tomato sauce   13.45

5. Woodland mushrooms, medley of cheeses, tomato sauce & fresh herbs   11.45

6. Black olive paste, grilled vegetables, grilled peppers, fresh basil & goat cheese   11.95

7. Smoked chicken, grilled eggplant, roasted red peppers, basil pesto & mozzarella cheese   12.95

8. Grilled black tiger shrimps, basil pesto, oyster mushrooms, artichoke hearts & Fontina cheese   13.45

9. Grilled chicken breast, Yukon gold puree, grilled leeks, fresh rosemary & mozzarella   12.95

Signatures

Hotel Inter-Continental
220 Bloor Street West
Toronto
416-960-5200

Global
MIDTOWN

Wheelchair
    access

valet parking

V / MC / AmEx / DC

Sunday brunch

lunch

dinner

beer/wine

cocktails

high chairs

live
    entertainment

private parties

non-smoking

reservations
    recommended

dress casual

menu changes
    seasonally

Signatures could be the biggest secret in town. Most Torontonians don't even know it exists. In the low-profile Hotel Inter-Continental, it's a handsome room, a little Frank Lloyd Wrightish, peering into a courtyard and offering a sensible slate of dishes from a global larder. The restaurant's secret weapon is chef Jack Lamont, whose solid, unfussy cuisine has a habit of sneaking up on you with the likes of chunky hummus in the breadbasket, surprising delicacy in a smidgeon of foie gras, a hint of Chinese five-spice in a sautéed mushroom, and jus that renders rack of lamb a carnivore's night out.

STARTERS

Shaved Artichoke and Grilled Fennel Salad with Organic Seedlings
Citrus Orange Vinaigrette and Toasted Pine Nuts
10

White Asparagus Soup with a Tiger Shrimp Soufflé, Padano Parmesan Tuille
10

Risi Bisi, Sweet Quebec Peas and Italian Rice with Parmesan Shavings
12

Baby Red and Gold Beet Salad with Crisp Hearts of Romaine Lettuce
Goat Cheese Shavings and Caper Vinaigrette
11

ENTRÉES

Oven Roasted Halibut with Wild Mushrooms Quinoa, Cpiquillo Peppers and Sweet Curry Sauce
26

Pan Seared Ontario Rack of Ontario Lamb Crusted with Mustard Seeds and Dill
Asparagus Strudel with Chanterelle Mushrooms, Minted Lamb Jus
28

Seafood Pot-au-Feu with Tiger Shrimp and Sea Scallops, Panache of Spring Vegetables
Herbed Lemongrass Tomato Broth
26

28 Day Aged Sterling Silver Beef Strip Loin, Golden Brown Turnip Roesti, Shallot Red Wine Jus
3.99 per ounce, minimum six ounce

Northern Arctic Char Glazed with Canadian Maple Syrup
Herb Roasted Artichokes and Wild Rice Fritters
24

Asian Style Barbecue Magret Duck Breast, Wilted Mustard Greens, Japanese Sweet Potato Crepes
28

Silver Spoon

390 Roncesvalles Avenue
Toronto
416-516-8112
www.silverspoon.ca

Italian
WEST TORONTO

V / MC / AmEx

dinner

late supper

take out

beer/wine

cocktails

booster seats

private parties

non-smoking

reservations
  recommended

dress casual

A gastronomic upheaval on Roncesvalles Avenue—
that artery of Little Poland (the Pope has indeed
dropped by) where pierogies and kolbasa normally
prevail—Silver Spoon is precisely the adrenalin
required to lure foodies back to a neglected part of
town. There are no false notes here. The marriage
of good looks (sea-green, scalloped banquettes
running the length of the room), intimacy (just
thirty-six seats), gracious service, and painstaking
cooking (chef Rocco Agostino at the stoves) culmi-
nates in a happy experience transcending neighborhood status. Signatures dishes include
crispy-skinned chicken, walloping rack of
lamb drizzled with balsamic syrup, and
whatever risotto Agostino fancies tonight.

il ristorante

*silver*spoon

Warm Herbed Woolwich Goat Cheese
crusted and served on a bed of mixed greens and grilled vegetables
9.00

Carpaccio of Beef
on a bed of arugula, drizzled with extra virgin olive oil, accompanied by
roasted red peppers and shaved parmesan cheese
9.50

Piatto di Antipasto
an assortment of marinated and grilled seasonal vegetables,
Italian meats and a variety of cheeses
(also available as a vegetarian dish)
• for one 8.50 • for two 13.00 • for four 18.00

Penne
Italian sausage, chilies, parmesan & pecorino cheese in a white wine, tomato basil sauce
11.00

Fusili
grilled chicken, sundried tomatoes, onions and red peppers, in a white wine cream sauce
12.00

Linguini di Mare
clams, scallops, mussels and tiger shrimp with white wine, olive oil and garlic
14.00

Spagettini
salmon, dill and green onion in a white wine cream sauce
13.00

Sintra

588 College Street
Toronto
416-533-1106
www.toronto.com/sintra

Portuguese
LITTLE ITALY

V / MC / AmEx /
  D / DC

dinner

late supper

take out

beer/wine

cocktails

private parties

non-smoking
  section

reservations
  recommended

dress casual

menu changes
  seasonally

On the hopping College strip, Sintra is yet another surge in a cuisine dismissed as coarse peasant fare before Chiado's Albino Silva shot it to the forefront of the city's restaurant scene. Intensely pretty in Provence blue-and-yellow and hung with suspended halogen orbs like flying saucers, Sintra sticks to its Iberian roots: Only racy *churrasco* rabbit distracts from a menu sagging with seafood. *Bacalhau,* salt cod, and steamed clams wafting with garlic and coriander salute a great mariner tradition. But be sure to order fish underdone or suffer the consequences; the kitchen can doze. And seek out proprietor Sergio Concalves's counsel on staggering lots of Portuguese wines.

Bacalhau a Sintra   **$16.95**
Pan Seared Salt Cod fillet with a ragout of Onions, Peppers and Tomatoes

Caldeirada na Cataplana   **$18.95**
A medley of Mussels & Fresh Fish steamed in a Cataplana dish, with Tomatoes, Garlic, White Wine, Olive Oil and Herbs

Garoupa Grelhada   **Market Price**
Grilled Fillet of Grouper on a warm Salad of Black Eyed Peas drizzled with a herb scented Lemon and Garlic Sauce & Chopped Egg

Carne de Porco Alentejana   **$16.95**
Marinated Cubes of Pork, Pan Seared with Clams, White Wine, Garlic & Coriander on a bed of Macedoine Potato accompanied by Portuguese Pickle

Coelho no Churrasco   **$21.95**
Grilled Marinated Rabbit with Madeira & Herb Sauce and Migas, a Hash of Kidney Beans, Chourico, Cornbread and Collards

Salmao Suado   **$16.95**
A Fillet of Fresh Atlantic Salmon steamed in Parchment on a bed of Julienne Vegetables with a Citrus & Coriander Butter.

Bife de Pimenta   **$19.95**
Grilled Rib Eye Steak with Aguardente & Peppercorn Cream Sauce, Rosemary Roast Potato & Seasonal Veg

Gambas Grelhadas   **$19.95**
Grilled Tiger Shrimps Sautéed with Fresh Herbs and Garlic in a White Wine Sauce

Bacalhau Grelhado   **$16.95**
Grilled Fillet of Salt Cod with Potato, Collards and Kidney Beans topped with Onion and Garlic seared in Extra Virgin Olive Oil

Sotto Sotto

116A Avenue Road (lower level)
Toronto
416-962-0011
www.toronto.com/sottosotto

**Italian
DOWNTOWN**

V / MC / AmEx / DC
dinner
late supper
take out
beer/wine
cocktails
private parties
reservations
  recommended
dress casual

Literally an underground success, Sotto Sotto dishes out Roman cooking in a contemporary catacomb, the subterranean stone walls and frescoes of the Ave-and-Dav location recalling the haunting archaeological vignette in Fellini's *Roma*. Marissa Rocca's pocket-sized restaurant fetches acclaim from visiting celebrities (Robert Duvall, Robin Williams, Sylvester Stallone, Anne Heche) for romance, fish, pasta, and wine, the latter unerringly chosen and sold at penthouse prices. Warm salad of shrimp and calamari and Provimi veal with artichokes are stars, but the ultimate specialty is saltimbocca, veal with prosciutto and sage, the way they do it in Rome, a dish I'd follow anywhere.

TRATTORIA
SOTTO SOTTO

BRESAOLA DELLA VALTELLINA $11.00
Cured beef topped with arugola and parmigiano, lemon and olive oil

POLENTA ALLA GAMBOLA $11.50
Grilled polenta topped with oyster mushrooms & gambola cheese

CASALINGO $8.50
A serving of Italian prosciutto with sliced bocconcini cheese

MIXED GRILLED VEGETABLES $8.50
A selection of vegetables, grilled with garlic, olive oil & balsamic vinager

SALMONE AFFUMICATO $12.95
Smoked salmon served with onions, capers & lemon

CARPACCIO DI MANZO $12.95
Beef carpaccio & parmesan shavings drizzled with olive oil & lemon on a bed of arugola salad

CARPACCIO DI TONNO $12.95
Tuna carpaccio drizzled with olive oil, garlic & lemon sauce & topped with capers on a bed of arugola

CARPACCIO DI PESCE SPADA $12.95
Swordfish carpaccio drizzled with olive oil, garlic, lemon sauce, capers on a bed of arugola salad

RADICCHIO E INDIVIA ALLA GRIGLIA $8.50
White Belgian endive, grilled with a balsamic, lemon ~ olive oil vinaigrette

GRILLED OYSTER MUSHROOMS $9.50
Oyster mushrooms, grilled with a balsamic, lemon & olive oil vinaigrette

CAPPESANTE ALLA GRIGLIA $12.50
Grilled sea scallops with garlic, olive oil, herbs and balsamic vinager

ANTIPASTO GORDONIA $17.00
Grilled tiger shrimp & calamari with mixed grilled vegetables

SARDINE ALLA GRIGLIA $12.95
Grilled fresh sardine (when available)

Southern Accent

595 Markham Street
Toronto
416-536-3211
www.southernaccent.com

American
WEST TORONTO

V / MC / AmEx /
  D / DC

dinner

late supper

beer/wine

cocktails

private parties
  and private
  booths

non-smoking
  section

reservations
  required

dress informal

menu changes
  monthly

In Mirvish Village—not Bourbon Street, but no bug-eyed voodoo queens and leering transvestites, either—American regional cooking of the N'Awlins persuasion has endured for two decades where other varieties (Tex-Mex, Southwestern) have blown in and out of town like tumbleweeds. The sultry sensibility of the Big Easy is as distant as the muddy Mississippi, but these quarters in a Victorian townhouse—the "Boo" Room is haunted, so watch out—cover a racy Cajun-Creole territory. Give me the dozen bourbons on the slate any time, house-baked hush puppies, blackened chicken livers, and that Jurassic-scale slab of juicy Louisiana catfish. True Grits Soul Shack up the street is Southern Accent's little sister restaurant.

'Southern' Accent
cajun & creole!

APPETIZERS

Our Nightly SOUP and GUMBO
...we'll tell you what's cookin'

Organic Baby GREENS and Seedlings
with Balsamic Soya Vinaigrette ... 5.50

HUSH PUPPIES (Cajun Corn Fritters) ...4.95

Piquant Black Tiger SHRIMP
Sauteed in Garlic Lime Hot Sauce, served with Beignets ...8.25

Blackened LIVERS
Napped with Lemon Beurre, served with Garlic Toast ... 6.95

Crispy CALAMARI Rings
with Ginger Remoulade and Blackened Tomato Coulis ... 8.75

Fresh OYSTERS
Served on the Half-shell with a Splash of Cajun Vodka
2.00 each   6 for 11.00 12 for 18.00

Crawfish BOIL
Whole crawfish, boiled in a Spicy Seafood Stock with Fresh
Corn and Potatoes ... 15.00

Ask for our instructions "How to best eat crawfish"
and share the experience with a loved one.

Special SALAD
Popcorn Shrimp on a Bed of Watercress with Steamed
Potatoes, Blackened Tomatoes, Marinated Purple Onion,
Boiled Eggs, Calamata Olives & an Herbed Vinaigrette... 12.00

MAIN COURSES

VEGETARIAN Special
Fried Green Tomatoes Napolean with Spinach and Goat's Cheese,
served with Sherry Mushroom Cream Sauce and
Grilled Asparagus ... 15.50

Blackened Free-Range CHICKEN BREAST
Breast of Chicken seasoned with Our Spices and Blackened on a
Cast Iron Skillet, then Napped with Fresh Lemon Beurre ...12.95

Aunt Fanny CRACKLING DUCK ROULADE
Moscovi Duck Breast filled with Andouille Corn Bread,
and served with Quince Glaze ... 24.00

Blackened DELMONICO
Blackened & Grilled N.Y. Steak, served with Smoked Tomato and
Roasted Garlic Butter ... 26.00

Creole Mixed Grill JAMBALAYA
A highly seasoned Rice Dish served with Blackened Chicken
Tenderloin, Grilled Andouille Sausage and Shrimp with Creole
Sauce atop Collard Greens ... 17.95

Cracker CATFISH
Farm Raised Louisiana Catfish Filet Coated in Crackers & Pecans,
Pan-fried and served with Pickled Jalapeno Tartar Sauce ... 17.50

CATCH of The Day
Ask your Server about how today's catch is prepared!!

Splendido

88 Harbord Street
Toronto
416-929-7788
www.splendidoonline.com

Global
DOWNTOWN WEST

Wheelchair
  access
valet parking
V / MC / AmEx / DC
dinner
late supper
beer/wine
cocktails
high chairs
private parties
non-smoking
reservations
  recommended
dress casual
menu changes
  weekly

Some argue that Splendido will never match the legend it forged in its decade under Arpi Magyar, but the current owners have made the room their own with muted colors, floral explosions, smart lighting, and colossal beveled mirrors dramatically expanding the space. Yannick Bigourdan brings huge Gallic charm and warmth to the front of the house, and David Lee, formerly of Centro, mans the symphonic open kitchen and woos a food-savvy crowd, beginning with a procession of impeccable pleasures from terrine marrying foie gras and duck confit all the way through to a formidable veal chop. Some of his sexiest dishes cast a spell on hopelessly addicted truffle-emulsion sniffers (including me).

SPLENDIDO
bar and grill

Ontario Pepper Squash Soup, Maritime Sea Scallop
Tamarind and Prune Compote   11

Imported Bufala Mozzarella, Vine Ripened Cherry Tomatoes
Niçoise Olive Vinaigrette   16

St-Benoit Quebec Blue Cheese Salad
Garden Arugula, Beets, Maple-Roasted Walnuts   12

Seasonal Selection of Oysters
Red Wine Mignonette   market price

Wood Burning Oven Roasted Whole Fish, Caper Nut Brown Butter
"Cookstown" Green Salad, Roasted Peppers   35

Slow Roasted "Queen Charlotte Island" Halibut Filet
Poached Nova Scotia Lobster, Butternut Squash Emulsion   39

Australian Rack of Lamb Seasoned with Sea Salt and Spices
Lima Beans, Savoy Cabbage Autumn Cassoulet, Rosemary-Garlic Jus   market price

Charcoal Grilled "AAA" Alberta Beef Tenderloin
Seared Quebec Foie Gras, Chanterelle Sauce   39

Crisp Provimi Veal Sweetbreads, "Pied de Cochon"
Quail Eggs, Bresaola, Duck Gizzard Mâche Salad   36

Salerno Sun-dried Tomato and Ricotta Striped Bauletti Pasta
Basil Pesto, Sautéed Rapini   21

Spring Rolls
on Yonge

689 Yonge Street
Toronto
416-972-7655
www.springrollsonline.com

Pan-Asian
DOWNTOWN

V / MC
lunch
dinner
late supper
take out
beer/wine
cocktails
high chairs
private parties
non-smoking
reservations
  recommended
dress informal

If Asianization is the best thing to hit honky-tonk Yonge Street since the Eaton Center, Spring Rolls leads the charge as Toronto's first pan-Asian restaurant, its menu pirouetting from Malasian satays to Singapore noodles, Vietnamese phos, Thai curries, Cantonese stir-fries, and Szechuan shrimps faster than Jackie Chan. The stylish room is watched over by replicas of the terra cotta warriors at the famous imperial tomb of Xi'an. The furious open kitchen proves competent with almost everything on the menu; the pity is, it compromises flavors to bland local tastes, defaulting to a complete loss of spirit. If you like it hot and spicy, say so, and keep your fingers crossed.

Also: 85 Front Street East
        Toronto
        416-365-7655

spring rolls
ON YONGE

FROM THE WOK

Chow Mein - The Crispy Chinese Egg Noodles
authentic Chinese style crispy egg noodles glazed in a garlic and onion sauce

- Cantonese (Tiger shrimp, scallops, bbq pork, beef, chicken breast, calamari & mixed vegetables) .... $ 8.95
- Vegetarian .... $ 6.95
- Beef .... $ 7.45
- Chicken .... $ 7.45
- Tiger Shrimp .... $ 9.95
- Seafood (Tiger shrimp, scallops & calamari) .... $ 9.95

Shanghai Noodles
thick wheat noodles stir-fried with cabbage, onion and pepper with a hint of "Hoi Sin" and mushroom soya sauce

- Vegetarian .... $ 6.95
- Beef .... $ 7.45
- Chicken .... $ 7.45
- BBQ Pork & Shrimp .... $ 7.95
- Shrimp .... $ 7.95

Spring Rolls .... $ 2.95
carrot, onion, ground chicken breast, taro, cabbage, shitake mushrooms and vegetables (2 rolls)

Shrimp Rolls .... $ 5.95
marinated Tiger shrimp (4 rolls)

House Spring Rolls .... $ 3.95
carrot, onion, ground chicken breast, taro, cabbage, shitake mushrooms and marinated Tiger shrimp (2 rolls)

Vegetable Spring Rolls .... $ 2.95
carrot, onion, taro, cabbage, shitake mushrooms and vegetables (2 rolls)

Cold Shrimp Rolls .... $ 3.95
shrimp, vermicelli, vegetables and coriander rolled in wheat wraps (3 rolls)

Cold Vegetable Spring Rolls .... $ 2.95
vegetables, vermicelli and coriander rolled in wheat wraps (3 rolls)

Cold Mango Rolls .... $ 3.95
vermicelli, julienned mango, vegetables and coriander rolled in wheat wraps (3 rolls)

Cold Grilled Chicken Rolls .... $ 3.95
grilled chicken, vermicelli, vegetables and coriander rolled in wheat wraps (3 rolls)

Spring Rolls Platter .... $ 8.95
Spring Roll, Shrimp Roll, House Spring Roll, and Cold Shrimp Roll served w/ mango salad

Starfish Oyster Bed & Grill

100 Adelaide Street East
Toronto
416-366-7827
www.starfishoysterbed.com

Seafood
DOWNTOWN

Wheelchair
  access
V / MC / AmEx / DC
lunch
dinner
late supper
take out
beer/wine
private parties
non-smoking
reservations
  recommended
dress casual
menu changes
  daily

It was only a question of time until somebody gave the incredibly successful Rodney Clark a run for his money. Right-hand man and world-champion oyster shucker Pat McMurray bolted Rodney's to open Starfish. The celestial hermaphrodite mollusks—sharp little Malpeques from P.E.I., and dreamy Kumamotos from Washington—star at the bar, but McMurray's also upgraded from Rodney rusticity to slick Manhattan ambience in which stocks and bonds (not foreplay) is the topic of hushed conversation. Beyond bivalves, the kitchen reaches out with first-rate surf (boiled lobster, black cod) and substantial turf (leg of lamb, grilled quails).

Starfish
OYSTER BED & GRILL

From the Oyster Bed

Malpeque – P.E.I.
Bras D'or Lakes - NS
Tatamagouche – NS
Newport Cups – RI
Prudence Is. – RI
Blue Point – Conn.

Kumamoto – WA
Olympia – WA
Royal Miyagi – B.C.
Littlenecks – CT
Live sea scallops – N.S.

Belon - France
Baie de Quiberon –France
Fines de Claire – France
Speciale – France

Market price

From the land

Classic whole-leaf caesar salad with shaved grana padano cheese	8-
Grilled Ontario farm-fresh quail on a roast parsnip puree and balsamic glazed pearl onions	10-
Watercress and duck confit salad with blood oranges and candied kumquats	12-
Roast leg of Ontario lamb in an herbed jus with oven roasted tomato and roasted garlic mashed potatoes	23-
Grilled U.S. Select rib-eye steak with parsley shallot butter and frites	27-

From the sea

Warm poached Langoustine with lemon ailoli	3.15 each
Daily soup	8-
Steamed P.E.I. mussels in a roasted garlic and smoked tomato broth	8-
Grilled calamari served on a warm salad of baby spinach, cherry tomatoes and double smoked bacon	10-
Salmon tartar with marinated oyster mushrooms and gingered beet puree	11-

Steakfrites

692 Mount Pleasant Road
Toronto
416-486-0090
www.oliverbonacini.com

Bistro
MIDTOWN

Wheelchair
  access

V / MC / AmEx / DC

Sunday brunch

dinner

late supper

take out

beer/wine

cocktails

high chairs

private parties

non-smoking

reservations
  recommended

dress casual

menu changes
  weekly

When Peter Oliver and Michael Bonacini, whose Jump, Canoe, Biff's, and Auberge du Pommier constitute the most successful restaurant oeuvre Toronto has ever seen, turn their hands to a neighborhood bistro, you know the neighborhood has arrived. Here they serve hand-cut, fresh frites golden-crisp from the fryer—the way they made 'em in Paris before the invasion of the freezer boxes. In the old Pronto location and stylishly designed by Ingrid Herczegh, who did Biff's, this bistro is about more than meat and taters, with starters that encourage mixing and matching and mains that veer off into pastas and polentas just to prove we're still in Toronto, Toto.

STEAKFRITES

APPETIZERS

Marinated chèvre and fresh artichoke salad with fine herbs	10.50
Romaine leaf salad with petites lentils and Caesar dressing	8.50
White asparagus wrapped in smoked salmon with an orange tarragon antiboise	11.25
Mixed lettuce with a French dressing	7.50
Pronto grilled calamari with capers and roasted garlic	9.50
Spinach, walnut and wilted grape salad with blue cheese and honey	9.00
Crispy roasted sweetbreads wrapped in bacon with Pommery mustard	11.00
The day's charcuterie with chutney and toast	9.50
Roasted sweet pepper salad with anchovies, capers and marjoram	8.50
Bruschetta du jour	7.50
Marinated tuna and white bean salad	8.00
Baked fresh ricotta on eggplant confit and dandelion leaves	8.50

SOUPS

French onion soup with duck confit and Gruyère cheese	7.00
Golden potato, leek and Stilton	7.00

PASTA AND POLENTA

Creamy polenta with Gorgonzola	10.50
Grilled polenta with Niçoise olives and capers	10.50
Penne all' amatriciana	13.50
Capellini with sautéed mushrooms, enriched chicken stock and cream	14.50

Stork
on the Roof

2009 Yonge Street
416-483-3747

**Bistro
MIDTOWN**

V / MC / AmEx

lunch (T-F)

dinner

beer/wine

cocktails

private parties

non-smoking

reservations
  recommended

dress informal

menu changes
  seasonally

Stork on the Roof's name derives from a Dutch children's story, signifying good fortune, and a Netherlands sensibility manifests itself in the Amsterdam canalscapes, and the East Indies cooking of Michael Van Den Winkel and Jennifer Gittens. Indonesian spices float through the room like a tropical breeze, imparting a hint of the piratical. Van Den Winkel and Gittens clearly have fun in the kitchen, with marriages as playful as tiger shrimp drizzled with black and white truffle oil. The famous Dutch attention to detail prevails throughout, even in lowly chicken livers, herein pink and creamy with hints of nutmeg and chile. Make reservations or join the long line.

Stork on the Roof
restaurant

Duck Leg Braised w/Orange, Star Anis and Port **Orange and Chicory Salad and Potato Cake**	**$18.50**
Baked Filo Parcel of Grilled Asparagus , Red Pepper, **Fresh Spinach, Oyster Mushrooms and Tallegio Cheese** **and a Tomato Caper Vinaigrette**	**$17.50**
Grilled Fillet of Salmon served **on a Potato Cake w/ Sauteed Vegetables** **w/a Lightly Spiced Enoki & Shitaki Mushroom Sauce**	**$18.00**
Sauteed Tiger Shrimps w/a Fresh Tarragon, **White & Black Truffle Jus w/ Sauteed Vegetables** **and Potato Cake**	**$20.00**
Grilled Filet of Chilean Sea Bass w/ Arugula, Golden Beets, **Pancetta and a Balsamic and Beet Reduction** **Sauteed Vegetables & Potato Cake**	**$20.00**
Oven Roasted Pork Tenderloin w/an Indonesian Style **Five Spice Sauce w/ Sauteed Vegetables & Nasi Goreng Rice**	**$18.50**
Oven Roasted Whole Cornish Hen **w/a Provencale Style Tomato, Fresh Herb Sauce** **Herb Roasted Vegetables and Mashed Potato**	**$19.50**
Pan Seared Lamb Tenderloin w/a Juniper Berry Jus **w/ Sauteed Vegetables and Mashed Potato**	**$21.50**

Studio Cafe

Four Seasons Hotel
21 Avenue Road
Toronto
416-928-7330
www.fourseasons.com

Global
YORKVILLE

Wheelchair
 access
valet parking
V / MC / AmEx / DC
Sunday brunch
breakfast
lunch
dinner
late supper
take out
beer/wine
cocktails
high chairs
non-smoking
dress casual
menu changes
 seasonally

Calls for "four burgers, three with fries, one with salad!" ring out along with those for apple-wood smoked salmon and lobster risotto. Painted wooden ceilings and old-fashioned moldings lend homey notes to the clattering open kitchen and exquisitely showcased Canadian glass sculpture. The busy room doubles as a forum for exec chef Lynn Crawford, whose notion of down and dirty encompasses Maryland crab cakes, chorizo pizza, and get this, sweetbread club sandwich. In the *When Harry Met Sally* mode, I expect ladies who lunch to purr, "We'll have what she's having."

Pizza and Bruschetta

◆ Portobello Mushroom Pizza, Smoked Scamorza Cheese, Oregano and Tomato   15.

◆ Margherita Pizza, Tomato Sauce, Basil and Mozzarella Cheese   14.

Potato and Prosciutto Pizza with Goat Cheese, Pommery Mustard and
Lemon Drizzling   15.

◆ Rocket Pizza with Sunchokes, Reggiano Cheese and Truffle Oil   15.

Assorted Bruschetta with Smoked Salmon, Tapenade, Ratatouille, Shrimp,
Grilled Vegetables and Avocado   14.

Pasta and Risotto

υ Cannelloni of Spinach and Ricotta Cheese, Melting Celery and Celeriac,
Black Truffle Scented Froth
Appetizer   14.   Entrée   22.

◆ Penne Pasta with Tomato-Basil Sauce   Appetizer   10.   Entrée   16.
Or Veal Bolognese   Appetizer   11.   Entrée   18.

◆ Sweet Potato Gnocchi with Caramelized Seasonal Vegetables, Wild Mushrooms, Sage Emulsion
Appetizer   14.   Entrée   22.

Seared Diver Scallops with Lemon Ginger Risotto, Sauce American   29.

Entrées

* Market Fish, Spinach Spätzle, Mixed Mushrooms, Pearl Onions
Choice of: Orange Green Peppercorn Sauce, Tartar Sauce or Aged Balsamic   29.

Pan-Roasted Fillet of Atlantic Salmon with Saffron-Vanilla Sauce and Fondant Potatoes   25.

Caramelized Marlin, Green Curry Vegetable Hash, Coconut-Chili Green Beans and
Basmati Rice   26.

Susur

601 King Street West
Toronto
416-603-9361

Fusion
DOWNTOWN WEST

Wheelchair
   access
V / MC / AmEx
dinner
beer/wine
cocktails
private parties
non-smoking
reservations
   recommended
dress informal
menu changes
   daily

Spurning moneybags from Manhattan—how many times did he have to say, "I wanna stay in Trawna?"—and bemused, if anything, by media fawning, Canada's most stellar chef, Susur Lee, lets no *gras* grow under his feet. The room tries to not take itself too seriously, but for the bucks here, foodies show up with expectations bordering on religion. At least the trendies have moved on, and Lee has been able to consolidate his standing as the Gandalf of the global village kitchen, pooling East and West in giddying flights of gastronomic fantasy. The tasting menu starts with the main course and winds down to soup before dessert. Leave all preconceived notions at home. Bring a sense of adventure and a fat wallet.

Lamb loin/green curry sauce, mint chutney/
rice cake   45

Roasted rare venison marinated in fresh green peppercorn/
black truffle sauce/gratin of Swiss chard & cauliflower   45

Smoked duck steak/spiced foie gras/sweet potato &
pineapple tart/chili lime confit   45

Roasted lobster/anchovy and garlic chili/
lobster dashi broth   45

Smoked sea bass/Thailandaise glaze/chanterelle
mushrooms/purée of lily bulb/cheriso   35

Roasted provimi veal loin/miso mustard/
marinated eggplant   45

Szechuan Szechuan

First Canadian Place
100 King Street West
Toronto
416-861-0124

Chinese
FINANCIAL DISTRICT

Wheelchair
  access

V / MC / AmEx / DC

lunch

dinner

take out

beer/wine

cocktails

high chairs

private parties

non-smoking

dress casual

A swank cherry wood–paneled dining room, servers ladling and spooning, and Szechuan fire— garlic and chiles ready to do business—bring substance to this skyscraping First Canadian Place. Wooing suits upstairs and shoppers from the mall below, the restaurant hedges its bets with Cantonese and Thai tokens, but Szechuan, which never really established much of a beachhead in Toronto, steals all the thunder with spicy hot-and-sour soup, and incendiary shrimps, tofu, and eggplant. Guinness, the great Irish bog beer, turns out to be a perfect accompaniment. Evening business remains dismally slack, so the kitchen closes at 9 P.M., a pity for post-performance crowds prowling for a bite.

SZECHUAN SZECHUAN
Fine Chinese Cuisine

Lemon Chicken...10.95

Sweet and Sour Chicken Ball 9.95

Stir Fried Sweet and Sour Pineapple Chicken 11.95

Cashewnut Chicken 11.95

Chicken in Black Bean Sauce...10.50

Chicken with Vegetable 10.95

Peking Chicken with Cashewnut 11.95

Curry Chicken..10.95

Thai Green Chicken Curry 10.95

Thai Basil Chicken...10.95

Crispy Duck (Seasoned with Spices)..............................15.95

Szechuan Duck 17.95
(Boneless Fried Duck with an Assortment of Fresh Vegetable in a Szechuan Sauce)

Peking Duck (Advance Order) served in two courses

a) Crispy Skin with Pancakes

b) Shredded Meat with Chinese Vegetable 38.95

Szechuan Beef...10.95

Crispy Ginger Beef 11.95

Orange Beef...11.95

Take Sushi

22 Front Street West
Toronto
416-862-1891

Japanese
DOWNTOWN

V / MC / AmEx / DC

lunch

dinner

take out

beer/wine

cocktails

high chairs

private parties

non-smoking

reservations
  recommended

dress casual

menu changes
  seasonally

When the owners of Nami bought and revamped the cavernous Front Street space—candlelight and blue a vast improvement on glare and blare—they prudently left chef Susumu Wada in charge. Wada does things his way, turning out flamboyant *omakase*, Osaka-style sushi pressed in a wooden box, riceless sushi "salad" roll, and tofu steak on a sizzling platter, juggling accents from fresh wasabi root to Thai spices. Drinks count here: Sakes from Japan, Oregon, and California preside at the bar, where the warmed rice wine may come afloat with a toasted *fugu* fin—that's right, the blowfish whose liver and ovaries contain a toxin 79,000 times more powerful than cyanide. Cheers.

ta
ke
sushi

SEAFOOD

Tempura Assorted <u>vegetables and three jumbo shrimps</u> deep   8.25
fried in light batter and served with tempura sauce

Gindara Saikyoyaki <u>Black cod</u> marinated in miso sauce   13.50

Tako Isobeage <u>Octopus</u> dipped in egg and deep fried in light   7.50
batter. Served in miso sauce

Namakaki Six <u>fresh oysters</u> with ponzu sauce   13.50

Soft Shell Crab Deep fried <u>soft shell crab</u> served with ponzu sauce   12.50

BEEF, CHICKEN AND EGG

Beef Sashimi Seared <u>strip loin</u> sliced paper thin. Served with   7.95
ponzu sauce

Yakitori Skewered grilled <u>chicken</u> in teriyaki sauce   5.75

Tori Karaage Japanese style deep fried <u>chicken</u> pieces   4.50

Chawanmushi Chicken, shrimp, ginko nuts, shiitake and enoki   6.50
mushrooms steamed in an <u>egg custard</u>

VEGETARIAN

Agedashi Tofu Deep fried <u>tofu</u> topped with chopped green onions   4.50
and ground radish mixed chili paste. Served with tempura sauce

Nasudengaku Broiled <u>eggplant</u> topped with our chef's own sweet   5.50
miso sauce

Edamame Boiled <u>soy beans</u> salted and served chilled   4.50

Imo Tempura <u>Yam potatos</u> deep fried in light vegetable oil.   4.50
Served with tempura sauce

Tasting Rooms

First Canadian Place
King Street West between
Bay and York
Toronto
416-362-2499

Global
FINANCIAL DISTRICT

Wheelchair
  access
V / MC / AmEx / DC
breakfast
lunch
dinner
take out
beer/wine
cocktails
private parties
non-smoking
  section
reservations
  recommended
dress informal

A weirdly comforting rusticity—the ambience of
Ontario cottage country, complete with crackling
fireplace, secreted away in a concrete colossus
of commerce—calls for a visit to Chris Boland's
experiment in orchestrated grazing. Half the
menu comes in "tasting" portions, the idea being
to play in the order of, say, Thai shrimp curry
followed by grilled quail followed by caribou pie.
The exploratory theme follows through with flights
of wines—light whites to big reds, everything in
two-ounce portions. After a few sips, you'll think
you're back in school, only the exams are a whole
lot more fun.

Tasting Rooms
RESTAURANT

Tortilla salad - mesclun greens, roasted red peppers,
Cambazola cheese, wrapped in tortilla with hummus (V)
$6.95

Shrimp jump-fried in garlic, lemon, vermouth and cream,
tossed with mixed greens
$8.95

Spicy mediterranean calamari with baby spinach, tossed
in Gorgonzola cream sauce (H)
$7.50

Smoked salmon tasting board - Canadian and Norwegian
with pickled ginger and sashimi dipping sauce
$7.25

Foie gras and chicken liver pate with Port preserve and
peach chutney
$6.25

Grilled chicken satay with spicy Thai peanut sauce (h,N)
$4.50

Fresh P.E.I. mussels simmered in white wine, garlic,
tomatoes and basil
$8.50

Seared sea scallops with fresh herbs, garlic butter and
asparagus risotto
$7.95

Terra

8199 Yonge Street
Thornhill
905-731-6161
www.terrarestaurant.ca

Global
SUBURBAN NORTH

Wheelchair
  access

V / MC / AmEx / DC

dinner

late supper

take out

beer/wine

cocktails

private parties

non-smoking

reservations
  recommended

dress smart
  casual

menu changes
  daily

Rodney Clarke's incomparable oysters, Beluga caviar, foie gras, and grilled ostrich among the strip malls and duck-tongue palaces of the northern burbs? No longer under the wing of the stellar Mark McEwan, but nonetheless rife with McEwanisms (designer trappings, painstaking detail, velvet-glove service, tightly focused preparations), Terra unclosets a vast pool of starving suburban and out-of-town sophisticates from as far afield as Woodbridge and Pickering. Congrats to restaurateurs Richard Cwynar and Ian Chase. A *Wine Spectator* award of excellence gives these guys a big lead hereabouts.

<u>Oysters</u>

Rodney's choice oysters served à la carte on shaved ice, with lemon, lime, freshly grated horseradish and gazpacho.

Acadian, Nova Scotia   **per piece**-2.75   or   **half dozen** - 15.30
Medium size, hint of watermelon rind in flavour, medium salt.

Malagash, Nova Scotia   **per piece**-2.95   or   **half dozen** - 17.70
Small, plump, low salt, medium soft texture with light finish.

Beau Soleil, New Brunswick   **per piece**-2.95   or   **half dozen** - 17.70
Very small size, salty, crisp texture, mild finish.

Raspberry Point, P.E.I.   **per piece**-3.50   or   **half dozen** - 21.00
Small size, firm with good flavour, somewhat similar to Aspy Bay oysters

Flats, Nova Scotia   **per piece**-3.75   or   **half dozen** - 22.50
Medium size, mild salt, buttery with a strong finish.

Oak Island, P.E.I.   **per piece**-3.95   or   **half dozen** - 23.70
Small to medium size, complex, briny, some similarity to Malpeque oysters.

<u>Vegetarian Selections</u>

* Grilled portobello steak with asparagus, green and yellow beans, sesame candy beets, spinach, mashed potatoes and sautéed onions
* An assortment of vegetables with ratatouille, hashed butternut squash and parsnip, sweet potato pureé, roasted baby tomatoes, fresh peas, honey mushrooms, asparagus, beans and steamed basmati rice
* Slow roasted eggplant stuffed with an assortment of wild mushrooms, shallots, roasted garlic, & roasted peppers and crusted with lemon-herb-sourdough breadcrumbs

✧ Our dining room can accomodate parties of 6 to 200 ✧
-Private rooms available for up to 40 guests -

Torch Bistro

253 Victoria Street
Toronto
416-364-7517

Bistro
DOWNTOWN

Wheelchair
  access
V / MC / AmEx / DC
lunch
dinner
late supper
beer/wine
cocktails
live
  entertainment
private parties
non-smoking
reservations
  required
dress casual
menu changes
  seasonally

High-backed banquettes, discreetly curtained cherry wood booths, aproned servers—welcome to a textbook bistro as it rarely exists even in the City of Light. For years, the room was a steakhouse, accommodating *Phantom of the Opera* hordes; the beef is reincarnated as steak frites. Only now, entrepreneur Bob Sniderman's baby fulfills its bistro destiny: Take a gander at that crispy-skinned duck thigh sided with certifiably addictive tomato tarte tatin. Also, check out Sniderman's lovingly preserved 1929 Senator Diner next door. Upstairs, the Top of the Senator jazz club is known for celebrity talent, including Diana Krall and Sheila Jordan.

BISTRO

DAILY SOUP / $7

SALAD OF ROMAINE HEARTS WITH GARLIC PARMESAN CROUTONS AND CAESAR DRESSING
/ $9

MIXED YOUNG GREEN SALAD WITH CITRUS MISO VINAIGRETTE AND SWEET POTATO CHIPS
/ $7

PUFF PASTRY WITH SHRIMPS, MUSHROOMS AND MUSSELS WITH WHITE WINE, TARRAGON
AND CREAM / $14

SENATORCH CRAB CAKES WITH TARTAR SAUCE / $7   TWO / $13

GRILLED MARINATED JUMBO QUAIL WITH AN ARUGULA SALAD, FRESHLY POACHED
PEARS AND A WALNUT OIL VINAIGRETTE / $12

HOUSE SMOKED ATLANTIC SALMON ON A CRISPY POTATO PANCAKE WITH CELERIAC
SALAD / $13

ENTRÉES

12 OZ GRILLED N. Y. STRIPLOIN STEAK WITH FRITES AND ROSEMARY SHALLOT JUS / $30

PAN SEARED ATLANTIC SALMON WITH WARM CALABRESE AND VEGETABLE SALAD WITH
CHAMPAGNE VINAIGRETTE / $25

ROAST BREAST OF CHICKEN WITH A SUNDRIED TOMATO JUS AND GRATIN DAUPHINOIS
$24

BEEF TENDERLOIN WITH ROASTED PORTOBELLO MUSHROOMS AND MASHED POTATOES
$32

GRILLED PROVIMI LIVER, BRAISED RED CABBAGE WITH APPLES AND BALSAMIC VINEGAR,
CRISP PANCHETTA AND ROASTED POTATOES / $23

SMOKED DUCK BREAST WITH ROSEMARY SHITAKE MUSHROOM RISOTTO, ROASTED
SHALLOT JUS / $28

Toula

Westin Harbour Castle Hotel
1 Harbour Square
Toronto
416-777-2002
www.toularestaurant.com

Italian
WATERFRONT

Wheelchair
  access

valet parking

V / MC / AmEx / DC

Sunday brunch

lunch

dinner

late supper

beer/wine

cocktails

live
  entertainment

private parties

non-smoking
  section

cigar lounge

reservations
  recommended

dress casual

menu changes
  seasonally

The North American beachhead for the Milan-based outfit whose empire reaches from La Scala to Kuala Lumpur and now Hogtown. The no-longer-revolving circular space atop the Harbour Castle Hotel, unlike the CN Tower's 360, is definitely not above it all: On the thirty-eighth floor level, Toula peers into the daunting Great Wall of condos (whoops, the woman on the twenty-fourth dropped the towel) that wreck Toronto's waterfront. Thankfully, the room's lavish burgundy-and-gold interior turns attention inwards. Acclaimed chef Oscar Turchi, bringing into play the gastronomic spectrum of Italy's twenty-one regions, may yet teach us a thing or two.

Soups / Minestre

Soup of the Day
Minestra del Giorno $9.00

Pasta and Borlotti Beans, Venetian Style
Pasta e Fagioli alla Veneta $9.00

Pearl Barley and Smoked Bacon Trentino Style
Minestra d'Orzo con Pancetta Affumicata alla Trentina $9.00

Cardamon scented Yam and Carrot Purée finsihed with Garlic Sour Cream
Purea di Carote e Patate Americane con Crema Acida All'aglio $9.00

Pasta / Paste

Spaghettini with fresh Tomato Sauce and Basil with Extra Virgin Olive Oil
Spaghettini al Filetto di Pomodoro e Basilico $15.00

Toulà Style Tagliolini with Parma Prosciutto in a light Cream Sauce
Tagliolini Verdi con Prosciotto Gratinati alla Moda del Toulà $23.00

Butternut Squash Tortelloni with Poppy Seeds and Asiago Cheese Sauce
Tortelli di Zucca con Semi di Papavero e Fonduta di Asiago $24.00

Tagliatelle tossed with Scampi, Baby Clams and Asparagus in a Saffron and Lemon Sauce
Tagliatelle con Scampi e Vongole in Salsa al Limone e Zafferano con Asparagi $29.00

Pennette with double Smoked Bacon and Onion Confit in a Tomato Coulis and aged Ricotta
Pennette all'Amatriciana con Ricotta Salata $18.00

Town Grill

243 Carlton Street
Toronto
416-963-9433

Bistro
CABBAGETOWN

V / MC / AmEx / DC

dinner

beer/wine

cocktails

private parties

non-smoking

reservations
recommended

dress casual

menu changes
seasonally
with daily
specials

The Town Grill is the quintessential neighbor-hood restaurant—unpretentious, cheerful, and consistent—a fave with the compulsive renovators of Cabbagetown's Victorian manses. Restaurateurs David Doherty and Scott Turner more often than not get it right, proffering "upscale comfort food" to a public increasingly needy in the comfort department. Mexican lanterns and gauze-wrapped overhead pipes accent the room, and the kitchen tarts up the menu with sexy ingredients, including spiced pecans, chickpea fries, and pomegranate-and-blood orange drizzle. Sometimes the boys go on an off-menu rip, serving items like rhea (South American ostrich), the profoundly phallic geoduck (pronounced "gooey-duck"), and lamb's testicles (which sell out with indecent haste).

THE
TOWN GRILL

supreme of chicken, stuffed with sundried tomatoes, spinach and garoxta cheese, served with roasted
artichokes, new potatoes and lemon-infused chicken jus
$18

"steak frites"-a grilled ribeye with bearnaise butter and thin-cut frites
$18

rabbit braised in white wine, pommery mustard & cream,
with a new potato-butternut squash cake and sauteed spinach
$19

lamb shank, slow-cooked in red wine and herbs, with chickpea fries
and a roasted celery root, carrot and parsnip salad
$19

grilled fillet of arctic char with braised dupuy lentils, oven-dried tomatoes,
sauteed spinach and a spruce tip and lemon butter sauce
$19

grilled applewood-smoked pork tenderloin with braised red cabbage and apples,
a potato and white turnip gratin and an apple-brandy sauce
$20

pan-roasted duck breast with a warm salad of toasted hazelnut, red onion and organic quinoa,
sauteed curly endive and a pomegranate and blood orange reduction
$21

dijon and horseradish-crusted beef tenderloin with roasted garlic mashed potatoes,
port-shallot jus and an onion-mushroom ragout
$23

Truffles

Four Seasons Hotel
21 Avenue Road
Toronto
416-928-7331
www.fourseasons.com

French
YORKVILLE

Wheelchair
  access
valet parking
V / MC / AmEx / DC
dinner
beer/wine
cocktails
non-smoking
reservations
  recommended
dress casual
menu changes
  seasonally

The showplace restaurant for Four Seasons Hotels and Resorts in the company's hometown ought to score close to 100 percent, but comes in at 110: Truffles is *the* special-occasion restaurant in Toronto. It glows with warmth and elegance trumpeted by sculptor Christina Luck's Uffizi boars, those legendary truffle hunters, at the door. Service is luxe, but also warm and witty. Chef Jason McLeod's menus—his eight-course seafood tasting menu is a breath-stealer—are cutting-edge. The eternal holdover from the ancien régime is spaghettini sauced in truffle emulsion, in which the "black queen of cuisine" struts her stuff and leaves me on the carpet, bowing and kowtowing.

Truffles

Sea

Poached Wild Salmon and Oyster Tempura,
Crab Bisque Scented with Cardamom   37.

* Roast Halibut and Braised Oxtail,
Balsamic Infused Braising Jus   38.

Crisp Yellow Tail Snapper, Seared Bay Scallop and Oscietra Caviar,
Vanilla Chervil Froth, Jerusalem Artichoke Ravioli   39.

Nova Scotia Lobster, Truffled Sauce, Finished with Vacherin Cheese,
Grilled Confit of Winter Mushrooms   40.

Land

Young Free Range Chicken "Under Pastry"
Truffled Sauce "Albufera"   37.

Braised Daube of Beef "Burgundy Style"
Whipped Potatoes   38.

* Loin of Venison, Bitter Chocolate Sauce,
Spiced Red Cabbage, Parsnip Purée   39.

Slow Roasted Rack of Alberta Lamb, Thyme Jus,
Tortellini of Ratatouille "Niçoise Garnish"   40.

Tundra

Hilton Toronto
145 Richmond Street West
Toronto
416-860-6800

Canadian
DOWNTOWN

Wheelchair
 access
V / MC / AmEx / DC
breakfast
lunch
dinner
take out
beer/wine
cocktails
high chairs
private parties
non-smoking
reservations
 recommended
dress casual
menu changes
 seasonally

Talk about nerve: high-concept *Canadian* cuisine in a restaurant off a hotel atrium? Hand it to Hilton for thinking big. A sweeping statement from trendy II BY IV Design Associates, Tundra miraculously evokes the stark, subtle hues and craggy majesty of the north in the Lawren Harris mode. Although the mission could be more daring, chef John Cirillo's kitchen sources indigenous products from tangerine-fleshed Arctic char to Quebec foie gras and imbues them with the mouth-filling flavors we associate with hotel dining. The wine list makes its case with expert choices from the vineyards of Ontario and the Okanagan Valley, and the results leave American and European visitors cheering.

TUNDRA

appetizers	small	large
crisp romaine hearts with warm pancetta, sourdough croutons and shaved pecorino	8	10
baby rocket leaves, crumbled gorgonzola, dried figs and peaches, toasted pine nuts, sherry vinaigrette	9	11
rare seared yellow fin tuna "nicoise" style, white skin potato and snap peas, arbequina olives	13	16
black and white angel hair pasta with shiitake mushrooms, arugula, cherry tomato and tossed in porcini oil	12	14
maple glazed "lakeland farms" quail with seared quebec foie gras, mascarpone flavored wild rice risotto		19
poached new brunswick lobster tail, lobster apricot and chive rillette with fennel, pepper slaw and chili lime emulsion		17
muscovy duck confit with thinly sliced crispy petit vegetables, tri color seaweed in rice wine and sesame seed infused dressing		16

main course

slow roasted pork tenderloin, glazed prunes with poppy seed spaeztle, cumin scented braised savoy cabbage in a dark ale jus	25
braised cornish game hen "coq au vin", red wine sauce cipollini onions, forest mushrooms, roseval potatoes	26
pan seared striped bass with herb scented creamy polenta and young turnips, sweet pea emulsion	29
oven roasted red deer loin with lemon sage dumpling, golden carrots, pickled beet root reduction	35

Vanipha Lanna

863 Street Clair Avenue West
Toronto
416-654-8068
www.vanipha.ca

Southeast Asian
WEST TORONTO

Wheelchair
   access

V / MC

lunch

dinner

take out

beer/wine

private parties

non-smoking

reservations
   recommended

dress casual

Vanipha Lanna, like its kin Ban Vanipha, offers the spicy, complex cuisine of Laos and Northern Thailand that renders the hot-and-sweet Southern Thai familiar to most of us mere titillation by comparison. Oddly located in a neighborhood of hole-in-the-wall Latin American eateries, it seems all the more exotic. Elevated, candlelit seating for twenty-six is reserved for romance and multi-course dinner packages. The kitchen takes its time, but for once, humbly endure: Coming your way are dishes explosively layered with kaffir lime, lemongrass, mint, coriander, and incendiary little chiles. A must is *laab gai*, a festive Laotian toss of chicken and spices sauced in seething chile-lime juices.

Meat and Poultry

PAAD GAI HOALAPHA (ck. with Thai basil)
  -stirfry chicken with bell peppers, fresh oyster
  mushrooms, fresh basil and chili lime
  sauce
          $9.25

PAAD GAI TOA DINH(smoky piquant ck)
  -stirfry chicken with bamboo shoots, mushrooms, whole peanuts in a smoky chili sauce
          $9.25

PAAD BHED KEE MAO (Thai duck strifry)
  -thin sliced roasted duck sauteed with scallions,
  mushrooms, baby corn, snowpeas with fresh basil
  and a touch of whiskey, spicy sauce
          $10.50

NUA YAHNG (Siamese B.B.Q)
  -tender beef lightly marinated, then grilled, sliced
  and served with hot dipping sauce
          $11.50

PAAD PRIG TOA YAAO (spicy ck. with
  long beans)
  -ck. with long beans, bell peppers, strifried in
  spicy kafir lime sauce
          $9.50

NUA NAAM MUN HOY.
  -sauteed tender beef with green onions, bell
  peppers in oyster sauce,on sizzling hot plate
          $12.50

SEAN NAM TOK (beef w/ herbs & lime)
  -grilled sliced flank steak tossed with fresh
  mint & corriander, chili, lime juice,
  chopped peanuts
          $9.95

OAR SEAN (spicy Northern beef dish)
  -spicy country sauteed beef stirfry, with
  assorted veg. and spicy herbs sauce
          $9.95

Curries

GANG PED (Thai famous red curry)
  ck. $9.25
  duck & lychee ... $10.95
  beef $9.75

PANANG NUA (Panang beef)
  -sauteed sliced beef in a dry curry lemon
  peanut sauce
          $9.95

GANG KEAW WHAAN (Emerald curry)
  ck. $9.25
  beef $9.75
  shr. $10.95

MAADSAMUN GAI (Thai chicken curry)
  -tender chicken in a tamarind curry
  coconut sauce
          $9.50

Verveine

1097 Queen Street East
Toronto
416-405-9906

Global
EAST TORONTO

V / MC / AmEx / DC

Sunday brunch

dinner

beer/wine

cocktails

non-smoking
section

reservations
recommended

dress casual

menu changes
seasonally

Perhaps the ultimate neighborhood restaurant, Verveine single-handedly rejuvenates a dreary stretch of Queen Street East and, energetically overseen by youngish proprietors Kim Saunders and Michael Larmon, proves good enough for any neighborhood. The pistachio-hued, tin-ceilinged room glows beguilingly after dark, practically stopping traffic in its tracks. The predominantly east-end crowd knows a good deal when it sees one. The kitchen rarely falters, delivering at neighborly prices supple tartares, nicely underdone fish and seafood, feathery deep-fry, and juicy strip loins with honest-to-goodness, hand-cut Yukon Gold fries, the way they were meant to be. And what's that about duck confit with foie gras bread pudding?

Salad of Fresh Organic Baby Lettuces with parsnip chips and black currant vinaigrette
$7

Egg Fettuccine with hedgehog mushrooms, green peas and fresh parmesan in light herbed broth
$9

Ragout of baby beets , carrot and turnip with braised scallions; beet and scallion emulsions
$8

Italian Prosciutto di Parma and Swiss Bunderflëisch with marinated artichokes, olives and tomato on fresh spinach
$10

Blue Cheese stuffed Bosc Pears, on fine French beans with pinenut butter and fresh lemon juice
$8

Lightly Poached East Coast Oysters, on garlic scented spinach with truffled white wine cream sauce
$12

Napoleon of Kristapson's Smoked Salmon , crisp Yukon gold chips, crème fraiche and arctic char caviar
with blood oranges, asparagus and dill
$10

Apple Braised smoked Octopus with arugula and multicoloured tomatoes,
rosemary croutons and apple-balsamic vinaigrette
$10

Crisp Polenta on braised greens, with broiled portobellos and sauce balsamella
$8

Grands

Crispy Skin Duck Confit with braised Belgian endive, poached quince, foie gras bread pudding and fino sherry sauce
$19

Whole Baked Highland Springs Trout, crusted with mustard and bread crumbs, with roasted fennel and garlic,
creamy fennel sauce
$18

Roast Sundried Tomato and Cheese Stuffed Breast of Chicken on carrot spaetzle
with slow roasted tomato and golden raisin sauce
$17

Winter Vegetable Risotto with oyster and shiitake mushrooms, rapini, parsnip and beets, with mushroom reduction
$16

Pan Seared Filet of Seabass with zucchini and pancetta wrapped wehani rice, cherry tomatoes,
basil oil and tomato essence
$18

Grilled Pork Rack Chop with eggplant and dried currant caponata, grilled new potatoes and red wine glaze
$18

Via Allegro

1750 The Queensway
Toronto
416-622-6677

Italian
WEST TORONTO

Wheelchair
  access
V / MC / AmEx / DC
lunch
dinner
late supper
take out
beer/wine
cocktails
high chairs
private parties
non-smoking
reservations
  recommended
dress business
  casual
menu changes
  seasonally

It sounds impossible, crazy, but the most dazzling wine cellar in Ontario sits in an Etobicoke strip mall west of Highway 427 (just about off the edge of the world). Consider at least 110 single malt whiskies, 160 grappas, more than 2,100 wines, the best collection of amarones in Canada, five sommeliers and an impressive *Wine Spectator* Best of Award of Excellence four years running—all this from what started life as a suburban pizza joint so long ago. The pizzas and pastas are still the best in the west, but under chef Lino Collevecchio, grilled seafood, veal, and venison hit the high notes, too.

Zuppa del Giorno: Please ask your server for the Chef's daily creation. Market Price

Zuppa di Funghi: A blend of woodland mushrooms, scented with truffle oil and finished with creme fraiche, presented with a mushroom duxelle pastry and light chevre goat cheese cream. $8.95

Cozze: Fresh cultivated Prince Edward Island mussels, simmered in a white wine tomato broth with double smoked bacon, roasted peppers and crostini. $8.95

Insalata Allegro Medley: Medley of fine field greens with grilled oyster mushroom, gorgonzola cheese, roasted spicy walnuts, wine poached pear, parmigiano grissini wrapped with proscuitto and drizzled with a balsamic-honey vinaigrette. $12.95

Insalata Caesar: Finest hearts of romaine _presented whole demonstrating freshness_, sprinkled with chives and spicy pumpkin seeds with a home-made vinaigrette dressing, crispy pancetta (Italian bacon), shaved parmigiano cheese and home-made croutons. $9.95

Insalata Mista: A medley of eleven organic field greens with cherry tomatoes, slivered bocconcini, vegetable crisps and organic seedlings tossed in a herbed balsamic vinegar and olive oil dressing. $8.95

Insalata Rossa: Crisp radicchio, baby arugula, shaved fennel, and Belgian endive with and aged _Grana Padano_ shards and a ruby grapefruit dressing. $8.95

Oven Baked Goat Cheese: Fine herb, peppercorn and hazelnut crusted Woolwich goat cheese baked in phyllo pastry drizzled with roasted pepper coulis. Accompanied by a fine cut grilled vegetable salad and wilted baby greens. $11.95

Duck Prosciutto: Delicate slices of in-house cured Hudson Valley duck breast with grappa marinated peach and dried blueberry compote, pickled onion and Arborio rice salad, drizzled with a fig infused vincotto. $15.95

Carpaccio: Fine cured Alberta beef tenderloin with aged parmigiano shards, lemon preserve, extra virgin olive oil, baby arugula and a Tuscan panzanella salad. $14.95

Calamari Fritti: Tender calamari cut daily, marinated in white wine, seasoned with sea salt and floured then flash fried and sprinkled with finely diced mediterranean vegetable brunoise. Served with a lemon-Pommery vinaigrette and grilled lemon wedge. $12.95

Agnolotti di Zucca: In-house freshly prepared butternut squash and walnut stuffed pasta with honey roasted Abati pears Proscuitto di Parma and gorgonzola cream sauce. $14.95

Whistling Oyster

11 Duncan Street
Toronto
416-598-7707
www.fredsnothere.com

Seafood
ENTERTAINMENT
DISTRICT

V / MC / AmEx / DC

lunch

dinner

late supper

take out

beer/wine

cocktails

non-smoking
section

reservations
recommended

dress casual

menu changes
seasonally

My favorite address in Fred Luk's Entertainment District empire (Fred's Not Here, Red Tomato, Fillet of Sole, Cha Cha Cha), Whistling Oyster flourishes because its globe-hopping menu covers so much—Chinese dim sum, Louisiana Cajun, Southeast Asian stir-fries, pastas—all good and at bargain prices, especially during happy hours when Fred practically *gives* food away. His brigade of Chinese and Sri Lankan cooks toil furiously at nicely underdone fish and gossamer deep-fry with chile-garlic accents. Me, I settle for a mug of Guinness, a dozen large Malpeques on the half shell with a platter of the city's best fries—fish and chips for the twenty-first century.

Let's Do Lunch!

THE WHISTLING OYSTER

DIM SUM
* Fried Shrimp & Mango Spring Rolls w/ Dipping Sauce $ 5.99
* Baked Stuffed Curried Crab w/ Shrimp & Scallops ......$ 6.99
* Grilled Indonesian Chicken & Shrimp Satay w/
  Peanut Sauce $6.99
* Fried Coconut Shrimp w/ Thai Dipping Sauce $6.99
* Fried Chicken & Shrimp Spring Rolls w/ Hot &
  Sweet Sauce ....$ 6.29
*Fried Chinese B.B.Q. Chicken Quesadillas w/ Leeks,
  Pineapple & Brie $6.29

MEXICAN CORNER
* **Nachos** - Slow Cooked 12 Hour "Tijuana" Chicken
  Confit, Monterey & Cheddar Cheese, Smoked
  Jalapeno & Tomato Salsa (Small)............................$7.49
* **Steamed Mussels** in a Smokey Jalapeno Tomato
  Sauce (Small)..$6.99

"RIBS" AROUND THE WORLD
* **Garlic Kansas "Smoke King" Baby Back Ribs**..$ 10.99
  w/ Fries & Cole Slaw (Large) ....$ 18.99
* **Hong Kong B.B.Q. Prime Beef Ribs** $9.99
  w/ Steamed Lotus Leaf Wrapped Sticky Rice
  (Large) $14.99
* **5-Spiced Garlic & Chili Riblets** (Small)............$6.99

Xacutti

503 College Street
Toronto
416-323-3957
www.Xacutti.com

Fusion
LITTLE ITALY

V / MC / AmEx

dinner

take out

beer/wine

cocktails

private parties

non-smoking

reservations
required

dress casual

menu changes
seasonally

For incarnations, the multiple choice question has burned more hotly than jalapeños from Hell: When you tone down Indian spices to a degree they're ever so-subtle, is it (a) the long-awaited modernization of Mother India's kitchen, (b) the oxymoronic Anglo-Indian "cuisine," (c) Indian for timid palates? Answer: all of the above. Chef Brad Moore, who cut his pan-Asian teeth at Monsoon, reaches into the Subcontinental spice box perhaps too cautiously, but halibut crusted in cumin and smoked lamb with cardamom are notions whose time has come. Whatever, Xacutti (pronounced "sha-coot-ee") scores heavily for lightening up a traditionally oily cuisine, bringing high-ticket ingredients into play, substituting refined for rustic and plating in a style as chic as the surroundings.

xacutti [sha koo tee]

small

iced tindora soup with cracked pistachios	8
tali macchi sole with arugula seedlings	13
tikka roasted quail with pomegranate honey	12
pistachio crusted seared blue fin tuna with cardamom orange	14
sweet yam fries with soy chili sambola, ginger plum	7
steamed mussels with tomato kaffir curry,toasted naan	9
goan spiced duck salad with nappa, tatsoi and popcorn seedlings	12
b.b.q. cinnamon guava pork ribs with grilled starfruit	11
pan seared tandoori salmon rolls with tangerine miso	11
galangal prawns in a lime mint currry	14
baby greens with passionfruit vinaigrette	9

large

tamarind duck with jaggery syrup, buttermilk arugula pancakes, and ginger greens	23
zaffron indo snapper in a coconut lime curry, pappadum and steamed rice	27
aloo bound king prawns, sesame asparagus, butter rice and tamarind soy	33
cardamom smoked spring lamb with masala roasted squash, mango chutney and ginger frites	34
jeera halibut, panfried with new potatoes, spinach and coconut tomato curry	26

YYZ

345 Adelaide Street West
Toronto
416-599-3399
www.yyzrestaurant.com

**Global
ENTERTAINMENT
DISTRICT**

V / MC / AmEx / DC

dinner

late supper

beer/wine

cocktails

private parties

outdoor patio
& bar

non-smoking
section

reservations
recommended

dress informal

menu changes
weekly

Savvy restaurateur Simon Bower and his chef
Chris Zielinski, who trained under Susar Lee at
Lotus, knocked us flat with fusion at the mercurial
Mercer Street Grill. At YYZ, slyly named after
Toronto airport's call letters, the boys deck their
forum in designer cool—those pale-lime mono-
chromes are maybe too cool—and rein in their
sense of adventure, focusing on subtler pleasures
perfectly embodied in a terrine of raw yellowfin
tuna and Atlantic salmon bound in nori and
drizzled with wasabi cream. The adjoining wine
bar—one of Toronto's few serving good food until
1 A.M.—is right up there with Avenue among
in-crowd watering holes.

RESTAURANT AND WINE BAR

STARTERS

SOUP TODAY
MARKET PRICE

ROAST PEAR AND TOURNEVENT GOAT CHEESE SALAD
BEET BALSAMIC DRESSING AND PINE NUT CRACKER
11

SALMON CARPACCIO WITH PICKLED SHAVED FENNEL
LEMON, OLIVE OIL AND MUSTARD CRESS
10

SAUTEED RARE DUCK BREAST WITH A HOT AND SOUR
GOLDEN PINEAPPLE ON A BED OF BABY LETTUCE
12

ARUGULA AND ESCAROLE SALAD WITH A LEMON PARMESAN
DRESSING AND AN OLIVE AND WHITE BEAN CROUTON
9

SASHIMI YELLOWFIN TUNA TERRINE AND WASABI SOYA BEANS,
DAIKON AND CUCUMBER SALAD, YUZU VINAIGRETTE
15

PAN SEARED QUEBEC FOIE GRAS WITH 5 SPICE "FRENCH TOAST"
WARM MANGO AND A MAPLE GINGER GLAZE
14

ROASTED SQUASH GNOCCHI WITH SMOKED TOMATOES,
PANCETTA, SCALLIONS AND SAGE GORGONZOLA BUTTER
12

Zachary's

Wyndham Bristol Place Hotel
950 Dixon Road
Toronto
416-675-9444

French
AIRPORT

Wheelchair
    access

valet parking

V / MC / AmEx /
    D / DC

Sunday brunch

lunch

dinner

beer/wine

cocktails

high chairs

private parties

non-smoking

reservations
    required

dress casual

menu changes
    seasonally

Classy dining amid the gastronomic rubble of Toronto's airport strip: For a foodie takeoff, Zachary's is the only game in town, but it doesn't fall asleep on the job. Maître d' Jack McKay, who's managed the room with a velvet glove for more than thirty years, and his team boost the comfort level into high altitudes: Butter and garlic float unashamedly through the room. Zachary's foie gras, crisply seared, pink and yielding, was one of Toronto's best long before duck liver was all the rage. Rack of Washington lamb and venison are standards, awaiting flyers in revolt against the twaddle that passes for airline food.

Thai Chicken Stir Fry   16.50
crisp vegetables, shiitake mushrooms and sprouts
tossed with gingered yellow curry and lemon grass on steamed rice

Rosemary Roasted Chicken Supreme   17.00
on sunburst zucchini and herb mash potato
Balsamic bisque cream

Pan Seared Provimi Calf's Liver   18.00
thin sliced liver with sauteed onion rings, Granny Smith apples and rosti potato
red wine shallot sauce

Bristol Crab Cakes   18.00
golden fried crisp with sweet potato fries and grilled vegetables
lobster tarragon sauce

Pan Roasted Atlantic Salmon Fillet   21.00
honey mustard glaze, parslied mashed potato
and chive beurre blanc

Oven Baked Chilean Sea Bass   24.00
with herb mashed potato and sauteed spinach
roasted bell pepper cream

Sesame Crusted Pork Tenderloin   23.00
pan seared with bok choy, steamed rice and crispy spring roll
ginger soya reduction

Zee Grill

641 Mount Pleasant Road
Toronto
416-484-6428
www.zeegrill.com

Bistro
MIDTOWN

V / MC / AmEx / DC

dinner

late supper

beer/wine

cocktails

private parties

non-smoking
  section

reservations
  recommended

dress casual

menu changes
  seasonally

A rollicking room overseen by a buxom ship's figurehead, the "Zee" a play on the Dutch for sea, Zee Grill (also known as Phebe's) has been teaching uptowners to respect fish and seafood for a remarkable two decades. Chef Jac Eckhardt, originally from The Hague, knows his stuff: There's no wincing at overcooked, wizened fish here. The Dutchman smokes lowly mussels and presents them as aristocrats on the half shell. He dallies with Asian fantasia via sea bass in crisp Japanese bread crumbs and rare tuna spiked with ponzu-wasabi. Regulars can't keep away from seafood stews, variations of cioppino with Chinese or Jamaican notes. Ahoy, Jac.

ZEE GRILL

CLAM CHOWDER - 4.95
* new england style

ORGANIC BABY GREENS - 6.95
* sesame garlic vinaigrette

ROMAINE SALAD - 6.95
* tomatoes / cucumbers / raspberry wine vinaigrette

CRISPY CALAMARI - 7.50
* pickled daikon / red currant chili-mint sauce

GRILLED ATLANTIC SALMON - 19.95
* sauteed spinach / fingerling potatoes /
  coriander broth / mango salsa

CRAB CAKES - 22.95
* pickled daikon and carrot salad /
  potato frites / watercress aioli / salsa

PAN ROASTED CHILEAN SEA BASS - 23.50
* julienne of mixed vegetables /
  grilled fingerling potatoes

Zen

2803 Eglinton Avenue East
Toronto
416-265-7111

Japanese
EAST TORONTO

V / MC / AmEx

lunch

dinner

take out

beer/wine

cocktails

non-smoking

reservations
recommended

dress casual

No way I'd find my way to a minimalist space in a mall in bleakest Scarborough if it weren't for owner Seiichi Kashiwabara, who long ago transformed Masa into one of the city's first great, pathfinding Japanese restaurants. Kashiwabara isn't taking too many chances in this neck of the woods—don't expect the creative play of Omi or Lily—but the sushi-sashimi lover, gawking at the bar as the chef so deftly orchestrates every detail, may well drift to heaven on a silken swatch of deep-fried tofu and the purity and beauty of Kashiwabara's yellowtail, salmon, and sea urchin.

SUSHI

☆ Served with Soy bean soup or clear soup ☆

1. 上寿司 （JYO ZUSHI） $18.50
   (Tuna, salmon, white fish, yellow tail, shrimp,
   cuttle fish, flying fish roe, mackerel & 6pcs, tuna roll)

2. 特上寿司 （TOKUJYO ZUSHI） $25.50
   (Tuna, salmon, white fish, Clam, cuttle fish,
   B.B.Q. Eel, yellow tail, salmon roe, & 4pce. Tuna Roll)

3. ちらし寿司 （CHIRASHI ZUSHI） $19.50
   (Tuna, salmon, yellow tail, white fish, shrimp, mackerel, octopus,
   Egg, clam cuttle fish, On a bowl of Sushi Rice)

NOODLES

1. かけうどん
   KAKE UDON $9.00
   (Noodles in soup)

2. 天麩羅うどん
   TENPURA UDON $10.50
   (Noodles in soup with shrimp tempura)

3. 肉うどん
   NIKU UDON $9.80
   (Noodles in soup topped with meat)

4. かけそば
   KAKE SOBA $9.00
   (Buckwheat noodles in soup)

Zucca

2150 Yonge Street
Toronto
416-488-5774

Italian
MIDTOWN

V / MC / AmEx / DC

dinner

take out

beer/wine

cocktails

private parties

non-smoking

reservations
  recommended

dress casual

menu changes
  seasonally

Andrew Milne-Allan seems an unlikely moniker for a top-ranking Italian chef in this most Italian of North American cities, but at Zucca, he shows 'em. Intricately sauced pastas, flawlessly grilled fish, and unerringly juicy fowl garner a repeat clientele including celebrated chefs (is that Avalon's Chris McDonald?) on their off nights. A hot spot and haven of Mediterranean sensibility in an aesthetically chilly midtown neighborhood, often looking south to Calabria and Sicily for power-house flavors, its aromas are nothing short of a spell, its service warm, its consistency assured. Zucca remains one of Toronto's most underrated and overlooked *ristorantes.*

Lucca

TRATTORIA

'Mpepata di Cozze
saute of string-cultured mussels with lemon, virgin olive oil, cracked black pepper, garlic *bruschetta*   9

Polpo alla Griglia
marinated & grilled octopus with warm salad of potato, winter cabbage and caperberries   12

all fresh pastas made in house
Ciriole al Pomodoro Piccante
thick-cut semolina noodles with sauce of tomato, basil, *peperoncino*   12

Gnocchi di Patate con Sugo di Brasato
potato gnocchi with braised lamb shank sauce, pecorino cheese   14

Maccheroni Autunnale
short pasta with saute of radicchio, fennel, savoy, chanterelles, *pancetta*, ricotta, parmesan   15

Strangozzi ai Tartufi Neri
hand-cut truffle flavoured noodles with chanterelles, fresh herbs, butter, parmesan   16

Straccetti al Ragu di Cinghiale
chestnut flour fettuccine with long-simmered *ragu* of wild boar, spices, red wine   17

Tagliolini al Nero ai Frutti di Mare
squid-ink pasta ribbons with clams, mussels, shrimp, calamari, tomato, white wine   17

Gallinella al Mattone
whole cornish hen (*) pressed on the grill with lemon, rosemary, black pepper; roast potatoes   19

Stinco d'Agnello Brasato
lamb shanks long-braised with tomato, herbs, *balsamico,* white wine, served with soft white polenta   20

Braciole di Vitello
veal rolls stuffed with artichokes, raisins, pinenuts, pecorino, braised with white wine, tomato,
served with yukon mash & steamed greens   22

Costola di Maiale al Vincotto
pork loin chop (*) marinated with sage, orange peel, toasted coriander, pan-roasted, with *vincotto sauce,*
yukon mash, braised winter cabbage, puree of butternut squash   22

cuisine

Fusion

Blowfish • 64
(DOWNTOWN WEST)

Rain • 262
(DOWNTOWN WEST)

Rosedale Diner • 276
(MIDTOWN)

Sen5es • 296
(DOWNTOWN WEST)

Susur • 322
(DOWNTOWN WEST)

Xacutti • 350
(LITTLE ITALY)

Global

360 Restaurant • 12
(DOWNTOWN)

Accents • 14
(DOWNTOWN)

Acqua • 16
(FINANCIAL DISTRICT)

Across the Road • 18
(MIDTOWN)

Agora • 24
(DOWNTOWN WEST)

Annona • 30
(MIDTOWN)

Avalon • 36
(DOWNTOWN WEST)

Avenue • 38
(YORKVILLE)

Boba • 66
(YORKVILLE)

Bymark • 76
(FINANCIAL DISTRICT)

Centro • 80
(UPTOWN)

Courthouse Market Grille • 94
(DOWNTOWN)

Epic • 108
(DOWNTOWN)

Fat Cat • 114
(MIDTOWN WEST)

Focaccia • 118
(DOWNTOWN)

Fred's Not Here • 120
(ENTERTAINMENT DISTRICT)

Hemispheres • 138
(DOWNTOWN)

JOV Bistro • 164
(MIDTOWN)

Jump • 166
(FINANCIAL DISTRICT)

Le Continental • 188
(NORTHEAST TORONTO)

Mildred Pierce • 210
(WEST TORONTO)

Mizzen • 216
(WATERFRONT)

North 44 • 230
(UPTOWN)

Opus • 236
(YORKVILLE)

Oro • 238
(DOWNTOWN)

Pangaea • 246
(MIDTOWN)

Sassafraz • 288
(YORKVILLE)

Scaramouche Pasta Bar • 292
(MIDTOWN)

Signatures • 300
(MIDTOWN)

Splendido • 310
(DOWNTOWN WEST)

Studio Cafe • 320
(YORKVILLE)

Tasting Rooms • 328
(FINANCIAL DISTRICT)

Terra • 330
(SUBURBAN NORTH)

The Corner House • 92
(MIDTOWN WEST)

Japanese

Benihana • 52
(DOWNTOWN)

Edo • 104
(MIDTOWN WEST)

Ematei • 106
(DOWNTOWN WEST)

Hiro Sushi • 142
(DOWNTOWN)

**Kaiseki Yu-Zen
Hashimoto** • 168
(SUBURBAN WEST)

Kaji • 170
(WEST TORONTO)

Katsura • 172
(NORTHEAST TORONTO)

Lily • 196
(DANFORTH)

Nami • 222
(DOWNTOWN)

Omi • 234
(DOWNTOWN)

Take Sushi • 326
(DOWNTOWN)

Zen • 358
(EAST TORONTO)

Korean

Korea • House 178
(LITTLE KOREA)

Mexican

Jalapeño • 158
(WEST TORONTO)

Middle Eastern

Jerusalem • 160
(WEST TORONTO)

Moroccan

Boujadi • 70
(MIDTOWN WEST)

Pan-Asian

Lalot • 184
(DOWNTOWN WEST)

Mata Hari Grill • 206
(DOWNTOWN WEST)

Monsoon • 218
(ENTERTAINMENT DISTRICT)

Spring Rolls on Yonge • 312
(DOWNTOWN)

Polish

Izba • 154
(WEST TORONTO)

Portuguese

Adega • 20
(DOWNTOWN)

Sintra • 304
(LITTLE ITALY)

Seafood

Adriatico • 22
(MIDTOWN)

Chiado • 84
(LITTLE ITALY)

Joso's • 162
(MIDTOWN)

Oyster Boy • 242
(WEST TORONTO)

Rodney's Oyster House • 270
(DOWNTOWN WEST)

**Starfish Oyster Bed
& Grill** • 314
(DOWNTOWN)

Whistling Oyster • 348
(ENTERTAINMENT DISTRICT)

Southeast Asian

Ban Vanipha • 44
(DOWNTOWN WEST)

Bangkok Garden • 46
(DOWNTOWN)

Golden Thai • 130
(DOWNTOWN)

Pho Hung • 252
(SPADINA CHINATOWN)

Vanipha Lanna • 342
(WEST TORONTO)

Spanish

Segovia • 294
(DOWNTOWN)

Steakhouse

Barberian's • 48
(DOWNTOWN)

George Bigliardi's • 126
(DOWNTOWN)

**Ruth's Chris
Steak House • 284**
(DOWNTOWN)

Turkish

Anatolia • 28
(WEST TORONTO)

Ukrainian

LVIV • 200
(BLOOR WEST VILLAGE)

neighborhood

Airport

Zachary's • 354
(FRENCH)

Annex

Bistro Tournesol • 62
(FRENCH-ITALIAN)

Goldfish • 132
(BISTRO)

Indian Rice Factory • 150
(INDIAN)

Natarãj • 224
(INDIAN)

Rouge • 280
(BISTRO)

Serra • 298
(BISTRO)

Bloor West Village

Lemon Meringue • 194
(BISTRO)

LVIV • 200
(UKRAINIAN)

Cabbagetown

Provence • 258
(FRENCH)

Town Grill • 336
(BISTRO)

Chinatown East

Pearl Court • 250
(CHINESE)

Danforth

Avli • 40
(GREEK)

Lily • 196
(JAPANESE)

Myth • 220
(GREEK)

Ouzeri • 240
(GREEK)

Pan on the Danforth • 244
(GREEK)

Downtown

360 Restaurant • 12
(GLOBAL)

Accents • 14
(GLOBAL)

Spadina Chinatown

Lee Garden • 192
(CHINESE)

Pho Hung • 252
(SOUTHEAST ASIAN)

Suburban North

Ambassador • 26
(CHINESE)

**Golden Court
Abalone Restaurant • 128**
(CHINESE)

Grand Yatt • 134
(CHINESE)

Rhapsody • 264
(HUNGARIAN)

Terra • 330
(GLOBAL)

Suburban Northeast

Chung King Garden • 88
(CHINESE)

Dragon Dynasty • 100
(CHINESE)

Magic Wok • 202
(CHINESE)

**Rich Congee
Chinese Restaurant • 266**
(CHINESE)

Sam Woo Seafood • 286
(CHINESE)

Suburban West

**Kaiseki Yu-Zen
Hashimoto • 168**
(JAPANESE)

Piatto • 254
(ITALIAN)

Rogues • 272
(ITALIAN)

The Beach

Arax • 32
(BISTRO)

Uptown

Auberge du Pommier • 34
(FRENCH)

Centro • 80
(GLOBAL)

Coppi • 90
(ITALIAN)

Herbs • 140
(BISTRO)

Millie's • 212
(BISTRO)

New Orleans Desire • 226
(BISTRO)

North 44 • 230
(GLOBAL)

Richlee's • 268
(BISTRO)

Waterfront

Mizzen • 216
(GLOBAL)

Toula • 334
(ITALIAN)

West Toronto

Anatolia • 28
(TURKISH)

Gamelle • 124
(FRENCH)

Il Mulino • 146
(ITALIAN)

Izba • 154
(POLISH)

Jalapeño • 158
(MEXICAN)

West Toronto, *continued*

Jerusalem • 160
(MIDDLE EASTERN)

Kaji • 170
(JAPANESE)

Little Tibet • 198
(HIMALAYAN)

Mildred Pierce • 210
(GLOBAL)

Noce • 228
(ITALIAN)

Oyster Boy • 242
(SEAFOOD)

Silver Spoon • 302
(ITALIAN)

Southern Accent • 308
(AMERICAN)

Vanipha Lanna • 342
(SOUTHEAST ASIAN)

Via Allegro • 346
(ITALIAN)

Yorkville

Avenue • 38
(GLOBAL)

Boba • 66
(GLOBAL)

Il Posto Nuovo • 148
(ITALIAN)

Jacques Bistro du Parc • 156
(FRENCH)

Opus • 236
(GLOBAL)

Prego della Piazza • 256
(ITALIAN)

Sassafraz • 288
(GLOBAL)

Studio Cafe • 320
(GLOBAL)

The Host • 144
(INDIAN)

Truffles • 338
(FRENCH)